HEIDEGGER'S ONTOLOGICAL PROJECT

THE COLLECTED WRITINGS OF JOHN SALLIS
Volume III/8

HEIDEGGER'S ONTOLOGICAL PROJECT
On Being and Time

John Sallis

Edited by Jeffrey Powell

Indiana University Press

This book is a publication of

Indiana University Press
Office of Scholarly Publishing
Herman B Wells Library 350
1320 East 10th Street
Bloomington, Indiana 47405 USA

iupress.org

© 2024 by Indiana University Press

All rights reserved
No part of this book may be reproduced or utilized in any form or by any means, electronic or mechanical, including photocopying and recording, or by any information storage and retrieval system, without permission in writing from the publisher.

Collected Writings of John Sallis Printing 2024

Cataloging information is available from the Library of Congress.

ISBN 978-0-253-07058-6 (hdbk.)
ISBN 978-0-253-07059-3 (pbk.)
ISBN 978-0-253-07060-9 (web PDF)

Contents

    Key to the Citations of Heidegger's Works   *vii*

    Introduction   *1*

  1 The Untitled First Page to *Being and Time*   *3*

  2 The First Introduction to *Being and Time*: The Necessity of an Explicit Renewal (*Wiederholung*) of the Question of Being   *10*

  3 The Second Introduction to *Being and Time*: The Double Task in Working Out the Question of Being: The Method of the Investigation and Its Outline   *25*

Division One: The Preparatory Fundamental Analysis of Dasein   *53*

  1 The Exposition of the Task of a Preparatory Analysis of Dasein   *55*

  2 Being-in-the-World in General as the Fundamental Constitution of Dasein   *59*

  3 The Worldliness of the World   *64*

  4 Being-in-the-World as Being-with and Being a Self: The "They"   *77*

  5 Being-in as Such   *84*

  6 Care as the Being of Dasein   *104*

Division Two: Dasein and Temporality   *115*

  1 The Possible Being-a-Whole of Dasein and Being-toward-Death   *119*

  2 The Attestation of Dasein of an Authentic Potentiality-of-Being and Resoluteness   *135*

  3 The Authentic Potentiality-for-Being-a-Whole of Dasein, and Temporality as the Ontological Meaning of Care   *150*

4	Temporality and Everydayness	*160*
5	Temporality and Historicity	*168*
6	Temporality and Within-Timeness as the Origin of the Ordinary Concept of Time	*174*
	Conclusion	*180*
	Appendix	*181*
	Editor's Afterword	*187*
	Index	*189*

Key to the Citations of Heidegger's Works

HEIDEGGER'S WORKS ARE cited with the following abbreviations followed by the original German page numbers and then the page numbers of the English translations. The page numbers provided for the English translation of *Sein und Zeit* will be the second edition of the SUNY Press translation by Joan Stambaugh and revised by Dennis J. Schmidt. Where there occurs a discrepancy between the SUNY translation and the translation provided, this is due to an alteration of the translation by the editor.

BT: *Sein und Zeit*, 15th ed. Tübingen: Max Niemeyer, 1979. *Being and Time*, 2nd rev. ed., trans. Joan Stambaugh, rev. Dennis J. Schmidt. Albany: SUNY Press, 2010.

HCT: *Prolegomena zur Geschichte des Zeitbegriffs*, ed. Petra Jaeger. Vol. 20 of Heidegger *Gesamtausgabe*. Frankfurt am Main: Vittorio Klostermann, 1979. *History of the Concept of Time: Prolegomena*, trans. Theodore Kisiel. Bloomington: Indiana University Press, 1985.

BPP: *Die Grundprobleme der Phänomenologie*, ed. Friedrich-Wilhelm von Herrmann. Vol. 24 of Heidegger *Gesamtausgabe*. Frankfurt am Main: Vittorio Klostermann, 1975.

HEIDEGGER'S ONTOLOGICAL PROJECT

Introduction: The Exposition of the Question of the Meaning of Being

Our main concern is the following: to read Heidegger's *Being and Time* carefully and thoughtfully. That is, to try to read it with the same attentiveness that Heidegger himself brought to his readings of Aristotle, Kant, Hegel, Schelling, Nietzsche, and so on. That is, to try to read it in such a way as to *think through the matters at issue* in it, to let them become genuinely questionable.

There are two characteristics of *Being and Time* on which we need to focus at the very outset.

(1) Its incompleteness.

According to the outline in section 8, *Being and Time* was to consist of two principal parts, each containing three divisions. Of these, only the first two divisions of part 1 were actually published.

In particular, the third division of part 1 ("Time and Being")—the division in which the basic question would finally have been taken up at its proper level—has never appeared.

So: *Being and Time* (as published) is all preliminary—

That is, radically incomplete.

That is, a torso!

(2) Its rootedness in the tradition—that it is in dialogue and an encounter with the tradition. A more appropriate metaphor: *Being and Time* is the tip of an iceberg.

What we do not see is the extended confrontation with the tradition that Heidegger carried out in his lectures. They throw considerable light on *Being and Time*, and we should compare the chronology with Sheehan's essay "Heidegger's Early Years."[1] We look at two lecture courses—those occurring just before and after *Being and Time*. But, for now, we need to get on as quickly as possible to the text of *Being and Time*.

It was in this confrontation that most of the basic issues of *Being and Time* were worked out, but in *Being and Time* itself, this dimension is mostly only alluded to.

By way of introduction, let me simply offer three quotations so as to situate Heidegger's project in the most global terms.

---

1. Thomas Sheehan, "Heidegger's Early Years: Fragments for a Philosophical Biography," in *Heidegger, the Man and the Thinker*, ed. Thomas Sheehan (Chicago: Precedent, 1981), 3–19.

(1) From Plato's *Sophist*. Heidegger cites on the first page of *Being and Time*. "For manifestly you have long been aware of what you mean when you use the expression 'being.' We, however, who used to think we understood it, have now become perplexed."²

This indicates the relation of Heidegger's work to Greek thought (Plato, Aristotle): from Greek thought, he takes over the fundamental question of his work—the question of the meaning of being.

(2) From Nietzsche's *Twilight of the Idols*, subtitled "How One Philosophizes with a Hammer."

"In fact, nothing has yet had a more naïve power of persuasion than the error of Being."³

This says: Being is an error.

Furthermore, in the same context, Nietzsche says of all such "highest concepts" that they are "the most general, the emptiest concepts, the last vapor of evaporating reality."

This text indicates the state into which the question of Being has come: Being is no longer even (as Hegel said) the same as nothing but rather sheer error, an idol whose twilight, whose demise, Nietzsche would announce.

This is the "situation" from which Heidegger seeks to renew the question of Being.

(3) From Husserl (Heidegger's teacher, to whom *Being and Time* is dedicated); specifically, from the foreword to the second edition of *Logical Investigations*, where Husserl characterizes the *Investigations* thus: "They are attempts at genuinely executed fundamental work on the immediately envisaged and seized things themselves. Even where they proceed critically, they do not lose themselves in discussions of standpoint, but rather leave the last word to the things themselves and to one's work upon such things."⁴

This indicates the *way* in which Heidegger seeks to renew the question of Being—by phenomenology, by going to the things themselves.

With this being said, let us go to the text of *Being and Time*.

---

2. Plato, *Sophist*, 244a. This reference occurs on the untitled first page of *Being and Time*. Note: throughout the manuscript, Sallis only provides line numbers for the material cited from Plato, and all translations from the Greek are his own. The citation of the Greek texts from the Loeb Classical Library (Harvard University Press) are provided by the editor; the corresponding Loeb translations are not intended to replace Sallis's translations.

3. Friedrich Nietzsche, *Kritische Studienausgabe*, vol. 6, eds. Giorgio Colli and Mazzino Montinari (Munich: Walter de Gruyter, 1980), 78.

4. Edmund Husserl, *Logische Untersuchungen*, Erster Band (Tübingen: Max Niemeyer, 1968), x. In English, *Logical Investigations*, vol. 1, trans. J. N. Findlay (New York: Humanities, 1970), 45.

1. The Untitled First Page to *Being and Time*

LET US TRY to formulate a preliminary question with which to make our first approach to *Being and Time*.

Philosophical thinking is *directed* toward a certain matter at issue (*Sache*, certain things themselves). It seeks to disclose that matter, to let it show itself.

However, in order for us to be able to take up such direction, the matter must *already* somehow be disclosed—that is, it must already somehow stand before us in such a way that we can direct our thinking toward it. In other words, it must already be "granted"; it must have already announced itself. (We should recall the *Meno*: one cannot go searching for an answer to the question "What is virtue?" unless one already knows what virtue is.)

So, in formal terms, philosophical thought already takes for granted precisely that which it would disclose. One way of expressing this: philosophical thought is *circular*—that is, in order to disclose the matter, we must already take it for granted, *but* it can be taken for granted only to the extent that it has already been disclosed. Heidegger writes: "What is decisive is not to get out of the circle, but to come into it in the right way" (BT 153/148).

So: Our preliminary question is what is the right way into the circle? That is, how does the project initiated in *Being and Time* come into the circle?

That is: where does *Being and Time* begin?

If one turns to the untitled first page of *Being and Time*, one sees, literally, where it begins: it begins with a passage from Plato's *Sophist*. This beginning is not mere decoration, not mere citing of authority. Rather, this statement belongs to the beginning of *Being and Time*—it has something important to do with its way of beginning. Rather than just passing over it, one should *wonder* at the fact that the first words of Heidegger's work are not his own but rather words spoken in a Platonic dialogue.

So: Where does *Being and Time* begin?

It begins in the middle of a Platonic dialogue. Its first words are those of the Stranger from Elea.

What is the context in which these words are spoken in the dialogue? The Stranger is speaking with Theaetetus, but he pretends to be addressing a certain group of men (thus it is a dialogue within the dialogue). He identifies them as those who seek to understand "how many and of what nature the beings [τὰ ὄντα] are" (*Sophist*, 242c).

The Stranger gives a second characterization of these men. Here one begins to hear the ironic tone, which will be amplified as the passage continues, and this indicates more clearly what the issue is in this part of the *Sophist*: he says that they always seem to tell us a story [μῦθος]—as if we were children. They tell of such things as the love and strife in which beings come to be from other beings and pass away into still others. There are several allusions to earlier thinkers. Most explicit is his reference to the Ionian and Sicilian Muses—that is, Heraclitus and Empedocles. As Heidegger puts it in the introduction (p. 6): they determine "beings as beings by tracing them back in their origin to some other beings, as if Being [*Sein*] had the character of a possible being [*Seienden*]" (BT 6/5). This says, they are aware only of beings and the relations between beings, but they are oblivious to the Being of these beings, which is not itself one of these beings.

In the sentence that immediately precedes the passage cited by Heidegger, the Stranger continues the dialogue within the dialogue. His irony becomes more audible. "Well, then, since we are in a state of perplexity, you [the 'storytellers'] go ahead and make them [i.e., beings] evident to us adequately, whatever you want to signify whenever you utter being [ὄν]." It is to these storytellers about beings that the Stranger speaks in that passage cited at/as the beginning of *Being and Time*. "For manifestly you have long been aware of what you mean when you use the expression 'being.' We, however, who once thought we understood it, have now become perplexed."

Here there are linguistic accounts that are needed.

(1) The phrase translated as "have become perplexed" (*in Verlegenheit gekommen*)—specifically, the word *perplexed*, *perplexity* plays an important role here and elsewhere. It is repeated several times in this one section of the *Sophist*. The word (*perplexed*) is ἀπορέω. The root word is πόρος. It designates a means of passing (e.g., across a river by means of ferry) as well as a way through or over, passage. If we add the privative ἀπορός (adjective), then we have that which is without passage, impassable, hard to see one's way through. The noun is ἀπορία, and it means a place that is impassable, a place where it is hard to see one's way through. Heidegger, in effect, describes where we are today regarding what is meant by Being *as an* ἀπορία. Immediately following the citation from the *Sophist*, he writes, "Do we in our time have an answer to the question of what we really mean by the word 'being'? Not at all [*Keineswegs*]" (BT 1/xxix).

(2) The word translated as "being" is ὄν. Heidegger translates this as *seiend* (the present participle, as in "being hungry"). This should be distinguished from several other forms:

sein: the infinitive (to be).

Sein: the noun derived from the infinitive (Being). It is neuter, so, *das Sein*. When Heidegger writes of the meaning of Being, he uses this form.

das Seiende: the noun derived from the participle, which means "that which is." This is generally used collectively and expresses beings in the plural. Macquarrie and Robinson translate this as "entity" or "entities," but this loses the connection with "sein" and "seiend." The practice now is to translate this as "beings."

ein Seiendes: a being. This is the same form but with the indefinite article.

To return to the passage from the *Sophist* that is cited in *Being and Time* along with its immediate context, the Stranger confronts the "storytellers" and criticizes the kind of stories that they tell about beings. He formulates his refutation in arithmetic terms, which was common among earlier philosophers. Briefly, there are those who declare the beings—all beings—to be two (e.g., hot and cold), but if each is said to be, then the "to be," Being, will be a third thing. Then the all is not two (as they maintained) but three.

The Stranger refers to further points in the refutation. But what he really wants to make evident is that these stories about beings will inevitably lead to perplexity—into the perplexity with which his and Theaetetus's condition is ironically contrasted—or rather, to an *entirely* different kind of perplexity.

At the end of the Stranger's refutation of the storytellers, he comes to the conclusion that if both of the two *are*, then (since they have Being in common) they are not two but one. This prepares (with a bit of comedy) the basis for a new discussion that begins just after the passage in which the citation by Heidegger occurs. Though his name is not mentioned, it is clearly Parmenides who is being discussed. (Recall that the Stranger is from Elea.) What the Stranger and Theaetetus take up is the Parmenidean thesis that the all is one. Although there seem to be criticisms, the tone is very different. In fact, some of the apparent criticisms point to the way in which Plato appropriates Parmenides's thought. For example, the distinction between the one (which Plato will think as ιδέα) and the name of the one (which Plato will think as λόγος).

So, more generally: the Stranger enacts (in one λόγος) the transition:

from: the level of the mere determining of beings through other beings—that is, of a determining that is oblivious to Being as such, which cannot say what Being means—

to: a Parmenidean level at which a genuine discussion of what Being means is possible.

Thus: In its original context, the passage with which *Being and Time* begins occurs within the transition:

from: the level of those who are oblivious to Being

to: the level of those who, like Parmenides and the Stranger, are alive to the questioning about Being.

Heidegger's first words in *Being and Time*, the first words of his own, essentially repeat what the passage from the *Sophist* says. That is, he refers to the question regarding what Being means and confesses an ignorance of this meaning, confesses perplexity: "Do we today have an answer to the question of what we really [properly, *eigentlich*] mean by the word 'being'? Not at all" (BT 1/xxix).

We should note that this repetition poses the question not to the ancient storytellers but to *we today* (*wir heute*).

This is the only personal pronoun construction on the entire page—though the *we* is repeated in this sentence and the *we today* occurs again a few lines later. We should not pass this by too quickly. We should at least pose the question: Who is this *we today*? Who is this *we* in whose name Heidegger here speaks? How is this *we* related to the questioning and analysis that this text will undertake?

In any case, since we today have no answer to the question of what "being" means, "it is fitting to pose anew [Heidegger does *not* use the personal construction] *the question of the meaning of Being* [Und so gilt es denn, *die Frage nach dem Sinn von Sein* erneut zu stellen]" (BT 1/xxix).

Thus, beginning in Plato's *Sophist*, *Being and Time* is to repeat (pose anew) the question that the Platonic text posed—up to this point called simply: the question of the meaning of Being.

Again, Heidegger asks about the *we today*, asks in the name of the *we today*. He asks whether we today are in that perplexity (by which the Stranger was driven on to genuine questioning regarding the meaning of Being) or whether, on the contrary, we today belong on the side of those storytellers who are untouched by perplexity and hence closed off to questioning about Being. "But are we today even perplexed [*in der Verlegenheit*] at not understanding the expression 'Being'?" (BT 1/xxix). Again, Heidegger answers: "Not at all" (BT 1/xxix). "And so it is fitting first of all to awaken again an understanding of the meaning of this question" (BT 1/xxix). So for *we today*, it is necessary not only to pose the question again but to awaken an understanding of the very sense of the question—for, like the ancient storytellers, *we today* are not even in perplexity regarding the meaning of Being.

So where does *Being and Time* begin? It begins at the place where *we today* are (in the beginning), a place like that of the unperplexed storytellers.

But by posing again the question of the meaning of Being, and even the very sense of the question, *Being and Time* would launch that movement that the Stranger enacted; namely, the movement through perplexity into the unfolding of the sense of the question of the meaning of Being. That is, *Being and Time* is to *reenact* the movement into perplexity and into the questioning about Being thus opened up. One might suppose, recalling another Platonic text (*Theaetetus*), that this movement is like the awakening of the original *wonder* with which, as Theaetetus says, philosophy itself begins.

Following this brief indication of the character of the beginning of *Being and Time*, Heidegger goes on to state the aim of the work as a whole: "The aim of the following treatise is to work out concretely the question of the meaning of '*Being*'" (BT 1/xxix).

This statement provokes a number of questions.

(1) What does it mean to *work out* a question? What is an *Ausarbeitung*?

Does it mean to ask the question—perhaps in the sense of unfolding and developing it as a question?

Or does it mean to *answer* the question?

Or is this question (and any questioning engaged in it) perhaps so radical that the very distinction between asking and answering gets called into question? That is, that the very character and structure of questioning get brought into question?

Already, in fact, we have gotten a glimpse of just how unstable this distinction is through the example from the *Meno*: in order to ask about virtue so as to eventually get an answer to the question "What is virtue?," one must already know what it is, one must already have an answer.

(2) What does it mean to work out the question of the meaning of Being *concretely*?

It would seem to be one of the most *abstract* questions. In *Twilight of the Idols*, Nietzsche says that Being is among "the most general, one of the emptiest concepts, the last vapor of evaporating reality."[1]

So how is the question about Being to be worked out *concretely*?—that is, by reference to the concrete, to that which presents itself (stands before us) in its full sensuous actuality? That is, how is *ontological* questioning to be carried through *phenomenologically*?

Heidegger adds, finally, a statement of the preliminary goal of *Being and Time*: "The provisional aim is the interpretation of *time* as the possible horizon for any understanding whatsoever of Being" (BT 1/xxix).

This results in two questions, which we might now briefly state:

(1) What does it mean to speak of a *horizon* of understanding? How is it that understanding has something like a horizon? How does its horizon belong to it, and how does understanding operate in relation to (within) its horizon?

(2) In particular, what does it mean for time to serve as a horizon of the understanding of Being?

We should make note of one thing: the understanding of Being by reference to time is *not* something simply introduced here by Heidegger. Rather, it is already operative throughout the history of philosophy in the distinction between

---

1. Friedrich Nietzsche, *Kritische Studienausgabe*, vol. 6, eds. Giorgio Colli and Mazzino Montinari (Munich: Walter de Gruyter, 1980), 76.

the temporal and the eternal, which is equivalent to the basic demarcation of beings in terms of time. In a much more intricate way, it is in play in Kant's *Critique of Pure Reason*, in the doctrine of the schematism: here, the articulations of Being (which are the categories) come to be determined by time (in an a priori synthesis).

We might, then, say: Heidegger wants to carry out explicitly (thematically) that understanding of Being by reference to time that, in the history of philosophy, remained implicit.

Two final remarks are in order:

(1) *Being and Time* is a difficult book. It requires patient reading and rereading, especially if one is to enter into the movement of the work itself and experience its radical and reflexive character, rather than just looking on from the outside. In this connection, Heidegger remarks near the end of the introduction: "With regard to the awkwardness and 'inelegance' of expression in the following analyses, we may remark that it is one thing to report narratively about *beings* and another to grasp beings in their Being. For the latter task not only most of the words are lacking but above all the 'grammar'" (BT 38–39/36).

(2) I have said (and will say) almost nothing biographical—only this—

- He was born in a village, Messkirch, in the Black Forest in 1889.
- Beginning in 1909, he studied theology in Freiburg.
- In 1911, he gave up his theological studies and began studying philosophy. During this time, two books were decisive: Franz Brentano's *On the Multiple Meanings of Being in Aristotle* and Husserl's *Logical Investigations*.
- From 1922 to 1928, he was a professor in Marburg. In 1927, *Being and Time* was published; also, the lecture courses related to *Being and Time* were delivered (though the publication of them began only in the 1970s).
- In 1928, he succeeded Husserl as Professor of Philosophy at the University of Freiburg.

One should see Heidegger's brief account of his development in "My Way to Phenomenology" in *On Time and Being*.

These biographical details tell us very little about Heidegger the philosopher.

So I would like to read some extended passages from an open letter published in 1971 in the *New York Review of Books*—"Martin Heidegger at 80." The voice that speaks in the letter is that of someone who can speak with authority: Hannah Arendt.

> Heidegger's "fame" predates by about eight years the publication of *Being and Time* in 1927; indeed it is open to question whether the unusual success of this book—not just the immediate impact it had inside and outside the academic world but also its extraordinarily lasting influence, with which few of the

century's publications can compare—would have been possible if it had not been preceded by the teacher's reputation among the students, in whose opinion, at any rate, the book's success merely confirmed what they had known for many years. . . . There was hardly more than a name, but the name traveled all over Germany like the rumor of the hidden king. . . . The rumor that attracted them [students] to Freiburg and to the Privatdozent who taught there, as somewhat later they were attracted to the young professor at Marburg, had it that there was someone who was actually attaining "the things" that Husserl had proclaimed, someone who knew that these things were not academic matters but the concerns of thinking men—concerns not just of yesterday, but from time immemorial—and who, precisely because he knew that the tradition was broken, was uncovering the past anew. . . . The rumor about Heidegger put it quite simply: Thinking has come to life again; the cultural treasures of the past, believed to be dead, are being made to speak, in the course of which it turns out that they propose things altogether different from the familiar, worn-out trivialities they had been presumed to say. There exists a teacher; one can perhaps learn to think.[2]

---

2. Cited in Walter Biemel, *Martin Heidegger: An Illustrated Study*, trans. J. L. Mehta (London: Routledge & Kegan Paul, 1976), 3, 5–6.

2. The First Introduction to *Being and Time*

The Necessity of an Explicit Renewal (Wiederholung) of the Question of Being

LET US NOW return to the question of the beginning of *Being and Time* and one of the most comprehensive goals of the work.

Being and Time begins in the middle of a Platonic dialogue; specifically, the *Sophist*. More specifically, it begins with the transition from those storytellers about being to the Eleatic questioning about Being. In the *Sophist*, this transition is followed by another similar discussion, which the Stranger describes as a γιγαντομαχία περὶ τῆς οὐσίας (battle of giants concerning Being). Heidegger cites this phrase and says, ironically, that we believe we are spared the exertion of rekindling a γιγαντομαχία περὶ τῆς οὐσίας. Of course, it is just the opposite: this is precisely what is necessary today.

So *Being and Time* is to engage anew in a γιγαντομαχία—that is, it is to carry out a repetition (*Wiederholung*) of the transition in the *Sophist*: from obliviousness to Being, to perplexity (ἀπορία), to a genuine questioning about Being. Heidegger gives a preliminary, very general indication of the terms in which this repetition is to be carried out: it will undertake to interpret time as the horizon of the understanding of Being.

When *Being and Time* appeared in early 1927, it remained incomplete (and has remained so since then). Of the two major parts, only the first was published, and even in the first part, the crucial third division was lacking.

In the summer semester of 1927, Heidegger presented the course *Basic Problems of Phenomenology*, in which he attempted to work out some of the analyses that would have belonged to the third division. But also—indeed, in the major part of the course—he developed many of the themes in *Being and Time* (divisions 1 and 2) not as he had in *Being and Time* but rather out of a discussion and critique of the history of philosophy.

One such development occurs in a chapter (chap. 1 of part II) entitled "The Problem of the Ontological Difference." The problem is that of differentiating properly, in a rigorous way, between beings and Being (*das Seiende/das Sein*). What Heidegger shows is that this differentiation must be carried out by way of a determining of the *meaning* of Being. That is, by a passage beyond Being to the meaning (horizon) from which (in terms of which, on the basis of which) it becomes understandable in its difference from beings.

Heidegger compares this to the movement of the prisoner out of the cave as portrayed in the *Republic*. The focus is especially on the culmination of the ascent: here the former prisoner's vision extends to the "idea of the good," which Socrates says is "ἐπέκεινα τῆς οὐσίας" (beyond Being). Such a passage beyond Being (to its meaning, to that from which it becomes understandable) is also precisely what *Being and Time* undertakes. From *Basic Problems of Phenomenology*: "We, too, with this apparently quite abstract question about the conditions of the possibility of the understanding of Being, want to do nothing but bring ourselves out of the cave into the light" (BPP 404/285).

So: *Being and Time* is to repeat the Platonic ascent, to reenact the passage beyond Being.

Section 1: The Necessity of an Explicit Renewal (*Wiederholung*) of the Question of Being

Heidegger has said that we today are not even perplexed about the meaning of Being. That is, measured against the demands exhibited in the *Sophist*, we today are in *need of perplexity* regarding the meaning of Being. This is to say, we need to undergo the *movement into perplexity*. However, for us, this movement into perplexity (what it requires) is not quite the same as it was with the ancient "storytellers"; because we are moderns, not ancients, there is a difference.

What, then, is this difference?

The relevant difference can be seen in the title of section 1 and its first sentence.

Section 1 begins: "This question has today been forgotten" (BT 2/1)—and thus there is a need for a renewal (*Wiederholung*) of the question. So the difference results from the fact that for us, the question *has already been posed* by Plato and Aristotle. For us, the movement into perplexity is a matter of regaining something already once and decisively accomplished. It is a matter of *re*enacting that movement into perplexity and that posing of the question of Being that was accomplished by Plato and Aristotle, and thus a newly rekindled γιγαντομαχία περὶ τῆς οὐσίας (BT 2/1).

Today, in "our time," this question has literally "come into forgottenness." But it is a question that was once posed, taken up, and worked out—namely, by Plato and Aristotle. As we have seen, it was posed in Plato's *Republic* and especially in the *Sophist*, in γιγαντομαχία περὶ τῆς οὐσίας (*Sophist* 246a). It was developed even further in Aristotle's *Metaphysics*, in his analysis of the multiple ways that being is said and so can be articulated—"Being is said in many ways"

(*Metaphysics* Γ, 2)—and in the idea of the analogy of Being; that is, it is from οὐσια that all other categories are determined (cf. Aristotle's *Metaphysics* Θ1–3, introduction). However, after Plato and Aristotle, this question subsided "*as a thematic question for actual investigation*" (BT 2/1). That is, the question lost its questionableness, and subsequent thinkers failed to hold themselves in that provocative perplexity about Being. Heidegger continues: what Plato and Aristotle "wrested from phenomena by the highest exertion of thought, albeit in fragments and first beginnings, has long since been trivialized" (BT 2/1). Because it has lost its connection with the perplexity of questioning from out of which it came, it has become a free-floating result, a doctrine. Thus this question (uprooted from the questioning) is handed down to us—or, better, *traces* of the question are handed down—for example, in such texts as Plato's *Sophist*. Because we have these traces, *less* is demanded of us than of the ancients. So in our time, it is a matter of recovering (repeating) that questioning that was inaugurated by Plato and Aristotle; that is, a matter of a newly rekindled "battle of giants."

In a sense, one might suppose that this recovery of the question is less demanding than the original posing of it by Plato and Aristotle. However, this recovery must confront a difficulty that the Greeks did not have to confront. This is because not only has the question become empty, trivialized; *also* a dogma has been developed that sanctions the complete neglect of the question; that is, which *positively conceals* the need for posing the question again; that is, which covers over what is genuinely questionable in that about which the question asks, which thus inhibits the movement into perplexity, into the aporia. Furthermore, this concealment is all the more radical by virtue of having its roots in ancient ontology itself. That is, the very way in which the question gets taken up by the ancients provided, at the same time, the ground for that concealment of the question (forgottenness) into which subsequent Western thought came.

So to reawaken a sense for the question, Heidegger needs to confront the dogma, the prejudices that serve to conceal the need to pose the question and so to sanction its neglect. Heidegger's strategy is to *invert* these prejudices in such a way that instead of concealing what is questionable, they come to point to that very questionableness (in reference to which the question needs then to be taken up). One could say Heidegger inverts them in such a way as to draw "we today" into perplexity (aporia), thus provoking a renewal of the question.

The three prejudices are the following.

I. The Universality of Being.

A. Being is said to be the most universal concept because its extension is unlimited. That is, whereas most concepts apply only to a limited domain of things, Being applies without limits, applies to everything that is, to all beings. This is taken to entail that it is empty, "the last vapor of evaporating reality" (TI 76) and hence that there is no need to ask further about it.

B. However, the universality of Being is not a universality in the usual sense. It is not the universality of a genus. In Aristotle (*Metaphysics* B3), this is explained. Being is not a highest genus, because a genus must, as such, be divisible into species. Such division proceeds by means of a specific difference, which is brought from outside the genus. Aristotle: "It is not possible for a genus to be predicated of its proper differences" (*Metaphysics* 998b26). *But* there is no "difference" outside the concept of Being since Being can be predicated of everything. *So* Being cannot be divided into species, and thus is not a genus.

The universality of Being *transcends* any universality of genus, which is to say that Being is a "transcendental." (Remark: in his early work on Duns Scotus, Heidegger carefully worked out the distinction between the categories and transcendentals and investigated two other transcendentals: the one [*unum*] and the true [*verum*].)

C. The identification of Being as a transcendental rather than dissolving the question only serves to show just how questionable the universality of Being is. To indicate this, Heidegger gives a brief discussion of the history of the problem. This nongeneric universality is what Aristotle tried to grasp as the unity of analogy, and with this, he put the problem of Being on a new basis. Heidegger is referring to Aristotle's discussion (for example, *Metaphysics* γ) of Being as πρὸς ἕν equivocal: the unity of the concept of Being (ὄν) lies in the fact that everything that *is* in any way (whether as quality, quantity, etc.) has reference to one and the same kind of thing, which is οὐσία (substance).

But even Aristotle "did not clarify the obscurity of these categorial connections" (BT 3/2). His efforts, as well as the Scholastics' attempt to grasp the universality of Being as a transcendental, only point out more profoundly how questionable this universality of Being remains. But, finally, when Hegel defines Being as the "indeterminate immediate," the Aristotelian problem of the unity of Being has been lost sight of. Thus "If one says accordingly that 'Being' is the most universal concept, that cannot mean that it is the clearest and that it needs no further discussion. The concept of 'Being' is rather the most obscure of all" (BT 3/2).

II. The Indefinability of Being.

The concept of Being is indefinable, which follows from its supreme universality. It follows in two ways.

A. As indicated in a quote (fn. 4) from Pascal: "In order to define *Being*, one must say 'It is ...' and hence employ the word to be defined in its definition" (BT 4/3).

B. Most obviously, if the definition is by means of genus and specific difference, "Being" cannot be defined since there is no higher (more universal) genus in which it could be placed. And yet, "The indefinability of Being does not dispense with the question of its meaning but forces it upon us" (BT 4/3).

Heidegger thus draws the conclusion that "'Being' cannot indeed be conceived as a being" (BT 4/3). How this follows from the indefinability of Being is clearer if we consider another statement: "'Being' cannot be so determined by attributing beings to it" (*'Sein' kann nicht so zur Bestimmheit kommen, daß ihm Seiendes zugesprochen wird*) (BT 4/3). The point is this: all beings (particular beings, genera, species) have a certain *determinateness*, which can be expressed in definition. *But* this is not so for Being (since indefinable). Thus, rather than eliminating the question of the meaning of Being, this indefinability only makes this meaning more questionable, more perplexing.

There is a marginal note keyed to the statement "We can infer only that 'Being' is not some kind of being." The note says: "*Nein! sondern: über Seyn kann nicht mit Hilfe solcher Begrifflichkeit entschieden werden.*" (No! rather: with the help of such conceptuality nothing can be decided regarding Being). Presumably, this means: from indefinability, we cannot even draw the inference: Being is not a being—that is, even this goes too far. In other words, the indefinability of Being leaves matters even more questionable than Heidegger's 1927 text allowed.

III. The Self-Evidence of Being.

"'Being' is the self-evident [obvious, *selbstverständlich*] concept" (BT 4/3). This is indisputably so, for we use the word "Being" constantly and understand what we mean. However, what we have here is an "average comprehensibility" (BT 4/3). That is, we operate with and within a certain understanding of Being *without* its being explicit, without ever raising the question regarding what Being means. Or, if the question were to be raised, we would not be able to say what we understand by "Being."

What is crucial is the *tension*: we live always already in an understanding of Being—*yet* the meaning of Being remains obscure, so much so that we do not even raise the question regarding what "Being" means. Like the ancient "storytellers," we talk constantly about beings and thus already understand what it means to be—*yet* we are unable to say what we mean in using the word "Being." This tension points to the need to take up the question of the meaning of Being.

Like the ancient "storytellers," we talk constantly about beings and thus already understand what it means to be, *yet* we are unable to say what we mean in using the word "Being."

Thus: these three prejudices, *as inverted*, indicate how very questionable the meaning of Being is—*so questionable* that the question itself "is obscure and without direction" (BT 4/3).

So from out of perplexity regarding the meaning of Being, there arises the need to work out an adequate way of formulating the question.

Section 2: The Formal Structure of the Question

One must begin with the formal structure; that is, with Heidegger's sketch of the formal structure of questioning, as such.

Heidegger says: "Every questioning is a seeking. Every seeking takes its direction beforehand from what is sought" (BT 5/4). So the first distinction (structural articulation) is between: the questioning-seeking and what is sought.

Heidegger proceeds to articulate what is sought into three structural moments.

1. What is asked about (*das Gefragte*).
2. What is questioned or interrogated (*das Befragte*); that is, that which is made directly subject to interrogation, what is submitted to investigation.
3. What is to be found out or ascertained by the questioning (*das Erfragte*). It is this that is really *intended* in that which is asked about. Thus its disclosure constitutes the *fulfillment* of what is more or less emptily intended at the outset of the questioning (Husserlian Schema).

Questioning – Seeking ———— What is sought { *Gefragte*—what is asked about / *Befragte*—what is interrogated / *Erfragte*—what is about to be ascertained

Heidegger stresses a certain connection between the two sides of the question (between questioning-seeking *and* what-is-sought). He repeatedly says the questioning-seeking must be guided beforehand by what-is-sought; that is, only if one has some understanding of it in advance. This is again the classical circle, as in the Platonic dialogues.

This connotation holds, even preeminently, in the case of the question of Being. Any questioning about Being, as a seeking, must be guided in advance by what is sought. *And so* the meaning of Being, which is what is sought, must already somehow be available to us. Indeed, such "availability" was already referred to when Heidegger discussed the self-evidence of the concept of Being: we always already live within a vague, average understanding of Being.

But now, however, Heidegger relates this already granted understanding of Being more explicitly to the posing of the question of Being: "We do not *know* what 'Being' means. But already when we ask, 'What *is* Being [*Sein*]?' we stand in an understanding of the 'is' without being able to determine conceptually what the 'is' means" (BT 5/4).

So the very asking of the question (even in that almost empty form in which it is handed over to "we today") attests to that vague, average understanding of Being that is always already granted. That is, we can take up the question only because we have an already granted understanding of Being. Here we begin to discern still another answer to our question "Where does *Being and Time* begin?" It begins within the already granted understanding of Being.

We should again consider how Heidegger specifies the three structural moments of "what is sought" in the question of Being.

(1) *das Gefragte* (that which is asked about), which is Being. At this point, little can be said about what this *means*. But there is indicated at least a kind of formal preunderstanding that is operative: Being is "that which determines beings as beings" (BT 6/5). This formal conception is also expressed by saying that Being is "that in terms of which (on the basis of which, *woraufhin*, [out] on which) beings have always been understood no matter how they are discussed" (BT 6/5). This means Being is the a priori in the broadest sense: it is that which must always be understood in advance in order for beings to be accessible as such; it is preunderstood in a way that accords with the almost empty form that the question of Being has for us. That is, in its utmost formality, it is preunderstood merely in its character as the Being *of beings*, which is to say as "that which determines beings as beings."

(2) *das Erfragte* (that which is to be ascertained or found out by the questioning) is the meaning of Being (*der Sinn von Sein*). Heidegger says this requires its own conceptuality in distinction from the concepts appropriate to the determination of beings. Already, Heidegger has here indicated that this conceptuality has something to do with one way in which *time* can serve as the *horizon* for the understanding of Being.

(3) The other moment, *das Befragte* (that which is questioned) is, to some degree, determined by the formal preunderstanding of Being operative here: "Insofar as Being constitutes what is asked about, and insofar as Being means the Being of beings, beings themselves turn out to be what is *interrogated* in the question of Being" (BT 6/5). *So* Being is to be asked about by interrogating beings. Or, more fully, by interrogating beings, *Being and Time* will ask about Being in such a way as to find out about its meaning.

Still, one could ask: Why the approach to Being *through* beings? Though Heidegger does not say so (at least not here), one would assume that it is precisely beings (not Being) that are *present* in such a way that one *can* interrogate them directly, concretely; that is, phenomenologically.

In any case, the immediate problem is this: Which being, which kind of being is to be questioned? That is, from which being is one able to learn about the meaning of Being, to read it off (*ablesen*)? Or, in terms of our initial question, which being provides a place where *Being and Time* can appropriately begin its questioning about Being?

Finally, Heidegger focuses on still another structure or structural connection, one of a somewhat different sort. He begins by asking how must the question of Being be worked out (what kind of *Ausarbeitung*?) so as to be *posed in its full transparency*?

What does he mean by this: posed in its full transparency? He means posed in such a way that what is in play in the questioning (what structures it, gives it its perspectives) gets made explicit, transparent, rather than remaining only implicit.

What is, in this sense, in play in questioning about Being? Heidegger answers in three ways: a certain conceptual means for understanding its meaning, the choice of a certain being as exemplary, and a certain way of access to that exemplary being. Now, most importantly, all of these are simply modes of comportment *of the questioner*. That is, they are modes of *Being* of the questioner. "Regarding, understanding, and grasping, choosing, and gaining access to, are constitutive ways of comportment of the questioning and are thus modes of Being of a particular being, of *the* being which we, the questioners, are ourselves" (BT 7/6).

So what is required in order that the question be posed in its full transparency; that is, in order that the *Fragestellung* (posing, deployment) be transparent? "Thus to work out the question of Being means to make a being—one who questions—transparent in its Being" (BT 7/6). So a transparent *Fragestellung* requires an explication of the Being of the questioner, though the full justification (if there can be such) comes only in section 4. It is precisely at this point that Heidegger introduces the word *Dasein*.

This calls for two comments:

(1) Here one finds still another answer to the initial question "Where does *Being and Time* begin?" It begins (that is, in the very deployment of the question) with Dasein.

(2) What does Heidegger mean by *Dasein*? Precisely what he says—and no more. It is the being that we ourselves are. That is, it is that being that is our *own*. That is, it is a being that has the character of being someone's own (ownness).

It is the being that has inquiry, questioning as one of its possibilities of Being—or, more specifically, that has questioning about Being as one of its possibilities of Being. That is, Dasein is a being whose Being is such that it can question about Being.

The obvious question is: Why does Heidegger call this being "Dasein" rather than "man" (*Mensch*)? *Not* because there could be a being with the character of Dasein who were not men—nor conversely. Both words designate the same beings. The point here is, in thematizing this being as Dasein, Heidegger wants to consider it in a radically different way. *And* this requires, first of all, that he avoid presupposing all those characteristics of this being that we take for granted in calling him *man*. That is, he wants to avoid the presuppositions already operative in this designation. We should also note that he avoids another common philosophical designation for this being: as *subject*. The same holds for subjectivity or consciousness.

How, then, does he want to thematize this being by designating it as Dasein? For now, let us say only: he wants to thematize it with reference to Being—as the "*Da*" (there, place) of "*Sein*"—as the place of questioning about Being.

To return to the structural connection[1] on which Heidegger wants to focus, here is how he formulates it. "Asking this question, as a mode of *Being* of a being, is itself essentially determined by that about which it asks—by Being" (BT 7/6–7). This is to say that the asking is not simply distinct from that which is asked about but, rather, that the two sides of the question are intrinsically connected. Indeed, they are so connected that the very deployment of the question (that is, the "asking" in the full sense) already requires a certain "answering" of it, thus disrupting the simple opposition. Heidegger mentions that one might consider this a vicious circle: in order to determine the meaning of Being, in order even to deploy the question transparently, one must explicate the *Being* of Dasein, which one can do only if one knows already the meaning of Being. Heidegger's answer, of course, is: indeed, in a sense, one does already know the meaning of Being, even if only in a vague, average way. Heidegger then finally focuses on the structural connection: "'Circular reasoning' does not occur in the question of the meaning of Being. Rather, there is a remarkable 'relatedness backward and forward' of what is asked about (Being) [*Sein*] to questioning as a mode of Being of a being" (BT 8/7). Does this mean, then, that Dasein has a certain priority that entitles it to serve as the exemplary being? Though Heidegger grants that a certain priority has announced itself, he insists that Dasein's priority has *not yet* been demonstrated.

Section 3: The Ontological Priority of the Question of Being

What does this title mean? The question of Being has priority. But what kind of priority? A priority in the order of grounding. That is, the questioning about Being is the discipline that grounds other kinds of questioning. But why an "*ontological* priority"? Because what this discipline most directly grounds is all other ontological questioning, all other ontologies. Thus to say that the question of Being has ontological priority amounts to saying that the discipline in which this question is worked out constitutes *fundamental ontology*.

Within the introduction as a whole, section 3 (which exhibits this priority) may be regarded as a supplement or positive counterpart to section 1. Like section 1, it shows how important it is to take up again the question of Being. More specifically, it shows that the question of Being underlies the entire edifice of knowledge to such an extent that perplexity regarding the meaning of Being (as provided by section 1) must eventually spread to all scientific knowledge. Even more specifically, every science presupposes a demarcation of the *region* of beings to which it is directed, thus *also* a fixing of the basic structure of that region

---

1. Ed. note: The discussion that follows picks up on what begins at page 15 and concerns the connection between *Ausarbeitung*, what is meant by Dasein, and now the movement of the questioning.

by means of certain basic concepts. Initially, this is done "roughly and naïvely" in terms of our prescientific experience. But in the course of scientific research, the basic concepts of a science get brought into question by the results of that research, *and* it is precisely then that the most important kind of development takes place. Heidegger writes: "The real 'movement' of the sciences takes place in the revision of these basic concepts, a revision which is more or less radical and transparent with regard to itself. A science's level of development is determined by the extent to which it is *capable* of a crisis in its basic concepts" (BT 9/9).

Especially in the wake of such crises, the need is seen for a genuine *grounding* of science. Grounding means: a rigorous, ontological determination of those beings to which the science is directed—that is, a determination of those beings with regard to their Being, in such a way that the basic concepts of the science get genuinely established, in contrast to the rough and naïve way in which they first arise. Heidegger describes this grounding or laying of a foundation thus: "Laying the foundations for the sciences in this way is different in principle from the kind of 'logic' limping along behind, investigating the status of some science as it chances to find it, in terms of its 'method.' Such laying of foundations is productive logic in the sense that it leaps ahead, so to speak, into a particular realm of Being, discloses it for the first time in its constitutive Being, and makes the acquired structures available to the positive sciences as transparent directives for inquiry" (BT 10/9–10). Such a grounding discipline (productive logic) corresponds to what Husserl calls a regional ontology.

The crucial point is that such regional ontologies need themselves to be grounded in a discipline in which the meaning of Being as such is considered: "It is true that ontological inquiry is indeed more primordial than the ontical inquiry of the positive sciences. But it remains naïve and opaque if its investigations into the Being of beings leaves the meaning of Being in general undiscussed" (BT 11/10). So regional ontologies need to be grounded in a fundamental ontology. Thus we see that the task of grounding, intrinsic to the character of scientific research, points to the task of taking up the question of the meaning of Being.

Section 4: The Ontical Priority of the Question of Being

Presumably this is to be contrasted to the "Ontological Priority of the Question of Being" dealt with in section 3, a priority that turned out to consist in the fact that the discipline devoted to the question of Being *grounds* all other (regional) ontologies. However, on the surface, it is not clear why section 4 has this title. Despite the title, it is devoted primarily to demonstrating the priority *not* of the question of Being but of Dasein.

What is the general character of the priority that Dasein is here shown (or at least anticipated) to have? Dasein is shown to have priority over other beings by virtue of its peculiar relation to Being. In general, this relation is a *questioning comportment* to Being. This relation has two sides corresponding to the distinction between (I) Dasein's own Being and (II) the Being of beings other than Dasein. Heidegger deals with each in turn.

I. Why, then, is Dasein chosen as the exemplary being? The most direct answer provided by Heidegger is that it is because of the distinctive constitution of this being. Initially, Heidegger focuses especially on the peculiar and distinctive comportment of Dasein to its Being. What is especially important is that Dasein's comportment to itself is *not* a comporting of one being to another (with which it is or becomes identical). It is not, for example, like a comportment of the subject to itself (as in the case of *Cogito* or Spirit). Rather, Dasein's comportment to itself is a comportment *to its Being*.

But *how* does Dasein comport itself to its Being? What kind of comportment is this? Let me mention only two descriptions.

Heidegger says Dasein is "ontically distinctive in that in its Being [*Sein*] this being [*Seinenden*] itself is concerned *about* its very Being [*Sein*]" (BT 12/11). (Alternatively translated: "In its Being, its very Being is at issue for this being.") This says: Dasein is such that its Being is *at issue* (of concern). That is, Dasein is such that it comports itself to its Being *as* something at issue. That is, Dasein's comportment (to its Being) is permeated with the peculiar character of being "at issue." But to be at issue is to be problematic, questionable in the most concrete sense. *And so*: Dasein's comportment to its Being is a *questioning* comportment, not in the sense that Dasein continually raises explicit questions about its Being but rather in the sense that the questionableness of its Being is continually being *lived through*.

Heidegger continues by saying: "It belongs to the constitution of the Being of Dasein that in its Being it has a relation of Being to this Being [*dass es in seinem Sein zu diesem Sein ein Seinsverhältnis hat*]" (BT 12/11). Here Heidegger is saying that Dasein's Being is not something that it *merely has* (in some more or less indefinite sense of "possession"). That is, Dasein is not merely *in* its Being; rather, *in* its Being, it also (on the other hand) *relates itself to* that Being. More precisely, it relates to its Being in such a manner that its Being is *held at issue* for it—that is, held in question, held in a certain suspension. For example, a human being is not courageous in the same way that a desk is brown; rather, one's being-courageous is something constantly at issue, in every decision rather than just passively subsisting.

Heidegger says: "Dasein understands itself in its Being in some way and with some explicitness" [*Dasein versteht sich in irgendeiner Weise und Ausdrücklichkeit in seinem Sein*] (BT 12/11). Here Heidegger designates Dasein's comportment to its Being "understanding." It is especially important to observe what understanding is *not*: it is not an affair of thought or conceptual knowing, if for no other reason than that "distance" (detachment), which these words require, is lacking; it is not a relation of knowing between two beings but rather a relation (comportment) between a being (Dasein) and its Being.

Heidegger writes: "It is proper to this being that it be disclosed to itself with and through its Being" [*Diesem Seienden eignet, daßmit und durch sein Sein dieses ihm selbst erschlossen ist*] (BT 12/11). So we have still another designation of Dasein's relatedness to its Being: Dasein is such that its Being is *disclosed*. That is, the relatedness is one of disclosedness [*Erschlossenheit*].

Thus Dasein's relatedness to its Being has been characterized in four ways.

1. As Dasein's questioning comportment to its Being.
2. As Dasein's having its Being as something held at issue for it.
3. As Dasein's understanding its Being.
4. As Dasein's having its Being disclosed.

That is, in the very constitution of Dasein there is:

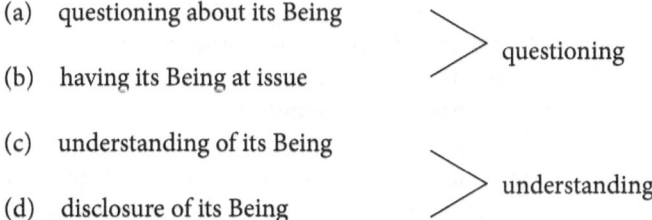

(a) questioning about its Being

(b) having its Being at issue

       questioning

(c) understanding of its Being

(d) disclosure of its Being

       understanding

If we put this together, it says: in Dasein, there is a preontological questioning of its Being in the full sense of questioning. That is to say, both a questioning comportment to its Being (having it at issue, calling it into question) **and** the correlative disclosure of its Being that such comportment presupposes (and in which it can also issue). This means, then, that in Dasein, the questioning of Being is already constituted, already (preontologically) contained, which is to say that Dasein's very comportment to its Being is a preontological form of questioning about its Being. This means, in turn, that explicit, philosophical questioning about the Being of Dasein will be merely a "developed" form of that comportment that Dasein always already has to its Being.

Heidegger consolidates these results terminologically with the term *existence*. At the end of the second paragraph in section 4, he focuses on one of the four characterizations; namely, that in terms of understanding when he writes "*Understanding of Being is itself a determinateness of Being of Dasein*"

[*Seinsverständnis ist selbst eine Seinsbestimmtheit des Daseins*] (BT 12/11). It is important to note that Dasein has a certain ontological determinateness, and it is precisely that determinateness ("structure") that is presented in the four characterizations. **But** this determinateness is *not* a matter of determinations (in the sense of properties or definite characteristics); that is, Dasein's essence is not a matter of it possessing a determinate character (a "what") or certain determinate features. Rather, its essence (its peculiar determinateness) lies in its peculiar comportment to its Being—that "it has its Being to be." Heidegger expresses this by saying: Dasein *exists*. Or, the Being of Dasein is *Existence* [*Existenz*].

In this connection, Heidegger draws an important distinction between:

- Existentiell understanding, which means concrete, ontic self-understanding in one's own particular situation. In this regard, he says: "We come to terms with the question of existence always only through existing itself" (BT 12/11). Heidegger also insists that such understanding does not necessarily require theoretical insight into ontological structures.
- Existential understanding, which means an understanding of the nexus of the ontological structures of existence, and that is the understanding of existentiality.

II. Dasein's comportment to the Being of other beings.

This second stage is perhaps most clearly indicated by the marginal note to the statement we cited earlier: "*Understanding of Being is itself a determinateness of Being of Dasein.*" The note reads (in part): "*Sein aber hier nicht nur als Sein des Menschen (Existenz)*" [But here Being not only as the Being of the human being (existence)] (BT 11). The point here is this: Dasein's preontological questioning comportment is a comportment not only to its own Being but also to the Being of beings other than Dasein. This comportment is attested to by the fact of science, that in science (at least initially) such comportment (with its inherent understanding) serves to allow Dasein to bring *into question* a certain region of beings with regard to their Being and delineate and conceptualize such a region.

We should take note of how Heidegger introduces this issue. "Sciences and disciplines are ways of Being of Dasein in which Dasein comports itself toward beings which it need not be itself. But to Dasein there belongs essentially: Being in a world. Thus the understanding of Being that belongs to Dasein pertains with equal primordiality both to an understanding of something like a 'world' and to the understanding of the Being of those beings which have become accessible within the world" (BT 13/12). This points ahead to the way the issue will be developed in the Analytic: Dasein's understanding of the Being of beings other than itself is somehow connected with an understanding of *world*, and thus it is in relation to the problem of the world that Dasein's understanding-comportment to such beings will be investigated.

Now we can bring these two stages together. Heidegger has shown that within the constitution of Dasein, there lies a preontological understanding of Being *as such*. This, then, means that the philosophical development of the question of being (that is, fundamental ontology) requires simply that this preontological questioning of Being be explicitly (theoretically) developed. That is to say, fundamental ontology develops the understanding of Being that is always already there in Dasein. As Heidegger says at the end of section 4: "But then the question of Being is nothing else than the radicalization of an essential tendency of Being that belongs to Dasein itself, namely, of the pre-ontological understanding of Being" (BT 15/13).

To come back finally to the title of section 4, what the section primarily shows is the ontical priority of Dasein, its priority over other beings. Why does Dasein have such priority? Because of its questioning comportment to Being—that is, because Dasein *is* (preontologically) the question(ing) of Being. In this sense, then, showing the ontical priority of the question of Dasein and showing the ontical priority of the question of Being amount to the same thing. Dasein *is* the question of Being—preontologically.

Thus one can say: in Dasein (in its very constitution) there is a preontological questioning of its Being. Hence in Dasein, the question of Being is already constituted, already (preontologically) contained. That is, Dasein's very comportment to its Being is a preontological form of questioning about Being. This means, in turn: explicit, philosophical questioning about the Being of Dasein will be merely a "developed" form of that comportment that Dasein always already has to its Being. In short, Dasein, in its very constitution, *is* preontologically the question(ing) of Being. This is why it is the exemplar being—*and not*, in the end, because the meaning of Being can be read off from it. There are two marginal notes that confirm this:

1. "But the meaning of Being is not read off from this being."
2. "Dasein is not an instance of beings [*von Seienden*] for the representational abstraction of Being, but rather the place [or site, *die Stätte*] of the understanding of Being."[2]

Conclusion

This relation of Dasein to its own Being is anything but simple, and it cannot be readily expressed in traditional concepts or in accord with traditional logic. To indicate its complexity, let us go back to a statement in section 4. "Thus it is

---

2. Ed. note: The two references noted here occur in the *Gesamtausgabe* edition of *Sein und Zeit* only. The first appears on p. 10 (p. 6 of the English translation), the second appears on p. 11 (p. 8 of the English translation).

constitutive of the Being of Dasein's Being [*Seinsverfassung des Daseins*] to have, in its very Being, a relation of Being [*Seinsverhältnis*] to this Being" (BT 12/11). The word *Being* occurs four times, and each time, it functions differently. We can see this if we simply ask: What (according to this statement) is Dasein's *Being*? Answers:

1. Dasein is *in its Being*; namely, in *being something* (for example, courageous). So Dasein's Being is simply what Dasein in a particular instance *is*.
2. But in its Being, it is at the same time *related* to its Being. So Dasein's Being is that to which it *relates*. That is, it is one term of the relation (over against Dasein).
3. But that relation is one of Being. That is to say, Dasein's Being consists in relating itself to its Being. That is, Dasein's Being is the *relation itself*.
4. The point is that Dasein's being is all of these things, and that is why Heidegger refers here to Dasein's *Seinsverfassung*.[3]

One thing is clear: traditional ontological categories cannot adequately express this *Seinsverfassung*.

Section 4 has established that Dasein is the exemplary being, which is to say that fundamental ontology is to proceed by way of interrogating Dasein; that is, by way of a certain regress to that being that modern philosophy calls *subject*. In this regard, it is helpful to refer to a discussion in *Basic Problems of Phenomenology* (part 1, chap. 1). Here, Heidegger begins with Kant's thesis about Being and shows how, in Kant, that thesis leads back to the problem of perception. That is, the determination of Being involves (for Kant) a *regress to the subject*. Heidegger goes on to point out that such a regress is characteristic not only of modern philosophy but also of ancient philosophy. He refers to the Greek regress to λόγος and to ψυχή. Then he says that "all philosophy, in whatever way it may view the 'subject' and place it in the center of philosophical investigation, returns to the soul, mind, consciousness, subject, ego in clarifying the basic ontological phenomena" (BPP 103–4/73). Then Heidegger explains that the analysis of Dasein is precisely the attempt to carry out this same regress *but* in the most radical way. Hence he says it has "become clear that the ontology of Dasein represents the latent goal and constant and more or less evident demand of the whole development of Western philosophy" (BPP 106/75). Thus *Being and Time* (fundamental ontology) is proposed as the fulfillment of the whole development of philosophy since the Greeks.

---

3. Ed. note: A marginal note in the manuscript reads: "Anticipates three moments of temporality: a) past, b) future, c) present."

3. The Second Introduction to *Being and Time*

The Double Task in Working Out the Question of Being: The Method of the Investigation and Its Outline

Introduction

The project of *Being and Time* is to carry out a recovery (repetition, *Wiederholung*) of the question of the meaning of Being. In taking up this question—in developing fundamental ontology—everything depends on the preontological understanding of Being. That is, we can take up the question only because we always already operate with (live and move within) a certain vague, implicit understanding of Being (attested to by the fact that we understand something of what is meant when we use the forms of the word *being*).

In recovering the question of the meaning of Being, *Being and Time* is to repeat (carry out anew) a movement found in the Platonic dialogues—*the* philosophical move as such.

In the *Sophist*: the move to a "battle of giants concerning Being"—or from the level of the storytellers about beings to the level of the Parmenidean discourse on Being as such.

In the *Republic*: the movement of the ascent that goes even beyond Being (to that from which it becomes understandable).

It is because *Being and Time* is to repeat this Platonic move that it can begin (appropriately) in the midst of a Platonic dialogue.

Being and Time is to repeat *also* another movement that has, from Plato on, always taken place within the compass of the "ontological" move: in asking about Being so as to determine its meaning, *Being and Time* is to interrogate *a* being—to turn to a certain kind of being—namely, the being that has been called the human being or subject. It is to this being that all philosophy has turned, ever since Plato, whether it spoke of ψυχή, λόγος, subject, consciousness, ego, spirit, or whatever.

So, in a sense, Heidegger is just repeating this classical move—turning to the human being as that being from which the meaning of Being can somehow be discussed or determined (in contrast to all others: animals, plants, stones, gods).

And yet Heidegger is carrying out this move to the human being *in the most radical way*—in such a way as to bring the entire development of philosophy since the Greeks to its fulfillment. He is carrying this out in the most radical way precisely by thematizing the human being *as Dasein*; that is, as the being whose fundamental mode of comportment is that of relating to its Being as *at issue*, of having its Being at issue, always at stake; that is, as the being in whose comportment the question(ing) of being is already (preontologically) contained; that is, as the being that *is* preontologically the question(ing) of Being. Thus when philosophy comes on the scene, when one sets out to develop fundamental ontology, it is a matter merely of taking up and developing that questioning about Being that Dasein always already (concretely) is.

Heidegger expresses this relatedness that Dasein has to its Being by saying: Dasein *exists*. Indeed—to the extent that one can continue to use the classical concept of essence—one can say that this relatedness, existence, is the essence of Dasein. In chapter 1, Heidegger thus says: "*The 'essence' [Wesen] of Dasein lies in its existence [Existenz]*" (BT 42/41).

The title of the second introduction reads: "The Double Task in Working Out the Question of Being: The Method of the Investigation and Its Outline." This title designates quite precisely the contents of introduction 2. In sections 5 and 6, Heidegger outlines the twofold task of *Being and Time*. The first part (§5) consists of the analytic of Dasein, which is to lead to the working-out of the question of Being in reference to time. This constitutes what Heidegger projected as part 1 of *Being and Time*. The second part (§6) consists of the task of sketching out the destruction of the history of ontology. This constitutes what he projected as part 2 of *Being and Time*. Section 7 presents the phenomenological method that the investigation is to employ. Section 8 presents the design, which is to say the outline of the entire investigation.

One might be tempted to regard this articulation (the basic one in *Being and Time*) as merely reproducing the traditional partition of philosophy into the systematic and historical. However, this would not capture the sense of the articulation Heidegger is proposing, as one can readily see from *History of the Concept of Time*. The question of Being "compels us to enter into an original arena of research which *precedes* the traditional partition of philosophical work into historiological and systematic knowledge. . . . This amounts to saying that the manner of research is *neither* historiological *nor* systematic, but instead *phenomenological*" (HCT 9–10/7).

For the moment, then, leave open the question of the sense of this articulation, of how the two parts projected for *Being and Time* would belong together. We should suggest merely that this sense has to do with the question of *phenomenology*. That is, the sense of the basic articulation of *Being and Time* is bound up with its methodological character as phenomenology.

Section 5: The Ontological Analysis of Dasein as Exposing the Horizon for an Interpretation of the Meaning of Being in General

In section 5, Heidegger sketches the first part of this twofold task by outlining the three main undertakings it involves, which corresponds to the three divisions projected for part 1.

But before developing the outline, he takes up the question of access to Dasein and of the horizon within which Dasein is to be approached. These are, of course, questions that bear on the character of the phenomenology operative in *Being and Time*. Heidegger raises the question: What is the appropriate way of access to Dasein? He goes on to indicate why this is a peculiarly difficult question—that is, why there is a peculiar difficulty involved in gaining appropriate access to Dasein. Heidegger formulates the difficulty thus: ontically Dasein is that which is closest (we *are* it)—and yet *for just this reason*, it is ontologically that which is farthest from us—that is, precisely because we are so close to Dasein (we *are* it—so there is an absolute proximity), it is what is *ontologically* most remote, what is least understood ontologically. Or, to put it the other way around: Dasein is what is most misunderstood ontologically—that is, Dasein has a tendency to misunderstand its own Being—that is to say, in Dasein, there is a tendency toward the concealment of its Being. What form does this concealment take concretely? Dasein's Being tends to get concealed (misunderstood, covered over) by being understood in reference to beings within-the-world. "Rather, in accordance with the kind of Being belonging to it, Dasein tends to understand its own Being [*Sein*] in terms of [literally: from, *aus*, in terms of] *the* being [*Seienden*] to which it is essentially, continually, and most closely comports itself—the 'world'" (BT 15/15–16). We should note two things here. First, Heidegger puts "world" in quotation marks as if it were simply the beings to which Dasein comports itself. *But* in his analysis of world (chap. 3), he will show that these are not the same. Rather, the difference will be decisive for the entire analysis. Second, Heidegger later attaches a note that says "*hier aus dem Vorhandenen*," which should not be translated as "i.e., here in terms of what is objectively present." In general, Heidegger is saying: Dasein tends to understand itself in terms of things (beings other than Dasein) and so misunderstands itself *as* Dasein. Here, of course, he is only indicating this in a preliminary way (as preunderstanding). Later, it will have to be demonstrated phenomenologically.

Because of Dasein's tendency to conceal its Being, there is a *problem* of gaining access to Dasein. That is, one cannot just go about understanding Dasein in a straightforward and uncritical way. Said differently, one cannot just go about understanding Dasein in terms of whatever categories happen to be available, one cannot apply to Dasein just any idea of Being, however self-evident it may seem. Rather than imposing something on Dasein, one must undertake to bring

Dasein to *show itself*. One must try to gain access to Dasein in just such a way as to bring Dasein to *show itself*. Heidegger: "The manner of access and interpretation must instead be chosen in such a way that this being can show itself in itself and from itself [*an ihm selbst von ihm selbst*]" (BT 16/16). Heidegger continues by specifying what, in the first instance, this requires: this way "should show this being as it is *initially* [*zunächst*: first in a double sense: first of all, above all; at first, to begin with, at the start of the analysis] *and for the most part*—in its average everydayness" (BT 16/16).

Thus Heidegger introduces everydayness as the *horizon* within which the Existential Analytic will proceed—at least initially. We should note the following: the analytic is placed within this horizon *not* because of some priority given to the ordinary and practical *but* as a way of ensuring that the analytic proceeds by letting Dasein show itself, *rather than* by imposing some special point of view on Dasein. (But we should also note that Heidegger will later indicate that the choice of this horizon is not in fact self-evident, and in section 71, he will return to investigate it.)

Next, Heidegger indicates two important features of this analytic of Dasein. First, it is *incomplete*. That is, it does not attempt to provide a complete ontology of Dasein such as would be necessary to ground a philosophical anthropology. On the contrary, "the analytic of Dasein thus understood is wholly oriented toward the guiding task of working out the question of Being" (BT 17/17). Second, it is *preliminary*, and thus leads over to two additional stages.

The structure of *Being and Time* is rigorously articulated. As originally projected, it was to consist of two parts; each part was to contain three divisions. Division One of part 1 is titled "The Preparatory Fundamental Analysis of Dasein." We can now look at the three main undertakings or stages corresponding to the three divisions projected for part 1 of *Being and Time*, and we should first note three points.

First, the analysis is carried out within the horizon of *everydayness*. It is set within this horizon to let Dasein show itself as we first encounter it and as it appears for the most part. In this way, Heidegger wants to avoid imposing some special point of view on Dasein.

Second, the concept of *horizon* plays an important role in all three divisions. This is a phenomenological concept corresponding to Husserl's outer horizon. As we will see, it is intimately linked to Heidegger's concepts of understanding and truth. For now, the horizon of something is that within which that thing (or concept) becomes understandable; that is, that from which, by recourse to which, by reference to which, on the basis of which, something is brought to light, disclosed. So in Division One, everydayness is that from which the Being of Dasein becomes to some degree understandable—though only preliminarily. For example, Dasein's relation to others (its *Mit-sein*) is considered (in Division One) only as it occurs in everydayness. The self as it occurs in everydayness is the "they-self" (*das Man*)—in contrast to the authentic self.

Third, Heidegger specifies the limited (preliminary) character of Division One: "It only brings out the Being of this being without interpreting its meaning" (BT 17/17). So: the analysis in Division One only determines the *Being* of Dasein—not the *meaning* of the Being of Dasein. We will see toward the end of Division One that the Being of Dasein is determined as *care* (*Sorge*).

Division Two is titled "Dasein and Temporality," and we should also note three points here. First, the analysis takes a further step: it determines the *meaning* of the Being of Dasein—*as* temporality. "The meaning of the Being [*Sein*] of that being [*Seienden*] we call Dasein will prove to be [will be pointed to as] *temporality*" (BT 17/17). In other words, temporality will prove to be the *horizon* of the understanding and interpretation of the Being of Dasein—that is, temporality will prove to be that from which (in reference to which) the Being of Dasein becomes understandable in a fundamental way.

Second, once temporality is disclosed as the meaning of the Being of Dasein, then the understanding and interpretation of the Being of Dasein must be carried through—that is, there must be a repetition of the preliminary analysis at this more fundamental level (that of temporality). That is to say, the various moments that make up the Being of Dasein—as disclosed in Division One—must be reinterpreted as modes of temporality. "We must repeat our interpretation of those structures of Dasein that shall have been indicated in a preliminary way—this time as modes of temporality" (BT 17/17). So the analysis of such moments (structures) must be repeated in order to reinterpret these moments as modes of temporality.

Third, however, not even the disclosure of temporality and the repetition this requires suffice for providing an *answer* to the question of the meaning of Being. "But with this interpretation of Dasein as temporality the answer is not yet given to the guiding question, that of the meaning of Being in general. But the basis for obtaining this answer is prepared" (BT 17/17).

So division 3 must go beyond the interpretation of Dasein and temporality to that of Being (as such) and time: "We must show that *time* is that from out of which [*von wo aus*, in regard to which, on the basis of which] Dasein tacitly understands and interprets something like Being at all. Time must be brought to light and genuinely grasped as the horizon of every understanding and interpretation of Being. For this to become clear we need a *primordial explication of time as the horizon for the understanding of Being, in terms of temporality as the Being of Dasein which understands Being*" (BT 17/17). Heidegger stresses that the conception of time as the horizon for the understanding of Being must be very different from the traditional concept of time (which has persisted—basically unchanged—since Aristotle). Heidegger points out that in fact such a concept of time (as the horizon for the understanding of Being) has been operative, tacitly and naïvely *throughout* the history of ontology: specifically, time has functioned as the criterion for discriminating various realms of beings (e.g., temporal/eternal)—thus for determining modes of Being. This means, then, that Being itself—and not only beings "in time"—has a temporal character. To mark this distinction terminologically, Heidegger introduces the word *Temporalität*, in distinction from *Zeitlichkeit* (*temporale/zeitlich*).

Heidegger then sums up the task of division 3: "We shall call the originary [*ürsprunglich*] determination of the meaning of Being and its characters and modes on the basis [*aus*, from out of] of time [*Zeit*] its *temporal* [*temporale*] determination. The fundamental ontological task of the interpretation of Being [*Sein*] as such thus includes in itself the working out [*Herausarbeitung*] of the *temporality of Being* [*Temporalität des Seins*]. In the exposition of the problematic of temporality, the concrete answer to the question of the meaning of Being is first given" (BT 19/18).

We can thus distinguish among three forms of time/temporality.

1. The time of beings ("worldly time"). This has been the traditional concept since Aristotle.
2. *Zeitlichkeit*: temporality as the meaning of the Being of Dasein.
3. *Temporalität*: temporality as the meaning of Being as such.

However, division 3 was never published. It is uncertain how much of it was actually written (there are rumors that Heidegger destroyed it). For understanding what division 3 might have involved, the most important source is *Basic Problems of Phenomenology* (summer semester 1927). At the very beginning, there is a note that reads: "A new elaboration of Division III of Part I of *Being and Time*." Indeed, in part 2 of *Basic Problems of Phenomenology*, Heidegger takes up and develops the question of *die Temporalität des Seins*, though he does not carry it through to completion. *Basic Problems of Phenomenology* is designated as a *new* elaboration. It is *new* (in contrast to what *Being and Time* proposed) in that it proceeds *not* from the outcome of Division Two but by way of an extensive discussion of four traditional theses about Being. It is then from (through the critique or destruction of) these theses that Heidegger moves to the proper task of division 3, which is to say, through a more originary appropriation of the history of Western philosophy. Here again, one sees how any simple separation between "historical" and "systematic" or analytic is precluded. In the shape that it was to have assumed in *Basic Problems of Phenomenology*, division 3 would have dealt with four basic problems, developing each by reference to *die Temporalität des Seins*:

1. The problem of the ontological difference, the difference between Being and beings. Here it would be shown how temporality makes it possible to distinguish between Being and beings.

2. The problem of the basic articulations of Being, proceeding from the traditional articulations into essence and existence.
3. The problem of the possible modifications (modalities) of being. This is developed through the critique of the modern thesis that the fundamental modalities are *res exstensa* and *res cogitans*. But behind this is Aristotle: the manifold senses of Being as expressed, for example, in the categories (cf. Heidegger's lectures on Aristotle's *Metaphysics*).
4. The problem of the truth character of Being. This is developed through a critique of logical theories of the copula (Hobbes, Mill, and Lotze). But here, too, it is especially Aristotle that is behind this (see *Metaphysics* Θ 10).

Section 6: The Task of Destroying the History of Ontology

Heidegger introduces a new reflexive dimension into the question of Being, which is focused in the word *Geschichtlichkeit, historicity,* the historical character of Dasein (from *Geschehen*, to happen). Heidegger introduces this dimension by anticipating the course that the Existential Analytic will follow: in the course of the analytic, Dasein (the questioner and the questioned) will eventually get understood in its temporality. In turn, it will be shown that temporality makes possible historicity, which is Dasein's "historical character." Thus at that point in the analytic, there is an essential reflection back from Dasein as questioned (and thus exhibited *as* historical) *to* Dasein as questioner (as hence also historical). That is, if Dasein, in the very constitution of its Being, is historical, then the questions that Dasein (as questioner) poses are essentially (and not just accidentally) historical. Thus if the question—the questioning—of the meaning of Being is to be genuinely worked out (made transparent to itself, allowed to be genuinely reflexive), its historical character must be exhibited, must be brought to light. Here we see more clearly how "systematic" and "historical" belong together; that is why fundamental ontology is situated prior to their separation. This is the task that was projected for part 2.

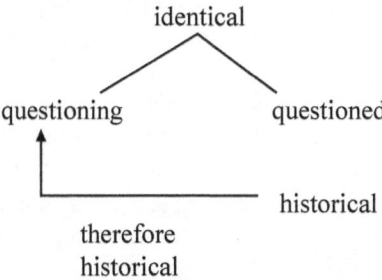

Again, this task of bringing to light the historical character of the question of the meaning of Being is the task Heidegger projected for part 2 of *Being and*

Time. But what, precisely, is the character of this task? What kind of exhibiting is called for? The task, according to Heidegger, needs to be seen over against (in its opposition to) a certain *concealment*. This concealment parallels at the level of history that concealment into which Dasein tends to fall by understanding itself on the basis of things in the world. More specifically, at the level of history, Dasein falls prey to tradition: "The tradition that hereby gains dominance makes what it 'transmits' so little accessible, that proximally and for the most part it covers it over instead. What has been handed down is handed over to obviousness; it bars access to those primordial 'sources' from out of which the traditional categories and concepts were in part genuinely drawn. The tradition even makes us forget such a provenance altogether. Indeed, it makes us wholly incapable of even understanding that such a return is necessary. The tradition uproots the historicity of Dasein" (BT 21/20–21).

The task is then to loosen up the hardened tradition in order to get back to the original experiences in which the meaning of Being was first determined; that is, in order to take up the *question* of Being by repeating (*wiederholen*) the *questioning* in which it first emerged and was brought to light. That is to say, to destroy the concealment that has covered over what was established in that originary questioning. "If the question of Being is to achieve clarity regarding its own history, then a loosening of the sclerotic tradition and a dissolution of the concealments produced by it is necessary. We understand this task as the *destruction* of the traditional content of ancient ontology which is to be carried out along the *guidelines of the question of Being*. This destruction is based upon the primordial experiences in which the first, and subsequently guiding, determinations of being were gained" (BT 22/21–22).

Heidegger stresses that this destruction does *not* have the sense of shaking off the ontological tradition, to merely leave it behind. It is a matter not of rejecting what was accomplished in the ontological tradition but rather of *recapturing* (*wiederholen*) it—and taking up "the positive possibilities in that tradition" (BT 22/22). What is to be destroyed in the destruction is the *concealment*, the covering over of genuine sources. The destruction, as Heidegger projects it, would involve three stages.

The first stage is devoted to Kant's theory of schematism. Why? Because it is only here that the problem of Being and the phenomenon of time have been brought together thematically. Nevertheless, Kant failed to gain access to this problematic for two reasons. First, he neglected the ontological side (that is, the problem of Being), or, more specifically, he failed to give an ontological analytic of the subject. That is to say, he failed to determine the Being of the subject. Second, his analysis of time remained oriented toward the traditional concept of time. So on both sides, there were *traditional* elements that served to conceal the fundamental domain of this problematic. Heidegger's task is to destroy this concealment so as to say what, because of it, Kant left unsaid.

The second stage is devoted to Descartes's *cogito sum*. Why? Because in failing to raise the question of the Being of the subject, Kant was proceeding in the same way that had already been established by Descartes, which is a carrying on of the Cartesian spirit. Despite the radical beginning that Descartes made with the *cogito, ergo sum*, he left undetermined the meaning of the Being of the *sum*. That is, he did not investigate the Being of the *res cogitans*. More precisely, he merely applied medieval ontology to his concept of *res cogitans* (which is equivalent to the subject). He took *res cogitans* to be *ens creatum*. He was unaware of the way in which createdness had been determined in ancient thought—as made or produced (*Herstellen*, ποίησις—see Plato's *Timaeus*). This is to say that Descartes was unaware that he was simply taking over a conception that, though determined in an originary way by the Greeks, had been thoroughly concealed.

The third stage is devoted to ancient thought. Why? To expose the ancient concept of being *and* its fundamental connection with the concept of time. This ancient conception of Being is oriented to the world or, more precisely, nature, *and* this conception is based on an understanding of Being in terms of time. This is attested to by the fact that the meaning of Being is designated by the Greeks as παρουσία, which Heidegger translates as *Anwesenheit* (presence). This alludes to the fact that the meaning of Being was here understood by reference to the Present. What is remarkable is that the Greeks interpreted Being in this way *without* really being aware of the fundamental ontological function being performed by time. On the contrary, they took time as itself merely a being and undertook to thematize it in its Being. That is, having (tacitly) understood Being through reference to time, they then set out to understand time in terms of this concept of Being. Thus Heidegger proposes to destroy this concealment that was operative, specifically through an interpretation of Aristotle's essay on time.

However, we should note that none of these divisions of part 2 ever appeared as such, but most of what Heidegger proposed is carried out in other works. Through his encounter with Kant in *Kant and the Problem of Metaphysics*. Nota bene: there Heidegger concludes by presenting *Being and Time* as a *Wiederholung* of what Kant undertook in *The Critique of Pure Reason*. For Descartes, compare *What Is a Thing?* and "Die Zeit des Weltbildes" ("The Age of the World Picture"). For ancient thought, see *Basic Problems of Phenomenology* for a discussion of the ancient conception of Being in relation to *Herstellen* and *Anwesenheit*; also, he gives there an interpretation of Aristotle's treatment on time.

Section 7: The Phenomenological Method of Investigation

In referring to the project of *Being and Time* as *fundamental ontology*, Heidegger does not mean to designate one philosophical discipline alongside others—for example, ontology as part of metaphysics, alongside logic, ethics, and so on—rather, because of the radicality with which fundamental ontology takes up the question of being, it cannot simply be submitted to a traditional delimitation of philosophical disciplines. On the contrary, it puts in question all these delimitations and so must itself be redetermined from the ground up. "In using the term ontology we do not specify any particular philosophical discipline standing in relation to others" (BT 27/26).

A major phase of this redetermination has to do with understanding the character of fundamental ontology *as phenomenology*. This character was already alluded to in the phrase "*concrete* working-out" and even more in Heidegger's insistence that the manner of access to Dasein must be such that Dasein can show itself in itself and from itself. In section 7, this becomes an explicit theme: "With the guiding question of the meaning of Being the investigation arrives at the fundamental question of philosophy in general. The treatment of this question is *phenomenological*. With this term the treatise dictates for itself neither a 'standpoint' nor a 'direction,' because phenomenology is neither of these and can never be as long as it understands itself. The expression 'phenomenology' signifies primarily a *concept of method*" (BT 27/26).

So *phenomenology* names the *method* of fundamental ontology. Heidegger says immediately what this method is, and from this statement, it becomes clear why phenomenology does not represent some particular standpoint or some specific philosophical direction. "The term 'phenomenology' expresses a maxim that can be formulated: 'To the things [matter] themselves' [*zu den Sachen selbst*]. It is opposed to all free-floating constructions and accidental findings; it is also opposed to taking over concepts only seemingly demonstrated." (BT 27–28/26). In *Basic Problems of Phenomenology*, Heidegger says phenomenology is simply the method of scientific philosophy as such (that is, required by the very concept of a scientific, rigorous philosophy). In other words, it is just the demand to proceed by reference to what is being investigated rather than in terms of preconceptions, empty speculation, or random observations.

However, there is in play from the outset a much richer background of phenomenological thought than Heidegger directly indicates in *Being and Time*. What we have in *Being and Time*—both in the account in section 7 and in the deployment of phenomenology throughout *Being and Time*—is the "outcome" of Heidegger's appropriation of Husserl's phenomenology. This is clearest in *History of the Concept of Time*, which moves directly from the discussion of phenomenology to analyses that almost coincide with those in *Being and Time*.

Heidegger's Account of Phenomenology (Marburg Lectures)

Heidegger always gave priority to Husserl's first major work *Logical Investigations* (1900–1901). This he calls "the initial breakthrough of phenomenological research," "*the basic book of phenomenology*" (HCT 30/24). He cites Dilthey's description of *Logical Investigations* as the first great scientific advance in philosophy since Kant's *Critique of Pure Reason*. It is primarily to the phenomenology of *Logical Investigations* that Heidegger's work is related in a positive way. He profoundly appropriates the insights and analyses of this work. However, there are major disagreements with the direction Husserl took in his later thought, although even there, Heidegger admired Husserl's concrete analyses.

This account begins with the famous injunction "*zu den Sachen selbst*," which says that phenomenology is to attend to the things themselves. We could easily take this to mean that what is required is that we just look at things, behold them; we could take it as prescribing a kind of immediacy and passivity. But Heidegger warns against this: "We must free ourselves from the prejudice that, because phenomenology calls upon us to apprehend the things themselves, these things must be apprehended all at once, without any preparation. Rather, the movement toward the things themselves is a long and involved process which, before anything else, has to remove the prejudices which obscure them" (HCT 36-37/29). Phenomenology has to make its way to the things themselves, to bring them to show themselves by clearing away the concealments.

Heidegger's account of phenomenology in *History of the Concept of Time* begins with intentionality. This is the first of the three "decisive discoveries" that he discusses (along with categorial intuition and the original sense of the a priori). I deal primarily with intentionality and mention only a few points in connection with the other two "discoveries."

I. *Intentionality*

In the most general terms, intentionality is the structure of lived experience. To say that experience is intentional means that every experience, every psychic comportment directs itself toward something, is a directing-itself-toward. If, like Husserl (but unlike Heidegger), we retain the concept of consciousness, then to say that consciousness is intentional means every consciousness is a consciousness *of*. In the account of intentionality given in *Basic Problems of Phenomenology* (pp. 80-94/58-67), Heidegger discusses two misinterpretations, and by correcting these, he shows what intentionality essentially is. This account closely parallels the account in *History of the Concept of Time*.

The first misinterpretation is suggested by common sense. It takes intentionality as a relation existing between two existing things, a psychic subject and a physical object. Here the mistake lies in taking intentionality to be something that the subject comes to have only when *and* because an existing object turns up. That is, it is, in effect, assumed that the subject is first isolated (i.e., in itself lacks intentionality) and only subsequently comes into an intentional relation when an object happens to turn up. Over against this, Heidegger insists that the subject is in itself intentionally structured, which is to say intentionality is the way of the Being of the subject, the way in which it *is* as a subject.

> It is not the case that a perception first becomes intentional by having something physical enter into relation with the psychic, and that it would no longer be intentional if this reality did not exist. It is rather the case that perception, correct or deceptive, is in itself intentional. Intentionality is not a property which would accrue to perception and belong to it in certain instances. As perception, it is *intrinsically intentional*, regardless of whether the perceived is in reality on hand or not. Indeed, it is really only because perception as such is a directing-itself-toward something, because intentionality constitutes the very structure of comportment itself, that there can be anything like deceptive perception and hallucination. (HCT 40/31)

The second misinterpretation comes from nonphenomenological philosophy. This misinterpretation is expressed in a question: How can the subject with its intentional experiences, which relate only to the immanent sphere, escape this sphere and take up a relation to the existing (objective) world? That is, how do experiences and that to which they relate (subjective sensations and presentations within the sphere of subjectivity) get related to the objective? Experiences—Presentations (ideas)—object within the subject. Heidegger's response: the subject, precisely because of its intentional character, is *not* in the first place confined to a sphere of immanence (encapsulated inside) so that it would be necessary to ask how it can escape and reach outside. Heidegger says that if we proceed phenomenologically (i.e., set all theories out of action and attend to natural perception), it is manifest that perception directs itself to things at hand, *not* to sensations. That is, what I perceive are things, *not* sensations, representations, or images in my mind.

> Let us take a natural perception without any theory, without any preconceived opinion about the relationship of subject to object and other such matters, and let us interrogate this concrete perception in which we live, say, the perception of the window. Toward what does it direct itself in correspondence with the peculiar sense of direction of its intention? Toward what is the perceiving directed in conformity with the peculiar sense by which it is guided? In everyday behavior, say, in moving around in this room, taking a look around my environment, I perceive the wall and the window. To what am I directed in this perception? To sensations? Or, when I avoid what is perceived, am I turning aside from representational images and taking care not to fall out of these representational images and sensations into the courtyard of the university building?
>
> To say that I am in the first place oriented toward sensations is all just pure theory. In conformity with its sense of direction, perception is directed toward a being that is present. It intends this precisely as present and knows nothing at all about sensations that it is apprehending. (BPP 88/63)

Earlier, in *History of the Concept of Time*, he writes:

> We will not look at the perceiving but at the perceived, and in fact at the *perceived of this perception*. What is this?
>
> If I answer without prejudice, I say the chair itself. I see no "representations" of the chair, register no image of the chair, sense no sensations of the chair. I simply see *it*—in itself. This is the most immediate sense that perceiving offers. (HCT 48/37)

We should note that it is in the context of the discussion of intentionality that Heidegger first introduces in *Basic Problems of Phenomenology* the term *Dasein*. Heidegger introduces it as a more appropriate expression for what up to that point had been called the *subject*. Why is it more appropriate? Because *subject* too easily suggests the misleading distinction between inner and outer, that very distinction to be overcome by the concept of intentionality. Heidegger thus says: "With a sufficient interpretation of intentionality the traditional concept of subject and subjectivity becomes questionable" (BPP 91/65).

If we grant the interconnection (belonging-together) of *intentio* (the comporting to) and the *intentum* (that to which one comports), then the description must proceed in terms of such an interconnection. More specifically, the description of the *intentum* must proceed in terms of the way it is intended, which is to say, it is to be characterized in the "how of its being intended." In this connection, we need to consider that there are various ways of intending (types of representation) *and* correspondingly various ways in which the *intentum* can be given.

A. The object may be intended in *perception*. Then it is *bodily given*, there in its *bodily presence*.

B. It may be merely envisaged (*Vergegenwärtigung*) in memory or phantasy. Then, too, it is in a sense given, but without being bodily present. "I can now envisage the Weidenhauser bridge; I place myself before it, as it were. Thus the bridge is itself given. I intend the bridge itself and not an image of it, no fantasy, but it itself. And yet it is not bodily given to me. It would be bodily given if I go down the hill and place myself before the bridge itself. This means that what is itself given need not be bodily given, while conversely anything which is bodily given is itself given. *Bodily presence is a superlative mode of the self-givenness of a being*" (HCT 54/41).

C. It may be given in an image-consciousness (*Bildwahrnehmung*); for example, in the apprehension of a picture. Here the structure is quite different from the other two, as there is something bodily present (the picture), and yet I do not simply perceive the picture as though it were a thing; rather, I see through the picture to what is pictured. Heidegger notes here that this analysis is especially important because of modern philosophy's tendency to take the apprehension of the picture as a paradigm for all perception, whereas a very simple phenomenological analysis shows that there is a fundamental difference between perception and image-consciousness. "In simple perception, by contrast, in the simple apprehension of an object, nothing like an image-consciousness can be found. It goes against all the plain and simple findings about the simple apprehension of an object to interpret them as if I first perceive an image in my consciousness when I see that house there, as if an image-thing were first given and thereupon apprehended as imaging that house out there. There would thus be a subjective image within and that which is imaged outside, transcendent. Nothing of the sort is to be found" (HCT 56/42).

D. From all these intentions in which *intentum* is given (in one way or another) *empty intending* (presuming *vermeinen*, to mean) must be distinguished; for example, when I speak of something without in any way bringing it intuitively to mind. "We mean the things themselves and not images or representations of them, yet we do not have them intuitively given. In empty intending as well, the intended is itself directly and simply intended, but merely emptily, which means without any intuitive fulfillment. Intuitive fulfillment is found once again in simple envisaging; this indeed gives it the entity itself but does not give it bodily" (HCT 54/41).

We should note one additional point with regard to the general analysis of intentionality. There is a peculiar feature of experience, most notably of perception: its profile or adumbrational character. The perceptual object is always given from some perspective, in a particular adumbration. Nevertheless, I never intend simply a profile but always the thing as a whole through a profile or series of profiles.

At the end of the discussion of intentionality in *History of the Concept of Time*, Heidegger insists that intentionality is not an ultimate explanation of the psyche but only an initial approach. He insists that certain basic questions about intentionality remain unanswered despite its development in phenomenology.

> Intentionality is not an ultimate explanation of the psychic but an initial approach toward overcoming the uncritical application of traditionally defined realities such as the psychic, consciousness, continuity of lived experience, reason. But if such a task is implicit in this basic concept of phenomenology, then "intentionality" is the very last word to be used as a phenomenological slogan. Quite the contrary, it identifies that whose disclosure would allow phenomenology to find itself in its possibilities. It must therefore be flatly stated that what the belonging of the intentum to the intentio implies is obscure. How the being-intended of an entity is related to that entity remains puzzling. It is even questionable whether one may question in this way at all. (HCT 63/47)

When we circle back to *Being and Time*, we shall see how these questions can be dealt with only when the concept of intentionality is appropriated in the more fundamental context of the Dasein-analysis.

II. *Categorial Intuition*

This is the second of the "decisive discoveries." At the beginning, Heidegger indicates in general what this involves and then goes on to show how the problem arises and how it is worked out. He begins with the general definition of *intention*: simply apprehending the bodily given as it shows itself. Especially important here is that this definition leaves open the question of whether intuition must be sense-perception; that is, whether the only objects of intuition are sensible particulars or whether there are other kinds of intuition. It leaves it open because this is precisely what is at issue in the question of categorial intuition. Specifically, the discovery of categorial intuition demonstrates (a) that there is a simple apprehension of the categorial and not only of sensible particulars, and (b) that such apprehension is involved in ordinary perception; that is, that all lived experience involves categorial intuition.

There are three basic issues in this discussion.

The first is intentional fulfillment. To show how the problem of categorial intuition arises, Heidegger resumes and extends the discussion of intentionality. We have already begun to see that there are interconnections among different types of intentions (e.g., image-consciousness and perception). The most important kind of interconnection is that between an empty intention *and* the intentional fulfillment that it can undergo through one of the other types of intention. This sense of fulfillment is this: in the fulfilling intention, there is intuitively given (present) precisely that which is intended in the empty intention. That is, the empty intended and the intuited come into coincidence; for example, (1) the chair and (2) the picture on the wall hanging askew. Such a bringing-into-coincidence can also be called an act of *identification*. We can also say that through the identifying fulfillment, I obtain insight into the matter itself. Such an act of obtaining insight can be called *evidence* (*Evidenz*, rendered/rendering self-evident).

The second is truth. The phenomenological concept of truth is based on intentional analyses and more specifically on fulfillment. If there is a thoroughgoing fulfillment, then that means that there is a certain agreement demonstrated between what is presumed (merely "thought") *and* the intuited thing itself. That is, what gets demonstrated is a certain adequation between *intellectus* (thought) and *res* (thing). But this is simply the traditional definition of truth. Hence the phenomenological concept of truth: truth is the subsistence of the identity of the presumed and the intuited. Thus phenomenology provides a means of determining the concept of truth, not just as the general, abstract concept but also through concrete, intentional analysis. Such an analysis forms the first part of Heidegger's analysis of truth in section 44 of *Being and Time*.

The third is assertion. Heidegger says assertions are acts of meaning. That is, assertions (e.g., in the form of propositions) are that in and through which I presume, emptily intend, that is, *mean*, something, *in a specific way*.

What, then, is categorial intuition? Instead of trying to retrace Heidegger's systematic development of this issue (to say nothing of Husserl's), let me simply take Heidegger's example and try to indicate what the basic issue is. Heidegger's example is this: the proposition "This chair is yellow and upholstered." This is what Heidegger calls an *assertion*. That is, the proposition expresses a complex meaning-intention, which is an empty intending of something *in a specific way* and not just as something globally meant or perceived. Heidegger anticipates what eventually he will show, which is that all our comportments are pervaded by the assertion. "It is not so much that we see the objects and things but rather that we first talk about them. To put it more precisely: we do not say what we see, but rather the reverse, we see what *one* says about the matter" (HCT 75/56). The full demonstration and sense of this will be worked out only in *Being and Time* (at least in the Dasein-analytic). But we can say that this is one of the main roots of the immense significance that *language* eventually comes to have for Heidegger.

So the question that Heidegger pursues is that of the *truth* of assertion. How can an assertion be called true when it is made within a concrete perception? This means: How can an assertion be fulfilled? Can it be fulfilled in the same way that a simple empty intuition is fulfilled? To answer this, Heidegger indicates more specifically what an assertion is—that is, how it functions in relation to the perception of a particular thing. He says: the thing is first apprehended directly and simply in its unarticulated totality. The assertion then makes certain relations stand out from the thing, draws them out; it accentuates them. For example, seeing the chair, I say: "This chair is yellow and upholstered." The question is: Is the intention that is expressed in the assertion perceptually fulfillable (demonstrable)? More precisely: Is *every* intention within the complex intention (expressed in assertion) capable of being fulfilled by a corresponding perception? Suppose I turn and look at the chair. Certain of the intentions will then be fulfilled. Heidegger notes: I can see the chair, that it is yellow (its being-yellow) and that it is upholstered (its being-upholstered). *But* I can never see the "this," the "is," or the "and" as I see the chair. In fact, strictly speaking, I cannot see even the *being-*yellow but only yellow (remember Kant: being is not a real predicate). *So*: in the assertion, there are intentions that cannot be fulfilled by perception; in the assertion, there is a *surplus of intentions*. What Husserl undertook to show (and Heidegger appropriates) is that along with sensible intuition (of the chair, yellow, upholstered), there are also acts of *categorial intuition*, which is to say, acts in which one intuits the categorial, syntactical, or universal moments (the "this," the "is," the "and") so as to fulfill those surplus intentions in the assertion.

Heidegger refers to the way modern philosophy has dealt with these nonsensory moments. Beginning with British empiricism and continuing into German idealism, the origin of these nonsensory moments is taken to lie in *immanent perception*. In Locke's phrase, if they are not "ideas of sensation," they must be "ideas of reflection," which is to say, derived from the mind's reflection on itself. Then he says: "Today we are in a position to move against idealism precisely on this front only because phenomenology has demonstrated that the non-sensory and ideal cannot without further ado be identified with the immanent, conscious subjective" (HCT 78–79/58). This "demonstration" lies in the discovery of categorial intuition. That is, phenomenology has shown that the nonsensory moments, though not demonstrable through sense perception, are demonstrable by way of a similar type of fulfillment, which is categorial intuition.

There are simple and founded acts. The paradigmatically simple act is perception. What is meant by saying that perception is a simple or single-level act?

Consider perception. As I see an object from various perspectives, each profile opens onto the object as a whole *and* links up with other profiles in a sequence. It is *not* as though I get several discrete profiles, which I then put together in order to get the whole object in view. That is, there is not in perception a higher-level *synthesis* that supervenes on profiles (as though they were mere matter in need of form). If one can speak of synthesis at all, it is a synthesis at the same level as the profiles it synthesizes.

Perception, though a single-level act, can become the foundation (i.e., the founding level) of multilevel acts. More specifically, perception can found *categorial acts*, which are acts that make the simply given accessible in a new way, in a new kind of "object."

Heidegger considers two kinds of categorial acts, acts of synthesis and acts of ideation.

A. Acts of synthesis.

For example, on the basis of my simple perception of the chair in its undifferentiated totality, I can come to see the chair *as being yellow*. The founded seeing is a kind of perceptual accentuating, and we should note several things about it. First, what is intended (namely, the state of affairs, being-yellow) is something *ideal*—the chair does not contain its being-yellow as a real (i.e., simply perceptible) property. Second, yet drawing out this ideal state-of-affairs, this *categorial form* allows the chair to *become* explicitly visible as it is, in what it is. So to say that the categorial form is not a real property of the chair does *not* mean that the form is not *objective*. Third, the perceptual accentuating is an act of synthesis or, more precisely, of σύνθεσις and διαίρεσις (joining together and taking apart). The categorial form (being-yellow) is taken apart from the perceptually given whole but then joined to it (the whole *as* being-yellow).

B. Acts of ideation.

These differ from acts of synthesis in the following way. In acts of synthesis (e.g., in perceptual accentuating: seeing the chair as being-yellow), I not only intend the categorial (ideal) object but also *cointend* the *founding object* (the object as undifferentiatedly perceived). But in the case of ideation, the founding object is *not* intended in the categorial act. Rather, I intend only the idea or species; for example, I bring the species "house" into relief within the multiplicity of individual houses. Here, too, there is a new objectivity constituted, which is generality. If, to go one step further, the ideal object excludes from its content not only everything individual but also everything *sensory*, then it is the object of a *pure categorial intuition*. It is such an intuition that the "this," "and," and presumably the "is" would fulfill.

One additional point in order to put into focus the significance of Husserl's theory of categorial intuition for Heidegger. Among the nonsensory moments is the "is"; that is to say, Being. Hence for Husserl, Being is not a mere empty abstraction (e.g., a mere copula of judgment) *but* is fulfillable through a categorial act (e.g., seeing the "being-yellow" of the chair). Also notable here is Heidegger's *Zähringen Seminar* (1973). Here he deals at some length with the significance of Husserl's work for his own.

> In order to be able to develop the question of the meaning of Being as such, Being would have to be *given*, in order to investigate its meaning. Husserl's achievement consists precisely in this envisagement of Being, which in the category is phenomenally present. Through this achievement, I finally had a basis: "Being" is no mere concept, is no pure abstraction yielded by way of derivation. The point, however, which Husserl does not work out, is the following: after obtaining Being as *given*, he failed to investigate it any further. He did not develop the question "What does Being mean?"[1]

III. *Original Sense of the A Priori*

This is the third of the "decisive discoveries." Here Heidegger's discussion is brief because a fundamental discussion of the a priori would presuppose precisely what the *History of the Concept of Time* is aiming at: the fundamental redetermination of the concept of *time*. This is evident in the word *a priori*, meaning "from earlier," which is to say something from which the earlier on already is. Short of this fundamental level, phenomenology has demonstrated three things with regard to the a priori.

A. The first is to be seen against the background of the modern philosophical understanding of the a priori. Since Kant, the a priori has been taken as characterizing knowledge and, more specifically, as that kind of knowledge that is not based on empirical experience. Such knowledge, since it does not come from without, must come from within—that is, is found only within the self-enclosed subject. Against this, phenomenology has shown that the a priori has universal scope and is not specifically limited to subjectivity. Heidegger is here referring to the question of the *material a priori*. What phenomenology demonstrates is that there are certain structures that pertain to the content of the matter itself (e.g., its color, materiality, spatiality), structures that are always already there in

---

1. Martin Heidegger, *Vier Seminare* (Frankfurt a.M.: Vittorio Klostermann, 1977), 116. In English, *Four Seminars*, trans. Andrew J. Mitchell and François Raffoul (Bloomington: Indiana University Press, 2003), 67.

any particular instance and hence are a priori. For example, (a) in the relation between color and extension, color presupposes extension, and (b) the adumbrational structure of perception.

B. Since the a priori is exhibited in the things themselves, the appropriate way of access to it is *direct intuition* (categorial, of course). That is, the a priori is not to be inferred, surmised, and so on—but *seen*.

C. The a priori, as the examples show, belongs exclusively neither to the subject (as modern philosophy supposed) nor to the side of the object (i.e., it does not simply express some relation; for example, a causal one, between things). Heidegger concludes, without yet elaborating: "Instead the *a priori* is a *feature of the structural sequence in the Being of beings, in the ontological structure of Being*" (HCT 102/74).

In conclusion to the principle of phenomenology, Heidegger undertakes finally to specify the principle "to the things themselves." That is, to indicate, in reference to the concrete discoveries of phenomenology, which things are the things themselves to which phenomenology is to turn and how it is to turn. More precisely, specifying the principle requires specifying three things. First is the field of the subject-matter (*Sachfeld*), and this is: intentionality. Second is the regard in which the subject is to be investigated. In phenomenology, one seeks out the structures that are always already in the given particulars. Hence that regard is: the a priori. That is, phenomenology is to investigate intentionality in its a priori. Third is the way of dealing with the subject-matter, the *method*. The method is simple originary apprehension, what is traditionally called *description*. More precisely, description is an accentuating articulation of what is intuited. Accentuating articulation is: *analysis*. Thus "Phenomenology is the analytic description *of intentionality in its a priori*" (HCT 108/79).

Heidegger's Critique of Husserl's Development of Phenomenology

In *Logical Investigations*, the breakthrough to phenomenology is accomplished. Still, in many ways, *Logical Investigations* remains preliminary and continues to use traditional language and concepts that are not entirely suitable. After *Logical Investigations*, Husserl undertook to develop phenomenology in a more rigorous way. Preeminently, this required a rigorous elaboration of the field of phenomenology. That is, it required a delimitation of "intentionality in its *a priori*" as an independent region, as the field of scientific research. This is what Husserl undertook in *Ideas* (1913). We cannot go into this development (or Heidegger's discussion of it) in any detail. But I do want to very briefly indicate the three main critical points that Heidegger makes with regard to it because these points serve to clarify why Heidegger, beginning also with *Logical Investigations*, undertook to develop phenomenology in a very different way, one that led to *Being and Time*.

What is the character of the development that Husserl carries out in *Ideas*? Husserl points out that the entire development, since it is aimed at the a priori, has a character similar to ideation. That is, there is an extended act of categorial intuition founded on a prior envisaging of a concrete individuation.

So then, the development involves three moments.

(1) The exemplary ground; that is, the concrete individuation, which is to say that form in which intentionality is first given in the natural attitude. Husserl identifies this as an individual stream of lived experiences, which are real occurrences in the world and in animal beings.

(2) The method by which from this ground the a priori structures (the rigorously determined region of phenomenological research) are to be brought into relief; that is, raised out of the exemplary ground. Husserl identifies this as the method of *reduction*—transcendental reduction—which puts into play phenomenological reflection on intentional acts and intentional objects (as intended). The eidetic reduction is that in which one disregards everything individual and focuses only on structure.

(3) Intentionality in its a priori *as* a rigorously determined region for phenomenological research. For Husserl, this is pure consciousness as absolute being.

The critical points for Heidegger are the following.

(1) Heidegger reviews in some detail the various determinations of the region of pure consciousness as worked out by Husserl. He shows that in each case, Husserl fails to really raise the question of the being of the region, of the being of consciousness. He then concludes: "The elaboration of pure consciousness as the thematic field of phenomenology is *not derived phenomenologically by going back to the matters themselves* but by going back to a traditional idea of philosophy. Thus none of the characters which emerge as determinations of the being of lived experiences is an original character" (HCT 147/107). Here we see, among other things, how important the *destruction* is, how utterly perilous it is to try to develop phenomenology in the relatively unhistorical way that Husserl did.

(2) But the basic difficulty that Heidegger sees is not in the determination of pure consciousness but rather in Husserl's starting point. That is, in the way in which the subject of intentional experiences is taken to be first given in the natural standpoint. "The basic difficulty with this determination of the reality of acts lies already in the starting position. What becomes fixed here as the datum of a natural attitude, namely, that man is given as a living being, as a zoological object, is this very attitude which is called natural" (HCT 155/112–13). Here we see why the question of everydayness is so important for Heidegger. It is his way of taking up the question of the natural attitude—of trying to get access to Dasein in a genuinely phenomenological way; that is, without simply taking a "well-defined theoretical position" (HCT 155/113) for granted.

(3) Heidegger points out that Husserl not only wants to delimit the region of pure consciousness but that in the process of doing so, he also draws what he considers the fundamental distinction among beings between, in Husserl's words, "being as consciousness and being as transcendent being manifesting itself in consciousness."[2] But what is remarkable is that this most radical distinction of being is drawn without any inquiry into what would have to direct the process of making any such distinction; namely, the meaning of being as such. Consequently, Husserl fails to raise the question not only of the Being of consciousness (subject) but also of Being as such. Here there is a fundamental neglect. Heidegger concludes: "In the basic task of determining its ownmost field, therefore, phenomenology is *unphenomenological!*—that is to say, *purportedly phenomenological!* But it is all this in a sense which is even more fundamental. *Not only is the being of the intentional*, hence the being of a particular entity, *left undetermined, but categorially primal separations in the entity* (consciousness and reality) *are presented without clarifying or even questioning the guiding regard*, that according to which they are distinguished, which is precisely *being in its sense*" (HCT 178/128–29).

Heidegger's Radicalization of Phenomenology

In what direction will Heidegger radicalize the phenomenological field? In general, beginning with intentionality, he will raise the question of the Being of that being that has intentional experiences. That is, how must that being be in order that it have intentionality as its basic structure? He attempts, then, to think intentionality to its ground. Heidegger explains: "To think intentionality to its ground means: to ground it on the ek-stasis of Da-sein. In other words, it must be recognized that consciousness is grounded in Da-sein."[3] In *Basic Problems of Phenomenology*, this is most clearly indicated. Here Heidegger begins with the Kantian thesis about Being and shows how it leads to the problem of perception; then he shows that the problem of perception can only be clarified by intentional analysis; finally, he shows "that not only do intentio and intentum belong to the intentionality of perception but so also does *the understanding of the mode of being of what is intended in the intentum*" (BPP 100–1/71). So Heidegger radicalizes phenomenology by introducing beneath the *intention-intentum* an understanding of Being. *And* this at the same time will amount to a determination of the Being of the subject insofar as (as *Being and Time* says) the Being of Dasein consists in its having always already an understanding of Being.[4]

---

2. Edmund Husserl, *Ideen zu einer reinen Phaenomenologie und Phaenomenoloischen Philosophie* (Hague: Martinus Nijhoff, 1950), sect. 42. In English, *Ideas: General Introduction to Pure Phenomenology*, trans. William Ralph Boyce Gibson (London: George Allen & Unwin, 1931).
3. *Vier Seminare* 122/67 in English.
4. Cf., *Vier Seminar* 122/67 in English.

Section 7: The Preliminary Concept of Phenomenology

We should now return to section 7 of *Being and Time* to see how Heidegger, independently of Husserl, formulates the concept of phenomenology, a discussion that is parallel to section 9 of *History of the Concept of Time*.

Heidegger stresses that he will provide *only* the "preliminary concept" (*Vorbgriff*) of phenomenology. Why only the preliminary concept? We should consider the following. As we have already seen, phenomenology demands that we go to the things themselves and let our research be directed by them. But, in turn, the things themselves get disclosed by such research. *And* to the extent that they get disclosed, we can approach them in a more appropriate way, let our research be more accurately directed by them, let it be more genuinely rooted in them. *So* the method and research are interrelated, mutually determining. This means, then, that the method is not to be entirely laid out before the research itself. That is, at best, only a preliminary concept of the method (i.e., of phenomenology) can be developed at the outset. Heidegger develops this preliminary concept by way of a reflection on the component words (λόγος, φαινόμενον) and the way they come together in "phenomenology."

I. *The Concept of Phenomenon*

Here Heidegger undertakes two tasks. (A) He distinguishes among several concepts related to that of phenomenon so as to show that the concept of phenomenon is most fundamental, that it is a founding concept. (B) He distinguishes among three different concepts of phenomenon.

A. The Distinction among Various Concepts.

1. *Phenomenon* [*Phänomen*]. In Greek, this is: φαινόμενον, which is derived from the verb φαίνεσθαι, which means "to show it itself" in the sense of bringing itself into the light—Middle-voice from φαίνω—to bring to light. So *phenomenon* means: that which shows itself in itself, the manifest (*das Sich-an-ihm-selbst-zueigende, das Offenbare*). Also, that which shows itself *from* itself (*von ihm selbst her*).

2. *Semblance* (*Schein*). Heidegger notes that a being can show itself in many ways depending on the kind of access we have to it. One such way is of special importance, which is that it can show itself as what in itself it is *not* (*sich als das zeigt, was es an ihm selbst* nicht *ist*). That is, it can show itself so as to look like (seem to be) something it is not. Such a self-showing is a seeming (*scheinen*), and what shows itself in this way is semblance (*Schein*).

How is semblance related to phenomenon? Only insofar as something makes a pretension of showing itself (i.e., of being a phenomenon) can it show itself *as something it is not*. So the concept of semblance can be defined only by reference to the concept of phenomenon, which is to say that the concept of semblance is *founded* on the concept of phenomenon. Semblance is the privative modification of phenomenon.

3. *Appearance* (*Erscheinung*). Heidegger illustrates this with an example: the symptoms of a disease (*Krankheitserscheinungen*). Here the point is the following: something shows itself (symptoms) in such a way as to indicate (announce) something else, which does not show itself (disease). So appearance means "the announcing itself by something, which does not show itself, through something that does show itself" (*das Sichmelden von etwas, das sich nicht zeigt, durch etwas, was sich zeigt*) (BT 29/28). Here Heidegger distinguishes three structural items: (i) that which appears (which does *not* show itself but only announces itself through something else), (ii) the appearance (which shows itself in such a way as to announce that which appears), and (iii) the appearing (which is an announcing). How is appearance related to semblance and phenomenon?

Semblance: with regard to semblance, appearing is a *not*-showing-itself. But the "not" is radically different from that involved in semblance. In the case of semblance, there is a privative mode of self-showing; in the case of appearance, what appears does not *show* itself at all, not even in a privative mode. Thus, appearance and semblance are fundamentally distinct.

Phenomenon: with regard to phenomenon, to appear is not to show itself (in the sense of phenomenon); that is, what appears does not show itself. Thus appearance and phenomenon are distinct concepts, yet appearing is only possible on the basis of a self-showing, specifically by the appearance, by that through which what appears announces itself. Thus the concept of appearance presupposes that of phenomenon.

4. *Mere Appearance* (*bloße Erscheinung*). This is a privative modification of appearance. The situation is this: that which does the announcing (which *does* show itself, the appearance proper) shines forth (radiates, *ausstrahlen*) from the nonmanifest (that which is announced, that which does not show itself) in such a way that the nonmanifest is something that can *never* become manifest. That is, that which announces shows itself in such a way as to keep that which is announced essentially veiled, covered up, sealed up in itself. Here the basic structure is the same as appearance, and that suffices to make mere appearance something distinct from semblance or the privative modification of phenomenon.

5. *Mere Semblant Appearance*. Here the situation is this: appearance involves a phenomenon, which is something that shows itself so as to announce something else. Such a phenomenon can undergo modification: it can take the privative form of semblance (show itself as it is not). Then appearance has become mere semblance. For example, in a certain lighting, someone's cheeks look red (semblance), and this may then be taken as announcing a feverish condition (as appearance).

B. The Three Concepts of Phenomenon.

1. The formal concept of phenomenon: if it is left indefinite which beings are considered phenomena (even left indefinite whether phenomena are beings or not).

2. The common or ordinary concept of phenomenon: if "phenomenon" is specified to mean those beings that are accessible through empirical intuition in Kant's sense (phenomenon is the same as objects of experience). *But* this is *not* the phenomenological concept of phenomenon.

3. The phenomenological concept of phenomenon: Heidegger illustrates this within the horizon of Kant's problematic: "In the horizon of the Kantian problematic what is understood phenomenologically by the term phenomenon (disregarding other differences) can be illustrated when we say that what already shows itself in appearances, prior to and always accompanying what we commonly understand as phenomena (though unthematically), can be brought thematically to self-showing. What thus shows itself in itself ('the forms of intuition') are the phenomena of phenomenology" (BT 31/29–30). Nota bene: the phenomena in the phenomenological sense do not *simply* show themselves. That is, their showing involves a certain negativity: they show themselves *un*thematically and so must be *brought* to self-showing in the full sense. In other words, for *such* phenomena, there is required a discipline by which they can be brought to a self-showing. *Thus* they are phenomena in the *phenomenological* sense. We should also note the following: their showing is somehow a priori linked up with another showing (in Kantian terms: the showing of objects of empirical intuition, of phenomena in the ordinary sense).

II. *The Concept of Logos*

In his consideration of λόγος, Heidegger's intent is threefold: (a) to maintain that the basic meaning of λόγος is discourse; (b) to explain what is meant by "discourse"; that is, to show what this basic sense of λόγος is; and (c) to explain how the other senses of λόγος are related back to its sense as discourse.

Heidegger identifies four senses of λόγος.

A. λόγος as discourse (*Rede*, ἀπόφανσις). The question is: What does "discourse" mean? Heidegger answers that discourse means δηλοῦν: to make manifest that about which one discourses in the discourse. That is, to make manifest that to which the discourse is directed. So the basic sense of λόγος is a making manifest of that about which it is a λόγος.

Heidegger elaborates on this issue by referring to Aristotle's *On Interpretation*. This function of λόγος (i.e., its function *as* discourse) was designated by Aristotle by the word ἀποφαίνεθαι. Φαίνεθαι means to let something be seen. So discourse lets something be seen; namely, that about which one discourses in the discourse, and it lets it be seen *for* the listener or the speaker. Ἀπο means "from." Thus ἀποφαίνεθαι means to let something be seen *from*... specifically, *from itself*. Discourse lets something be seen from itself. It lets that to which the discourse is directed be seen *from* itself. This means that in discourse, what is said is drawn from what the discourse is about *in such a way* that through the discourse it (what the discourse is about) gets made manifest.

B. λόγος as φωνή (sound). In its concrete execution, λόγος as discourse has a further characteristic: it is a speaking, a verbal sounding, a sounding of words. So λόγος has a second sense: φωνή. More specifically, λόγος is φωνή μετὰ φαντασίας. Heidegger translates this as "*stimmliche Verlautbarung in der je etwas gesichtet ist*" (verbal sounding in which something is sighted) (BT 33/31).

C. Λόγος as σύνθεσις (synthesis). The relevant sense of "synthesis" is based on the fundamental sense of λόγος (λόγος as discourse, as letting something be seen from itself). Specifically, "Here the συν [the 'together'] has a purely apophantical signification and means letting something be seen in its *togetherness* with something, letting something be seen *as* something" (BT 33/31). For example, suppose we say, "The table is brown." The putting-together (syn-thesis) that occurs in this λόγος is not some psychical connecting of representations, not a mere connecting of concepts in thought. Rather, if we consider it concretely, the putting-together makes something manifest *in* its togetherness with something else (the table together with the brown color); that is, it makes manifest the table *as* brown.

D. Λόγος as ἀληθεύειν (being-true). The character of λόγος (its character as true, i.e., the capacity of λόγος to be true or false) is likewise based on the fundamental sense of λόγος (discourse). That is, the meaning of truth (at least of "propositional truth") is to be determined in reference to the function of making manifest, which belongs to λόγος as discourse. "The 'Being-true' of λόγος as ἀληθεύειν means: to take beings that are being talked *about* in λέγειν as ἀποφαίνεθαι out of their concealment [*Verborgenheit*]; to let them be seen as something unconcealed (ἀληθές); to *discover* them. Similarly 'being-false,' ψευδεσθαι, is tantamount to deceiving in the sense of *covering up* [*verdecken*]" (BT 33/31). Here Heidegger points ahead: the primary sense of truth will prove to be not some abstract "correspondence" between propositions and things but rather uncoveredness, unhiddenness, *unconcealment*.

In conclusion, we should note the following. Heidegger's reflection on the meaning of truth (merely anticipated here) is one of the most important in *Being and Time* and beyond. For now, we can think of it in terms of the intentional analysis of truth in *History of the Concept of Time*. According to that analysis, a statement is demonstrated to be true when fulfillment takes place, which is to say, when a fulfilling intention presents intuitively what was merely intended in the statement. Now suppose a case in which there is fulfillment. What would, then, have been demonstrated about the statement? For example, "This chair is yellow." It would have been demonstrated that the statement *accentuates* the thing *as it is*. That is, that it draws out something about the thing that in a global, perceptual apprehension remains concealed. That is to say, that it lets the thing be seen in the sense of drawing out, tracing out, what can *then* be seen in the fulfilling act. The statement, by meaning the thing in a certain way, lets it be seen in that specific way.

III. The Preliminary Concept of Phenomenology

Heidegger puts together the meanings determined for "phenomenon" and "λόγος."

Phenomenology = λέγειν τὰ φαινόμενα
= ἀποφαίνεσθαι τὰ φαινόμενα
= "to let what shows itself be seen from itself, just as it shows itself from itself" (BT 34/32).

This is the *formal concept* of phenomenology. But it merely expresses more precisely the maxim "to the things themselves." That is, the formal concept of phenomenology simply expresses the demand that, whatever the subject matter, one proceed from the way that subject-matter shows itself from itself.

In this connection, Heidegger notes that the word *phenomenology* is different from words like *theology* and *biology*, in which the subject-matter is also named. *Phenomenology*, in its formal sense, has no reference to any subject-matter but rather indicates *how any* matter must be investigated *if* that investigation is to be one that is rigorous, genuinely scientific. "Science 'of' the phenomena means that it grasps its objects in *such* a way that everything about them to be discussed must be directly indicated and directly demonstrated" (BT 35/33). And so the phrase *descriptive phenomenology* is tautological. Thus phenomenology in the formal sense simply expresses the demand that, whatever the subject-matter, one proceed from the way the matter shows itself from itself.

But this is *merely* the *formal* concept of phenomenology, corresponding to the formal concept of phenomenon (i.e., that which shows itself). To move from this to the distinctively phenomenological concept of phenomenology, the formal concept of phenomenon must be *deformalized*. "Now what must be taken into account if the formal concept of phenomenon is to be deformalized to the phenomenological one, and how does this differ from the vulgar concept? What is it that phenomenology is to 'let be seen'? What is it that is to be called 'phenomenon' in a distinctive sense?" (BT 35/33) Heidegger has already touched on this by saying that phenomenon in the phenomenological sense is that which shows itself only *unthematically*. Now he elaborates: "Manifestly, it is something that does *not* show itself initially and for the most part, something that is *concealed* [*verborgen*] in contrast to what initially and for the most part does show itself. But, at the same time, it is something that essentially belongs to what initially and for the most part shows itself, indeed in such a way that it constitutes its meaning and ground" (BT 35/33). So phenomenon in the phenomenological sense does not simply show itself (is concealed), yet it belongs to what shows itself as its very meaning and ground. But what is it that belongs essentially to what shows itself as meaning and ground and yet is concealed? Heidegger's answer: the *Being* of beings (*das Sein des Seienden*). Being is what is concealed in the most distinctive—or, rather, radical—sense, in a way that beings could never be. This is attested to by the very forgottenness of the question of the meaning of Being that *Being and Time* addresses from its first page on.

Thus ontology requires phenomenology. "*Ontology is possible only as phenomenology.* The phenomenological concept of phenomenon, as self-showing, means the Being of beings—its meaning, modifications, and derivatives" (BT 35/33). Why does ontology require phenomenology? Because Being is *concealed* and so must be *brought* to show itself. Thus that which phenomenology is to let be seen is *not* merely to be gazed on in the sense of a straightforward description, it is not a matter of mere beholding. Rather, it "must first be *wrested* from the objects of phenomenology" (BT 36/34). But this, in turn, requires that phenomenology interrogate objects; that is, beings, which is to say, phenomena in the common sense manner. "Thus the common concept of phenomenon becomes phenomenologically relevant" (BT 37/35). Thus phenomenology involves two concepts of phenomenon, the common and the phenomenological: it interrogates phenomena in the common sense so as to wrest from them phenomena in the phenomenological sense.

Finally, we should note three additional points that "round out" the discussion of phenomenological method.

First is a merely terminological point. Heidegger distinguishes between *phenomenal* and *phenomenological*. *Phenomenal*: "What is given and is explicable in the way we encounter the phenomenon is called 'phenomenal'" (BT 37/34). Thus to say of something that it is phenomenal means that it shows itself, which is to say that the term *phenomenal* refers to its self-showing character. A "phenomenal structure" is a structure that shows itself, which is manifest. This is contrasted with *phenomenological*, which refers to "everything that belongs to the manner of indication and explication, and that constitutes the conceptuality [*Begrifflichkeit*] this research requires is called 'phenomenological'" (BT 37/34–35). That is, *phenomenological* refers to procedures or method.

Second, Heidegger brings the ordinary concept of phenomenon back into consideration. We have seen that the phenomena of phenomenology are Being and what pertains to it. But Being is the Being *of* beings, and if Being is to be exhibited, this can only be done by way of an exhibiting of beings (of an exemplary being). However, a being is a phenomenon in the *ordinary* sense and thus "in this way the ordinary concept of phenomenon becomes phenomenologically relevant" (BT 35).

Third, against this background, Heidegger indicates finally the specific form that the "letting be seen" (i.e., the λόγος of phenomenology) is to assume: "From the investigation itself we shall see that the methodological meaning of phenomenological description is *interpretation* [*Auslegung*]. The λόγος of the phenomenology of Dasein has the character of ἑρμηνεύειν . . . Phenomenology of Dasein is a *hermeneutics* in the primordial signification of that word, which designates the work of interpretation" (BT 37/35). Thus the analysis of Dasein is a hermeneutics of Dasein. Yet what this means (what hermeneutics is) can be genuinely worked out only through the investigation itself and through the reflection of that investigation *of* Dasein back on Dasein as the one who carries out the investigation, which is to say, by exploiting the double genitive in: hermeneutics of Dasein.

Finally, Heidegger brings the entire methodological reflection together, and to some extent the entire introduction, into a "definition" of philosophy. "Philosophy is universal phenomenological ontology, taking its departure from the hermeneutic of Dasein, which, as an analytic of *existence*, has secured the end of the guiding-line of all philosophical questioning at the place from which it *arises* and to which it *reverts* [falls back, *zurückschlägt*]" (BT 36). Just before Heidegger's definition of "Philosophy is universal phenomenological ontology," he indicates what this means: "Ontology and phenomenology are not two different disciplines which among others belong to philosophy. Both terms characterize philosophy itself, its object and procedure" (BT 38/36). So *ontology* names the object: Being. *Phenomenological* names the procedure: let it be seen from itself as it shows itself. *Universal* indicates that philosophy deals with Being as such, not in some special regard; that is, that it is *fundamental* ontology rather than regional ontology. This entire sentence calls for commentary.

By "proceeding from the hermeneutic of Dasein" (BT 38/36), Dasein is the exemplary being, the being to be questioned, the being in reference to which the procedure (phenomenology) is to be applied. As so applied, the procedure takes the form of a hermeneutic; that is, *hermeneutic* expresses the specific character of the λόγος of phenomenology.

In saying "which, as an analysis of *existence*" (BT 38/36), "existence" names the *Being* of Dasein. Dasein is to be questioned *about* its Being, and the elements of its Being, the "existentials" are to be laid out, let be seen. That is, there is to be an *analytic* in the sense that Heidegger takes over from Kant, which is a laying out of the elements. "Which . . . has fastened the end of the guideline of all philosophical questioning at the place" (BT 38/36). The direction and directives for all further philosophical questioning are to originate (to be developed) from the way philosophical questioning is attached to its place of beginning; that is, by the way the *ends* of the guideline are "fastened" to the beginning. That is to say, everything depends on philosophical questioning being attached to its proper place of beginning, which is Dasein. "The place from which it [philosophical questioning] *arises* and to which it *reverts*" (BT 38/36). Dasein is the place from which philosophical questioning arises, the place where it begins. That is, Dasein is the one who raises the question. But also, Dasein is that exemplary being that philosophical questioning is to interrogate. Thus Dasein is the place where the various strands of the questioning of Being are joined. That is to say, Dasein is the distinctive place of the question. Dasein is the place where *Being and Time* can appropriately begin; it is the site of its beginning.

Division One: The Preparatory Fundamental Analysis of Dasein

Introduction

Our previous discussions have, in effect, indicated how this title is to be understood. There is to be an *analysis* of Dasein. From *History of the Concept of Time*, we know that the analysis is an accentuating articulation. So Dasein as a whole is to be articulated in such a way as to accentuate certain structures, to make them stand out. We shall see that in fact there will be a series of such articulations, accentuating first one structure, then another.

The analysis is to be *fundamental*. This means the analysis is to be a matter of fundamental ontology. That is, Dasein is to be analyzed specifically with regard to its Being (in contrast to other ways in which it might be investigated).

This analysis, though fundamental, is to be *preparatory*. This means it will merely exhibit the *Being* of Dasein without interpreting it in a primordial way, which is to say, without referring it to its most proper horizon. It will only *prepare for* the disclosure of that horizon and the referral of the Being of Dasein to it.

The analysis is *of Dasein*. What is Dasein? When Dasein was first introduced (in the introduction), Heidegger identified two characters as the sole determinants of this exemplary being. Dasein is that being (a) that we ourselves are, which is to say, it is the being that is always one's own; and (b) to Dasein there belongs a questioning comportment to its own Being—that is, its Being is always in question, is always at issue. Said differently, Dasein is always engaged in questioning what and how it is to be. Hence Dasein has a unique kind of self-relation: it is not a relation of a being to a being (of one thing to another; for example, of the self to itself) *but* of a being (Dasein) to its Being. That is, Dasein is characterized by its questioning comportment to its Being.

1. The Exposition of the Task of a Preparatory Analysis of Dasein

In chapter 1, Heidegger gives an exposition of the *task* of this analytic in two ways: (1) by working out the twofold character of Dasein (especially section 9), and (2) by contrasting this analytic with other disciplines also directed at Dasein (§§ 10 and 11).

Section 9: The Theme of the Analytic of Dasein

Without doing a careful reading, let me briefly extract three points and elaborate them briefly.

I. "The 'essence' [*Wesen*] of this being lies in its to-be [*Zu-sein*]. The whatness [*Was-sein*] (*essentia*) of this being must be conceived in terms of its Being (*existentia*)" (BT 42/41). Dasein's questioning comportment to its Being Heidegger calls *existence*. What Dasein is (its essence) is not a matter of its possessing certain properties; rather, its essence (what it is) lies in its peculiar *comportment* (relatedness) to its Being. This is to be understood radically. It is not that Dasein first *is* in the sense of possessing certain characteristics or properties (e.g., rationality, embodiment) *and then* (on that basis) comports itself to its Being. On the contrary, only on the basis of its comportment to its Being could one begin to understand in what sense Dasein can be called rational or embodied. Existence has to do with "possible ways for it to be" (BT 42/41). That is, existence is Dasein's (questioning) engagement with its possibilities, with what and how it *can be*. If *existence* designates this comportment (in contrast to the traditional sense of existence that is appropriate only to things), then "*The 'essence' of Dasein lies in its existence*" (BT 42/41). Thus Heidegger draws a sharp distinction between two kinds of basic characters or determinations that beings may have.

A. Properties or categories, which are those determinations proper to beings encountered within-the-world; that is, beings other than Dasein. Such beings Heidegger calls *vorhandene*, or present, beings. They have the character of *Vorhandenheit*. (To translate this as "objective presence" is incorrect. This has nothing to do with objectivity, although it does have to do with presence or perhaps immediate or direct presence.) He notes that in ancient ontology, such beings were taken as the exemplary beings, and hence all determinations tended to be understood as properties (categories).

B. Existentials, which are those determinations (characters of Being) proper to Dasein, which are the various structural moments that belong to Dasein's comportment to its Being; that is, to its existence.

II. The other side of Heidegger's general twofold character has been expressed by saying that Dasein is that being that we ourselves are, which is to say, as always one's own. Heidegger reformulates this in terms of mineness (*Jemeinigkeit*). "The Being [*Sein*] which this being [*Seienden*] is *concerned about* [or, better: which is at issue, at stake, in question, for this being] is always my own [or, simply: mine, *meines*]" (BT 42/42). So the Being that is *at issue* also has the character of *mineness*, of always being my own. Here Heidegger is explicitly bringing together the two sides of the twofold: Dasein's Being is such that it is *at issue* (comported to, questioningly) *and* it is *mine*. It is in relation to mineness that Heidegger introduces *authenticity* (a concept that has had broad and notorious—not to say scandalous—effects on twentieth-century philosophy and that was thoroughly misconstrued by, for example, Sartre). *Eigentlichkeit*→*eigen* (own) as in, for example, "*ein eigenes Zimmer*" or "one's own room." So this has to do with Dasein's relation to its ownness, to its way of carrying out (or bearing) its mineness.

More specifically, the first moment of Dasein's twofold character lies in its comportment to its Being as something *at issue*; that is, as something that Dasein *can* be. So one can say that that to which Dasein comports itself has the character of *possibility* (in the most concrete sense). Furthermore, because of the character of mineness, because that Being is Dasein's *own*, such possibility is Dasein's *own* possibility; as Heidegger says, Dasein's "ownmost" possibility. The point, then, is this: Dasein's comportment to such possibility, specifically to its *ownmost* character, can develop in different ways. "And because Dasein is always essentially its possibility, it *can*, in its Being, 'choose' itself in its Being, it can win itself; it can lose itself, or it can never and only 'apparently' win itself" (BT 42/42). This means that Dasein can take up possibility *as its own*. Then it is *authentic*. Or Dasein can evade the ownmost character of its possibility. For example, Dasein can comport itself to its possibility in a way that conceals its ownmost character, which makes it look like "everyone's possibility." This is *inauthenticity*. "Both modes of Being, *authenticity* and *inauthenticity*—these expressions are terminologically chosen in the strictest sense of the word—are grounded in the fact that Dasein is in general determined by mineness" (BT 42–43/42). We should note that these words are linked etymologically with *eigen* (own). They refer to Dasein's relation to its ownness, to its way of fulfilling its mineness. For Heidegger, it is imperative to insist that authenticity is to be understood *strictly ontologically*, without importing any traditional ethical preconceptions.

III. Heidegger says that the peculiar twofold character of Dasein shows how the analytic of Dasein "is confronted with a unique phenomenal region" (BT 43/42). This says, recalling the sense of *phenomenal*, that in this region, the kind of self-showing we find is *unique, eigenartig*, meaning "a kind of its own"—though Heidegger is also playing on the word *eigen* and thus a kind of self-showing permeated by ownness. Confronted with such an *eigenartig* region, *method* becomes a problem: "This being does not and never has the kind of Being of what is merely objectively present within the world. Thus, it is also not to be thematically found in the manner of coming across some present thing" (BT 43/42). The question, then, is: What is the right way to present a being constituted by its *comportment* to its *ownmost* Being? Clearly, it would be wrong to present it by observing and then enumerating its properties as one might with a thing. Does one observe at all this comportment to Being so that one could describe it? And can one even get at what is another Dasein's ownmost? It is clear that these questions can be dealt with *only* by coming to understand more concretely what "comportment to its ownmost Being" really comes down to. That is, one must pursue the analysis by means of a provisional horizon, which is average everydayness, *and then* eventually let that analysis reflect back on these questions of method.

Sections 10–11

From sections 10 and 11, we will look briefly at two issues. First, Heidegger attempts to clarify the task of the Existential Analytic by reference to Descartes's *cogito sum*. The task is to work out the meaning of the *sum*, which is precisely what Descartes left undetermined. Only on this basis can the *cogito* be determined. This says, in effect, that the Being of man (sum) is more primordial than man's character as cogito, that is as a subject (as I). This is why Heidegger goes on to indicate his radical break with Descartes and the entire modern philosophy of the subject: "One of our first tasks will be to show that the point of departure from an initially given I and subject totally fails to see the phenomenal content [*Bestand*] of Dasein" (BT 46/45). This means that to proceed (like Descartes) from the understanding of man as subject (as I) is to miss what is really shown in this being's self-showing.

Second, in discussing how the question of the Being of Dasein has gotten closed off, waylaid, Heidegger says that what is really responsible for this is an unquestioned orientation toward a certain "traditional anthropology" composed from Christian and ancient conceptions about the human being. There are two main elements in this anthropology.

(1) The definition of the human as "rational animal" (ζῷον λόγον ἔχον). The problem is that the kind of being belonging to ζῷον is understood as being-present (*Vorhandensein*), as the kind of Being proper to beings other than Dasein (to "things"). Λόγος is then regarded as some "superior endowment," but its kind of Being is left just as obscure as is that of the being composed from ζῷον and λόγος.

(2) The other element is theological: the human being as created in the image of God. The problem here is that the Being of God gets understood by means of ancient ontology (oriented to "things"), and this tacit ontological interpretation is carried over to the human. Thus the ontological foundation of such a traditional anthropology remains inadequate, even undetermined. The same is true of psychology and biology, as here, too, the explicit ontological foundations are lacking. And it is true also (§11) of anthropology in the narrow sense, as the study of primitive people (ethnology). In all of these cases, there is a need for a fundamental ontological investigation, for an analytic of Dasein such as could provide them an adequate foundation. However, this does *not* mean that the work of such positive sciences should simply be postponed until the ontological foundation is worked out. The point is, rather, that such foundations are needed in order to determine the genuine sense of the scientific results, that when such foundations are laid, the scientific results must be reinterpreted in reference to that foundation. "But since the positive sciences neither 'can' nor should wait for the ontological work of philosophy, the continuation of research will not be accomplished as 'progress'; but, rather, as the *repetition* [*Wiederholung*] and the ontologically more transparent purification of what has been ontically uncovered" (BT 51/50).

2. Being-in-the-World in General as the Fundamental Constitution of Dasein

Section 12: The Preliminary Sketch of Being-in-the-World in Terms of the Orientation toward Being-in as Such

At the beginning of section 12, Heidegger introduces the concept of Being-in-the-world. We should note carefully how he does this. Before introducing it, he summarizes the issues from section 9, especially the two determinations, existence and mineness. Then he says that these determinations of Dasein's Being are to be understood a priori as grounded on Being-in-the-world. So Being-in-the-world is to be exhibited as the ground of existence and mineness. He designates it as the "constitution of Dasein's Being" (*Seinsverfassung des Daseins*).

Heidegger stresses that Being-in-the-world is a unified (unitary) structure. Yet, as was already noted, there are three constitutive moments in its structure. Each may be considered in relative independence of the others, although the whole must always be kept in view. These three moments are: (a) as expressed in the phrase *in-the-world*, and the constitutive moment is world and so the analysis is directed at the worldliness of the world and which deals with the relation between world and beings within-the-world, with signs, and with spatiality (chap. 3); (b) the *being* that is in the manner of Being-in-the-world, which is to say, the being asked about when one asks about the "who," and this moment concerns primarily the self-character of Dasein (chap. 4); and (c) Being-in as such (chap. 5), and this will converge on analyses of understanding, interpretation, and discourse. For the sake of orientation, Heidegger proposes to give a preliminary characterization of the third moment (Being-in), and here Heidegger considers five main points.

(1) Being-in is an existential. As such, it must be distinguished from all categorial-type relations; that is, from the type of relations that present things (things other than Dasein) have to one another. Thus to say that Being-in belongs to the constitution of Dasein does *not* mean that one present thing (e.g., the human body) is "in" another present thing (e.g., the world as totality, cosmos) as, for example, water is in the glass or clothes are in the closet. Being-in is not a spatial containment.

(2) *Sein-bei*, Being-with. And yet Dasein is alongside beings (*Sein-bei*). It is dispersed into various relations to things within-the-world. It is alongside them.

Heidegger expresses this engagement with the word *Besorgen* (taking care of, being concerned with, these beings). This engagement with things is an existential. It is founded on Being-in-the-world. On the other hand, Dasein's relation to its world is entirely different. It is that on the basis of which taking care (concern) is possible. That is, world is not something to which Dasein may or may not relate itself *but rather* is something to which Dasein is always already related: "According to what we have said, being-in is not a 'property' which Dasein sometimes has and sometimes does not have, *without* which it could *be* just as well as it could with it. It is not the case that the human being 'is,' and then on top of that has a relation of Being to the 'world' which it sometimes takes upon itself. Dasein is never 'initially' a sort of being which is free from being-in, but which at times is in the mood to take up a 'relation' to the world" (BT 57/57). In different terms, world is not just some being that Dasein happens to encounter, that just happens to meet up with Dasein; rather, any being can be encountered by Dasein only insofar as it can show itself within a world. That is, world is something that must always already be revealed in order that beings might become manifest from out of it and thus become accessible to Dasein.

(3) Facticity. Although Dasein is radically different in the constitution of its Being (in *Seinsverfassung*) from present things, it can with some justification and within certain limits be taken *as* merely present; namely, if one completely disregards Dasein's existential constitution. Roughly speaking, Dasein **can** be taken as merely a *thing*. However, this must be distinguished from a certain kind of presence that is Dasein's *own*, a kind that *belongs essentially* to Dasein (is its *own*) rather than resulting from a disregarding of Dasein's constitution. This proper way in which Dasein is present, Heidegger calls *facticity*. At this point, he says merely: "The concept of 'facticity' implies that a being 'within-the-world' has Being-in-the-world in such a way that it can understand itself as bound up in its 'destiny' with the Being of those beings which it encounters within its own world" (BT 56/56).

(4) Spatiality. By distinguishing Being-in from spatial containment (of the sort proper to present beings), Heidegger is *not* denying that Dasein is spatial. Rather, he wants to insist that Dasein has its *own* kind of spatiality (existential spatiality) and that this spatiality is founded on Being-in-the-world. "Dasein itself has its own 'Being-in-space,' which in its turn is possible only *on the basis of Being-in-the-world in general*" (BT 56/56). So facticity is the way in which Dasein is bound up with (bound to) the very Being of beings within-the-world. But this is a relation quite different from a mere taking-care.

(5) Here Heidegger introduces one of the first methodological reflections to be introduced in the course of *Being and Time* (which *must* be introduced since method cannot simply be decided in advance). Heidegger notes that the description given of Being-in has, at this point, been largely negative, and he has

mostly just said what Being-in is *not*. He explains why this is appropriate: "But the prevalence of negative characteristics is no accident. Rather, it makes known what is peculiar to this phenomenon, and is thus positive in a genuine sense—a sense appropriate to the phenomenon itself" (BT 58/58). The appropriateness of the negative procedure lies in the need of "rejecting dissimulations and obfuscations" (BT 58/58). Yet how is it that there are dissimulations and obfuscations, which must be rejected (exposed)? Heidegger's answer: because the phenomena are to be "seen" in some form in every Dasein. Dissimulation and obfuscation— that is, concealment—can be seen and are operative in every Dasein. In short, Dasein misunderstands itself, bears a certain concealment from itself. Heidegger identifies the character and origin of this self-concealment: "But the phenomenon has mostly been basically misinterpreted, or interpreted in an ontologically inadequate way. However, this 'seeing in a certain way and yet mostly misinterpreting' is itself based on nothing more than the constitution of the Being of Dasein itself. In accordance with that constitution, Dasein understands itself ontologically—and that means also its Being-in-the-world—initially in terms of *those* beings and their Being which it itself is *not*, but which it encounters 'within' its world" (BT 58/58–59). It should be noted that here we have what will prove to be the third constituent of care; namely, being-fallen, which goes together with existence and facticity to constitute care, which is the Being of Dasein.

It is highly significant that this tendency is the same as that which Heidegger identifies among the Greeks: Dasein gets understood in terms of determinations appropriate to things encountered in the world (i.e., in terms of categories, not existentials). This, more than anything else, contributed to the forgetting of—or obliviousness to—the question of Being. We begin to see that the misdirection of Greek philosophy was not just accidental but rather a "natural" misdirection, one to which Dasein, by its very constitution, is prone. At the same time, this gives us a kind of measure of the exertion (violence) that will be needed to resist this direction—as the Dasein analysis must do.

Section 13: The Exemplification of Being-in in a Founded Mode: Knowing the World

The task of the Existential Analytic, as it has emerged, is to exhibit Being-in-the-world as ground, in its function of grounding to bring it to show itself. Heidegger will do this with each of the constituent items in chapters 3–5: world, the who, and Being-in. But before he begins his detailed analyses, he gives in section 13 a preparatory analysis. Specifically, he sketches the way that Being-in-the-world serves as ground; that is, he gives a first glimpse of it in its character as grounding. His intent is to provide an orientation for more thorough analyses to come later, and that includes destroying in advance certain preconceptions.

Heidegger discusses the phenomenon of "knowing the world." He here shows how this phenomenon tends to get covered over, misunderstood. In its phenomenal character, as it shows itself, knowing is a way of being in and toward the world. However, when one *reflects about* knowing, it is noted that knowing is not to be found in the known (e.g., nature) but only in the being that knows. Yet even in this being, knowing is not present-at-hand; that is, it is not some external characteristic; for example, like bodily properties. Thus one concludes that knowing must be "inside." It is then that the *problem* of knowing arises. The problem is: "How this knowing subject comes out of its inner 'sphere' into one which is 'other and external'" (BT 60/60). That is, the problem becomes: How can a subject transcend its own sphere of immanence? The result is that the phenomenal character of knowledge gets covered over. In place of knowing as a mode of being in and toward world, knowing becomes an activity within a sphere of immanence. And, among other things, the positive sense of this "inner sphere" (immanence) remains undetermined.

Looking now at the more positive side of the discussion, Heidegger wants to understand knowing phenomenologically. That is, in a way that, rather than covering the phenomenal character of knowing (the way, the context in which it shows itself), he proceeds in constant reference to this. What is this phenomenal character? How does "knowing the world" show itself? As a way of being in and toward the world, as a particular way of having to do with what concerns us within the world. More precisely: knowing is to be regarded as founded on "being-already-alongside-the-world." This "being-already-alongside" is no mere staring at something merely "there" (i.e., present) but is rather a concernful dealing with the world, a being fascinated (captivated) by world. How, then, does knowing arise? What is characteristic of this founding relation? "In order for knowing to be possible as determining by observation what is present, there must first be a *deficiency* in our having-to-do with the world concernfully" (BT 61/61).

So knowing arises through a modification of our being-already-alongside-the-world; namely, as a deficiency, as a certain narrowing-down. What is this narrowing-down? "*On the basis* of this kind of Being toward the world which lets us encounter beings within-the-world solely in their pure *outward look* (εἶδος)" (BT 61/61). So knowing arises when we hold back from the manipulation and use of things, from our concernful dealings. Or, more precisely, a whole complex of higher level (founded) modes arise: the perception of the present thing, addressing of something *as* something, interpreting, determining, assertion in propositions. At this point, Heidegger does not yet undertake to exhibit the interconnections among these. For now, what is essential is this: that knowing is founded on Being-in-the-world. "The perception of what is known does not take place as a return with one's booty to the 'cabinet' of consciousness after one has gone out and grasped it" (BT 62/62). Again, "In directing itself toward . . . and in grasping something, Dasein does not first go outside of the inner sphere in which it is initially encapsulated, but, rather, in its primary kind of Being, it is always already 'outside' together with some being encountered in the world already uncovered" (BT 62/62).

We should take note that in this discussion, we see clearly how Heidegger is appropriating and developing the phenomenology of Husserl's *Logical Investigations*. Suppose we think of the act of knowing as: meaning-intention (capable of fulfillment). Then Heidegger's refusal to place knowing in a sphere of immanence corresponds precisely to Husserl's insistence of the intentional character of experience; that is, that what I intend is the thing itself and not some interior mental representation. But Heidegger is going one step further. Instead of merely analyzing the more or less isolated intentional acts, he is showing phenomenologically how such an act arises from a more global concern with things; that is, how it is grounded in Being-in-the-world.

3. The Worldliness of the World

Section 14: The Idea of the Worldliness of the World in General

Chapter 3 is devoted to a detailed analysis of the first of those three constitutive items that make up Being-in-the-world; namely, world. Heidegger begins by distinguishing four different meanings of *world*.

1. As used as an ontic concept to signify the totality of beings that can be present (*Vorhanden*) within the world (*innerhalb der Welt*).
2. As used as an ontological concept to signify the Being of those beings.
3. As used in another ontic sense to signify "that '*in which*' a factual Dasein 'lives'" (BT 65/65). Here it has a preontological, existentiell meaning. It is the world of life, a life-world; one could say the space of life.
4. As used to designate the ontological-existential concept of *worldliness* (*Weltlichkeit*). Heidegger says: "Worldliness itself can be modified [i.e., can be differentiated into various modes] into the respective structural totality of particular 'worlds' (=#3), and contains in itself the *a priori* of worldliness in general" (BT 65/65). Here Heidegger is using *a priori* in the sense developed in History of the Concept of Time, freed from the traditional affiliation with subjectivity.

How do these various senses enter into *Being and Time*? Neither number 1 nor number 2 constitutes the proper sense of *world*. Heidegger occasionally uses *world* in sense number 1, but then he always puts it in quotation marks. He never uses *world* in sense number 2 *because* one of the principal tasks is to determine the relation between the Being of beings within the world *and* world in its proper sense. The proper sense is number 3, and whenever Heidegger uses the word without quotation marks, it has this sense. Sense number 4 is always designated as *worldliness* rather than *world*. This is the ontological-existential concept—the existential (a priori existential structure belonging to every world). Worldliness is the primary theme of chapter 3.

Let us try to see, in a general, preliminary way, how the problem of world is to be taken up. The problem is to let worldliness show itself from itself. This *is* a problem because, for the most part, worldliness does *not* show itself. The best testimony to this is the history of ontology, in which worldliness gets continually passed over. This entails that the concept of world and hence of Being-in-the-world also gets passed over. So worldliness must be *brought* to show itself. How?

By an investigation of beings within-the-world. That is, beings must be allowed to show themselves in such a way that through them, worldliness is brought to show itself as connected up with these beings. The horizon for this questioning about world, the horizon for the showing of world has already been determined: everydayness. So the questioning will be directed to the world of *everyday* Dasein, which is the surrounding world (*Umwelt*, environment). The beings to be interrogated are beings within the surroundings, which are those beings that we encounter as closest to us. More precisely, they are to be *ontologically interpreted* (determined in their Being) in such a way as to bring the worldliness of the surrounding world (environmentality of the environment) to show itself.

Section 15: The Being of Beings Encountered in the Surrounding World

Here Heidegger undertakes such an ontological interpretation of beings within the surrounding world as they are encountered by Dasein in its everydayness—the beings that are closest to us. The first question that is raised is: Which beings are these? Heidegger answers that they are those with which we *deal*, have to do with (*Umgang*, go about) within the world, are engaged. Specifically, those with which we deal not by way of perceptual cognition but by handling, using, concerning ourselves with them (*Besorgen* does not mean "take care"). The next question is: How are these beings to be *designated* in general? Heidegger here observes that we must be very careful to put aside those interpretive tendencies that we bring with us and that easily end up concealing the phenomenon. In positive terms, the ontological interpretation, and even the language by which we designate these beings, must proceed *from* the phenomena, from the way these beings show themselves to our concernful dealings. These strictures would *not* be observed if these beings were designated as *things* and their ontological interpretation carried out as investigations of thingliness or reality. Why? Because this designation and the interpretation anticipated by it would miss precisely what is distinctive about beings as they show themselves to our concernful dealings, their pragmatic character. Thus Heidegger proposes to designate them: *Zeug*, as implement, tool, or equipment. The first task, then, is to determine what makes equipment be equipment—its equipmentality (*Zeughaftigkeit*).

Here there is a major translation problem. Heidegger excludes the designation *thing* (*Ding*, res), and yet it is difficult to find a good translation of certain key terms without using the word *thing*.

> *das Zuhandene*: the thing at hand (tool, equipment)
> *Zuhandenheit*: handiness (Macquarrie and Robinson: the ready-to-hand)
> *Das Vorhandene*: the present thing (just there before us)
> *Vorhandenheit*: presence (Macquarrie and Robinson: the present-at-hand)

So we will translate them as:

thing-at-hand (*Zuhandene/Zuhandenheit*, handiness)
present thing (*Vorhanden*)
Zeug: implement, tool, equipment; one could say "useful thing," but . . .

Let us now consider Heidegger's analysis of equipment in seven steps.

(1) The Being of equipment is such that any piece of equipment always belongs to a *totality of equipment*, which is to say that equipment can be what it is only within an equipment-totality. In specific terms, equipment is something in-order-to (*etwas um zu*); that is, equipment involves the "in-order-to" as its basic structure, *and* this structure is a kind of reference or assignment (*Verweisung*) of something to something. Through this reference, an item is bound up in a totality. For example, the shoemaker has his hammer in his shop *in order to* hammer or, more extendedly, *in order to* make shoes. So there is a reference or assignment of the hammer to the *work* of making shoes. But other pieces of equipment are also needed in order to make shoes (knife and scissors for cutting, needle and thread for sewing, etc.). So there is an equipment totality defined by reference of each item to the work of making shoes. Heidegger is saying that beings can show themselves *as* equipment only from out of an equipment totality. This means, in turn, that whenever an item of equipment shows itself to our concernful dealings, the equipment totality must already somehow have been uncovered, brought into view.

(2) Equipment can genuinely show itself only to an appropriate comportment; for example, hammering with a hammer rather than just staring at it as an occurring thing. "The less we just stare at the thing called hammer, the more we take hold of it and use it, the more originary our relation to it becomes and the more undisguisedly it is encountered as what it is, as equipment" (BT 69/69). Equipment *as* it shows itself originarily to our concernful dealings Heidegger calls *zuhanden* (handy or at hand). Or, in phenomenological-ontological terms: "The kind of Being of [i.e., that belongs to] equipment in which it reveals itself from itself, we call *handiness* [*Zuhandenheit*]" (BT 69/69).

(3) In our concernful dealings with equipment, the individual items of equipment are not grasped thematically. Rather, to be genuinely handy, such items must "withdraw," hold themselves back in a certain inconspicuousness. "What our everyday dealings initially dwell on [*aufhalten*, stay] is not the tools themselves, but the work. . . . The work bears with it the referential totality within which the equipment is encountered" (BT 69-70/69). For example, in hammering, the shoemaker is oriented not to the hammer (he just uses it) but to the *work* of making shoes, to which the hammer, as equipment, is referred. What he *dwells on* is the work. Heidegger is saying, then, that the work is what carries (bears, gathers) the equipment totality, and that is to say, the referential totality by which the items of equipment are related and form a totality. As we shall see,

this equipment totality is what constitutes the environment, the *world* of everyday Dasein, and the referential totality is what constitutes its structure, which is to say, its worldliness.

(4) In our concernful dealing, the equipment totality is, as with individual items, not known, not grasped thematically. Nevertheless, it must somehow be in view in order that items of equipment be able to show themselves as such. The point is that the "sight" operative here, the sight that guides our concernful dealings is of a distinctive kind and *not* just a privative form of theoretical seeing. "Our dealings with equipment subordinate themselves to the manifold of references of the 'in-order-to.' The sight with which they thus accommodate themselves is *circumspection [Umsicht]*" (BT 69/69).

(5) The work is the "what-for" (*Wozu*) of the items of equipment. But, in turn, the work has a reference beyond itself, a "what-for." For example, the shoes are made for wearing, for a certain *use*. So what is produced through the work has a useability; that is, the work has *reference* to use.

(6) The work (making/thing made) is also a using *of* something—of materials. The shoes require leather, thread, and so on. So the work also sustains reference to materials, and, through the reference to materials, there is reference to nature as the source of materials.

(7) The work sustains also a reference to a *user*. For example, the shoes are made to be worn *by someone*, even if this someone is indefinite. And, through the reference to a user, there is a further reference to the *public world* and to an environing nature.

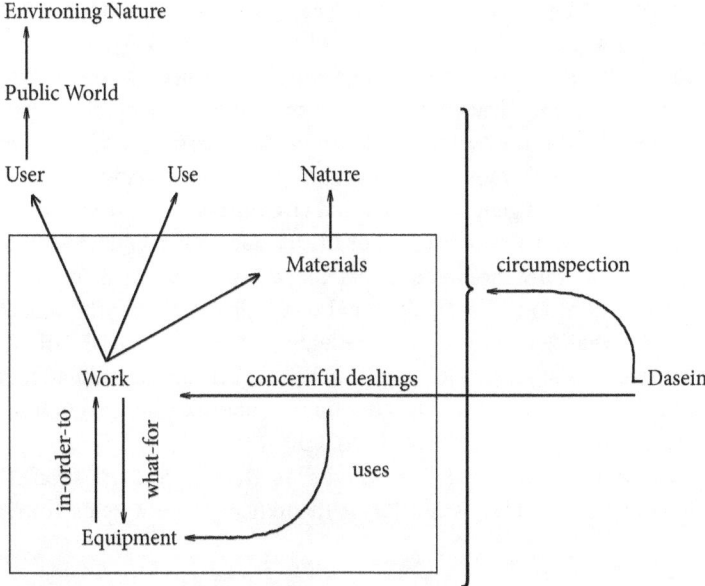

Thus here we have a first indication with regard to environmentality (i.e., the structure of environment, of world, and this is to say, worldliness): it is the totality of references borne by the work.

We should note, finally, that at the end of section 15, Heidegger returns to the concept of handiness in order to ward off a certain misunderstanding. Handiness is not just a certain way of taking things. That is, there are not, first, "neutral" things that are then given subjective coloring: things are not first simply present and then rendered handy by having certain subjective meanings cast over them. It is not even that things are first of all objectively present and then come to be set within a referential totality in relation to which they have the character of handiness. Rather, "*Handiness is the ontological categorial definition of beings as they are 'in themselves'*" (BT 71/71).

Section 16: The Worldly Character of the Surrounding World Announcing Itself in Innerworldly Beings

At this point, the task of the Existential Analytic is to thematize the equipment totality (i.e., the world of everyday Dasein). In fact, such a thematizing is already underway in section 15 where the various references sustained by the work are indicated. *However*, if this thematizing is to be fully and rigorously *phenomenological*, it must follow (subordinate itself to) the way in which such a totality *shows itself* prephilosophically. That is, the analytic must have a phenomenal basis, a basis in a showing of this totality *to* our concernful dealings.

What can provide such a basis? How does this totality show itself? Already, we have seen that in order for an item of equipment to show itself, the equipment totality must already be disclosed, which is to say, it must have already shown itself. However, this showing, and our circumspection attuned to it, is "submerged" in our practical dealings. It is the kind of showing/circumspection by which the shoemaker, where he has a specific thing to do, reaches for the right tool—without any deliberation. This pertains more to the hands than to mere seeing or abstract intelligence. In our usual circumspective concern, the equipment totality does *not* stand out, is not lit up, does not thematically (overtly) show itself but rather has the character of being taken for granted. Thus our usual concern is not sufficient as a phenomenal basis for the Existential Analytic of the world. So what does provide an adequate phenomenal basis? This is what Heidegger indicates in section 16 when he points to certain exceptional modes of concern in which the equipment totality does announce itself through items of equipment in which world gets brought to light.

We should note that there is here another methodological reflection. The existential/ontological analysis is not just a theoretical account apart from/above

Dasein's actual engagement with beings within-the-world. Rather, it must have a phenomenal/ontic basis. The analytic elevates (raises) this phenomenal basis to the level of theoretical reflection, which, however, never simply leaves the basis behind.

There are three such modes of concern in which the equipment totality announces itself.

(1) In our circumspective dealings, a tool may be encountered as *unusable* (e.g., the broken hammer). When so encountered, it becomes *conspicuous*, and this conspicuousness presents the otherwise handy tool as having a certain unhandiness. It merely lies there, like a "tool-thing." As Heidegger says, "Pure presence [*Vorhandenheit*] announces itself in such equipment only to withdraw again into the handiness [*Zuhandenheit*] of something with which one is concerned, that is, of what is being put back into repair" (BT 73/72).

(2) A tool may be encountered as *missing* (e.g., the missing hammer). Then what is still handy takes on the character of *obtrusiveness*. That is, it seems to lose its handiness and to reveal itself as something merely present, as what cannot be budged without the missing tool.

(3) A tool (or even a certain work) may be encountered as *unhandy* in the sense of standing in the way in the mode of *obstinacy*; that is, as something with which we must concern ourselves before doing anything else (e.g., repairing the hammer). Here, too, the presence of what is handy (cf. the handy: *das Zuhandene*) announces itself.

All three of these modes serve to bring out the character of presence in what has the mode of Being of handiness (in *das Zuhandene*). But how does this serve to light up the equipment totality? "Something is unusable. This means that the constitutive reference of the in-order-to to a what-for has been disturbed. The references themselves are not observed, rather they are 'there' in our concernful submissions to them. But in a *disturbance of reference*—in being unusable for . . .—the reference becomes explicit. . . . The context of equipment comes to light, not as a totality never seen before, but as a totality that has continually been seen beforehand in our circumspection. With this totality, however, the world announces itself" (BT 74–75/74). The point is this: when something handy proves unusable (missing or unhandy), a certain presence obtrudes in it or around where it would be. It does *not simply* become present; rather, there is a kind of vacillation between handiness and presence. In this vacillation, the references belonging to the handy are not simply obliterated—*but* they are *disturbed* insofar as a certain objective presence obtrudes. It is precisely then that the references become explicit; that is, when they remain to an extent in effect and yet cannot simply operate in their usual, covert way. Since these references are what gathers the equipment into a totality, this amounts to a lighting-up of the equipment totality—that is, of world.

Section 17: Reference and Signs

Heidegger next provides an analysis of signs in which he shows that they belong to the equipment totality *and* have the capacity to bring this totality (i.e., world) to light. We will look very briefly at section 17, in which the question of the phenomenal basis is developed in this other way through a detailed analysis of signs. We will mention only two points.

(1) Within the horizon of everydayness, a sign is an item of equipment. As an item of equipment, it belongs to an equipment totality. This means it is involved in the system of references that constitute the structure of the equipment totality—*and*, in particular, it has a *reference* to some work (an in-order-to). In the case of the sign, the reference becomes ontically concrete in the function of "indicating" [*zeigen*]. That is, this is its specific form, just as the reference that the hammer has takes the form of a hammering. *However*, in general, we must distinguish between referring and indicating; all tools are involved in referring, only signs indicate. This has a very important consequence: the system of references by which an equipment totality is structured can*not* be reduced to a system of signs.

(2) What is the character of the indicating (showing) that a sign performs? "Signs are not things that stand in an indicating relation to another thing; rather, they are *equipment which explicitly bring a totality of equipment to circumspection so that the worldly character of what is handy announces itself*" (BT 80/78). So signs serve to light up an equipment totality, to let the world announce itself—and thus they bear on the issue of the phenomenal basis for the existential-ontological analysis of world.

Here, in a very preliminary way—little more than a hint—we can anticipate the enormous significance that language will eventually have for Heidegger.

Section 18: Relevance and Significance: The Worldliness of the World

In section 18, Heidegger undertakes a *Wiederholung* of the analysis of world, but he does so in such a radical way that these six pages reach the deepest level of the Dasein-analytic. Each transition is a *Tigersprung*! I will try to make a few of these leaps, especially where the leap reveals an aporia that, up to this point, has remained concealed. To the extent that numeration is even relevant, we will traverse five stages of the analysis.

I. One recurrent difficulty is that Heidegger sometimes reaches very deeply into the German language by appealing to archaic words. The first transition in section 18 begins with the term *reference*. This (as already seen) designates the relations among the various moments that belong to an equipment totality (i.e., world). But then he replaces it with *Bewandtnis*—an unusual, probably archaic word. This is translated as *relevance* (we might perhaps translate it as *connection*). He explains that things that are referred are referred to something (e.g., work is referred to use). But things "are relevant *together with* something else. The character of Being of things at hand is *relevance*. To be relevant means to let something be together with something else" (BT 84/82).

This raises the question: Is there a difference between these two designations? Does *reference* designate a relation between two moments and *relevance* the entire complex? Or does relevance indicate a closer, more compact bond between various moments? Heidegger does not say. Perhaps we are to sense this in the word *Bewandtnis*.

II. Relevance always occurs and is determined within a totality of relevance, a total relevance. This was also shown in section 15: a piece of equipment belongs to a totality and can show itself as equipment only from out of this totality. Within a totality of relevance, there can be "reiteration" or a connected series of involvements. Heidegger's example:

The hammer has relevance for hammering.

Hammering has relevance for fastening something down.

Fastening something down has relevance for protecting against bad weather.

Protecting against bad weather has relevance for providing shelter for Dasein (i.e., a possibility of Dasein's Being).

So not only is there a series of relevances *but also* that series leads eventually to a "primary for-which," beyond which there is no further relevance, which is not for anything else. This "primary for-which" Heidegger calls a "for-the-sake-of-which" (*Worum-willen*). And it always pertains to the Being of Dasein. So here we have a first indication of how world is connected to Dasein.

III. Heidegger introduces two additional expressions.

A. Letting-be and, more specifically, letting be relevant (*Bewendenlassen*). "This '*a priori*' letting-be-relevant is the condition of the possibility that things at hand be encountered so that Dasein in its ontic association with the beings thus encountered can let them be relevant in an ontic sense. On the other hand, letting be relevant, understood in an ontological sense, concerns the freeing of *every* thing at hand as a thing at hand" (BT 85/83). So letting be relevant has a double sense. It has the ontic sense of letting particular things-at-hand function in accord with their character; for example, letting the hammer function as a hammer. It has the ontological sense of letting the entire referential totality hold sway. This is the condition of the possibility for letting-be in the ontic sense.

B. Freeing or releasing (*freigeben*). "Understood ontologically, letting be relevant is the previous freeing of beings for their innerworldly handiness" (BT 85/84).

The sense of both expressions is letting the totality of relevance (reference) be operative—that is, not binding it, for example, to a subject, not interrupting it. That is to say, *freeing* it *to* its character as the a priori condition for encountering beings within-the-world.

IV. Heidegger then introduces the concept of *understanding*. "The previous disclosure of that for which the freeing of things encountered in the world ensues is none other than the understanding of world to which Dasein as a being is always already related" (BT 86/84). This says: the freeing or letting-be of the referential (relevant) totality, which is presupposed for an encounter with beings, is the *understanding* of world.

To see what constitutes understanding, we need to go back to the character of Dasein as first introduced. Dasein comports itself to its Being as at issue (always in question). Now Heidegger reformulates this: Dasein comports itself to its Being *as possibility*. Further, in comporting itself to a particular possibility, Dasein refers itself to an in-order-to (i.e., that which must be done in order to realize the possibility). But, in turn, this requires equipment—perhaps a whole series of equipment.

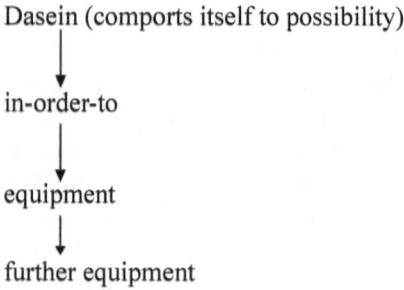

So there are two series that run in opposite directions. Previously, it began with equipment (the hammer) and traced this to Dasein (as the for-the-sake-of-which). Now the series begins with Dasein (with its comportment to possibilities) and traces this to equipment. (Note: this comportment to possibilities is equivalent to understanding.) The first series entails: Dasein presupposes world—that is, Dasein is always already in a world. The second series entails: Dasein unfolds (constitutes) world. More precisely, in existing, Dasein is always already in a world—*and yet* Dasein constitutes world (unfolds worldliness).

V. Heidegger introduces the concept of signifying and significance. Heidegger describes signifying as the relation between the various items in a relevant totality (such as an equipment totality). So signifying is the same as referring as relevance—but with a shade of difference. Heidegger says that we must avoid taking *signify* to refer to linguistic signs, as though the only things that signify are words. Rather, the significance that Heidegger refers to here is something prior to signs (in the linguistic sense). "But the significance itself with which Dasein is always already familiar contains the ontological condition of the possibility that Dasein, as understanding and interpreting, can disclose something akin to 'significations' [*Bedeutungen*] which in turn found the possible Being of words and language" (BT 87/86). But we should note here Heidegger's later marginal note that reads: "Untrue. Language is not imposed, but *is* the primordial essence of truth as there [Da]" (BT 87/86). This points to developments beyond *Being and Time*, especially "On the Essence of Truth."

We should note two brief points by way of conclusion.

(1) We have seen that Dasein's relation to world involves two sides: (a) Dasein presupposes world, which is to say that in existing, Dasein is always already in a world, and (b) Dasein unfolds the worldliness of world, Dasein constitutes world. In further development, Heidegger elaborates these two moments.

(a) Dasein's being always already in a world is characterized as its *thrownness*. Yet Dasein is not thrown into the world as a stone is thrown into a pond. Rather, Dasein has a certain "awareness" of world to which it is submitted and indeed of that submission itself. In Heidegger's language, these are revealed, disclosed to Dasein. Such disclosure occurs in *Befindlichkeit* (attunement); that is, in moods.

(b) Dasein's constitution of world is what Heidegger calls *understanding*. Understanding has the character of projection (throwing).

These moments (attunement, understanding), along with *Rede* (the existential foundation of language) constitute *Being-in*. So we can see how the moments of Being-in-the-world belong together, how they form a unity, how they make it (following *History of the Concept of Time*) an articulated unity.

(2) These analyses are complex. Heidegger's text is intricate and requires the utmost care and patience in following the interwoven, minute strands. Yet this complexity results not from a lack of clarity but from the phenomenological insistence of the text; that is, its binding itself to the complexities of the self-showing to which it is addressed. In this regard, one could appropriately say of Heidegger what Heidegger himself, in a 1935–1936 lecture course, said of Kant—that he "has something in common with the great Greek beginning, which at the same time distinguishes him from all German thinkers before and after him: this is the incorruptible clarity of his thought and his speech, which by no means excludes the questionable and the unstable and which does not feign light where there is darkness."[1]

Sections 22–24: Spatiality

We will give only a brief consideration to these sections.

When Heidegger introduced the concept of Being-in, he insisted that it does not mean spatial containment (Dasein is not *in* world as clothes are in a closet).

---

1. Martin Heidegger, *Die Frage nach dem Ding* (Tübingen: Max Niemeyer, 1962), 42. In English, *What Is a Thing?*, trans. W. B. Barton and Vera Deutsch (Chicago: Regnery, 1967), 56.

However, he insisted that Dasein has its own peculiar spatiality. Against the background analysis of world, Heidegger goes about exhibiting this spatiality. And, along with it, he exhibits the spatiality of things at hand and shows how it is founded on world.

In the spatiality of things at hand we have two spatial characters: (a) *nearness* (or *closeness*) (*Nähe*) and (b) direction (*Richtung*). (a) This is not a distance that could be determined by being measured. "Beings 'at hand' have their various nearnesses which are not ascertained by measuring distances" (BT 102/100). Rather, this is the kind of nearness that a tool at hand (within reach) has. "Their nearness regulates itself in terms of circumspectly 'calculative' handling and using" (BT 102/100). (b) *Direction* (directionality) (*Richtung*). "The circumspection of concern at the same time establishes what is thus near with respect to the direction in which equipment is always accessible" (BT 100/100). For example, the hammer not only is within reach (close) but is also within reach in a definite *direction*, a direction within (defined by) the equipment context.

These two spatial characters together constitute the *place* (*Platz*) of a piece of equipment. In turn, the place belongs to a totality of places (i.e., places of all the equipment in a particular equipment-totality). Furthermore, the structure of this totality of places corresponds to that of the totality of equipment. "Place is always the definite 'over there' and the 'there' of a useful thing *belonging there*. In each and every case belonging there corresponds to the useful character of what is at hand, that is, to its relevant belonging to a totality of useful things" (BT 102–103/100). (Cf. Biemel, *Le Concept de Monde chez Heidegger*: "The different places of a complex are among themselves in the same relation as the items of equipment").[2]

Finally, Heidegger introduces "the underlying condition" for any such places: *region* (*Gegend*). A region is a "whither" (*Wohin*) to which a totality of places (of an equipment-totality) gets allotted. "This 'whither' which makes it possible for equipment to belong somewhere and which we circumspectly keep in view in advance and in our concernful dealings, we call the *region*" (BT 103/100).

What does Heidegger mean by *region*? This is difficult to thematize precisely because, as he says, it is so inconspicuous. However, three points are mentioned. (a) Clearly, it is *not* a three-dimensional multiplicity of possible positions; that is, it is *not* the dimensional, isotropic, uniform space of geometry and modern physics. (b) Region or regional orientation (of places) is what makes up the "aroundness" (*das Umhafte*), the "round-about-us" (*das Um-uns-herum*) of things in the environment (*Umwelt*). This "aroundness" is what, at the more remote level of mathematical thematization, will be thematized as the dimensionality of space.

---

2. Walter Biemel, *Le Concept de Monde chez Heidegger* (Louvain: Nauwelaerts, 1950), 68.

"This regional orientation of the multiplicity of places of what is at hand constitutes the aroundness [*Umhafte*], the being around us [*Um-uns-herum*] of beings encountered initially in the surrounding world. There is never a three-dimensional multiplicity of possible positions initially given which is then filled out with present things. This dimensionality of space is still veiled in the spatiality of what is at hand" (BT 103/100–101). (c) Heidegger stresses the a priori character of the region, a priori in that nonsubjective sense developed by phenomenology (cf., *History of the Concept of Time*). "Something akin to a region must already be uncovered if there is to be any possibility of alloting or coming across places for a totality of equipment available to circumspection" (BT 103/100).

Regarding Dasein's spatiality, Heidegger writes: "And only because Dasein is spatial by way of de-distancing and directionality can things at hand in the surrounding world be encountered in their spatiality" (BT 110/107). This is to say that Dasein is spatial in a special way—its spatiality is *not* a mere occurring in space, *not* a being at hand at some *place*. Rather, its spatiality is constituted by certain characters pertaining to its concernful dealings, which is to say, its character as Being-in-the-world. These characters correspond precisely, are fitted to the spatial characters what is at hand, *and thus* allow at hand things to be encountered in their spatiality. The two spatial characteristics of Dasein are, then, briefly, as follows.

(1) De-distancing (*Entfernung*). This means to make the farness (remoteness) of something vanish, to draw it near; that is, to let it be *close* with that kind of closeness that the at hand has, a closeness regulated by circumspective concern.

(2) Directionality (*Ausrichtung*). The point here is that in our concernful dealings, in drawing equipment close, Dasein is *directed* (takes a direction) toward a region and toward places from which beings are brought close. From this directionality arises the "bodily" directions of left and right. "But we must observe that the directionality that belongs to de-distancing is grounded in Being-in-the-world. Left and right are not something 'subjective' for which the subject has a feeling, but they are directions of orientation in a world which is always already at hand. I could never find my way around in a world 'through a mere feeling of a difference between my two sides'" (BT 109/106).[3]

In conclusion, let me cite part of a statement in which Heidegger sums up his results as regards the nature of space as such:

> *Space is neither in the subject nor is the world in space*. Rather, space is "in" the world since the Being-in-the-world constitutive for Dasein has disclosed space. . . . And because Dasein is spatial in the way described, space shows

---

3. Ed. note: Heidegger is here citing Kant's essay "Was Heisst: Sich im Denken orientieren?" (1786) from *Werke* (Akademie Ausgabe), vol. 8, 131–47.

itself as *a priori*. This term does not mean something like belonging beforehand to an initially worldless subject which spins a space out of itself. Here, apriority means the previousness of encountering space (as region) in the actual encountering of things at hand in the surrounding world (BT 111/108).

The essential point is that space must be understood in reference to *world*. As Heidegger says at the end of the chapter, "Space can only be conceived by going back to the world" (BT 111/110).

4. Being-in-the-World as Being-with and Being a Self: The "They"

CHAPTER 4 BEGINS with two important methodological reflections: the first pertains primarily to analyses of the previous chapter; the second (§25) serves to orient the analyses in this chapter.

The first reflection takes up again the question of the beginning of *Being and Time*. But now, more specifically, Heidegger asks about the beginning of the Existential Analytic proper (in distinction from the preliminary sketches in chaps. 1 and 2). Still more specifically, the question is why the Existential Analytic began as it did in chapter 3; that is, why it began with the problem of world. Heidegger answers: because everyday Dasein is "taken over by its world" [*benommen*, dazed, benumbed], "absorbed in the world" (BT 113/111). That is, world is the focal point for everyday Dasein, the point where it is anchored, involved, takes its bearings. So the Existential Analytic begins where Dasein is: the analysis is directed toward that toward which everyday Dasein is primarily directed (oriented). Furthermore, through the Existential Analytic, this directedness of everyday Dasein toward world gets brought more fully to light, so that the Existential Analytic comes to disclose its point of beginning and the appropriateness of that beginning. One further point: since everyday Dasein is absorbed in the world, its other modes of comportment (e.g., toward itself) will be determined by this orientation to world. Specifically, everyday Dasein's way of being itself, the "who" of everyday Dasein, the "self" of everydayness, will be determined by this absorption in the world. In chapter 4, the Existential Analytic will thematize this determination.

The second methodological reflection is given in section 25. Heidegger observes that it would seem that the question "Who is Dasein?" has already been answered: in section 9, it was said that a basic character of Dasein is its "mineness." And so, presumably, Dasein is an I, a subject, a self, in the sense of what maintains itself as identical throughout changes in its experiences (*subjectum*, ὑποκείμενον). However, such a conception of the "who" moves in the wrong direction. Why? Because, in effect, it takes *substantiality* as the basic ontological clue for understanding the "who." That is, "Dasein is tacitly conceived in advance as a present thing" (BT 114/112). *However*, the Being of Dasein is not presence but rather existence. Heidegger stresses that in this domain, we must resist the

77

"obvious" answers and the ways of formulating the problem that are derived from those answers. For example, we must avoid taking the ontically obvious assertion that Dasein is an I *as* prescribing a way of developing the ontological question about the "who." Rather: the issue must be developed phenomenologically, which is to say, from the things themselves, which is to also say, through a phenomenal demonstration that proceeds from the mode of Being of Dasein. And thus it must be questioned (wondered about, doubted) whether reflective awareness of the I provides genuine access to Dasein and hence to the "who." "In the present context of an existential analytic of factical Dasein, the question arises whether the way of the giving of the I which we mentioned discloses Dasein in its everydayness, if it discloses it at all. Is it then *a priori* self-evident that the access to Dasein must be simple perceiving reflection of the I of acts?" (BT 115/113) The question, in effect, calls into question the entire modern philosophical tradition since Descartes and especially Husserl after the *Logical Investigations* (cf. *History of the Concept of Time*, p. 90ff). In fact, what has been shown in the analysis of world is already sufficient to forbid taking reflective awareness of the I as a point of departure for the question of the "who." "The clarification of Being-in-the-world showed that a mere subject without a world 'is' not initially and is also never given. And, thus, an isolated I without the others is in the end just as far from being given initially" (BT 116/113). Why is a bare subject never given? Because *in existing*, Dasein is always implicated in world. Why is there no I without others? Because others are already implicated in the referential structure of Dasein's world (i.e., worldliness). So the "who" is *not* to be ontologically understood in terms of the "I." Rather, it is to be understood in terms of *existence*—that is, existentially interpreted. This, then, means that the character of the "who" must be determined in terms of Dasein's way of comporting itself to its own Being.

In section 26, Heidegger turns more directly to the task of giving a phenomenological demonstration of the "who" of Dasein, one that proceeds from the character of Dasein as existence. Almost the entire analysis in section 26 is contained in this statement: "The world of Dasein is a *with-world* [*Mitwelt*]. Being-in is *being-with* [*Mitsein*] others. The innerworldly Being-in-itself of others is *with-Dasein* [*Mitdasein*]" (BT 118/116). Thus the issues are: (1) World as with-world, (2) Being-in as Being-with others, (3) Being of others as with-Dasein.

(1) In section 25, Heidegger had already referred to the involvement of others in world. Now he elaborates the issue descriptively. In the work-world of the craftsman, there are always already *references* to others. For example, there is the reference of the work to a *user* (shoes→possible wearers). With material, there is a reference not only to nature but also to the one who supplies or produces the material. More generally, things are loaded with references to others and so render others present with Dasein. For example, the book is written by someone, bought from someone, recommended by someone, already read by someone. Each such

thing "spreads round about it an atmosphere of humanity."[1] So in the environment, others are always already encountered in terms of their involvement in the world. It is *not* a matter of inferring from things to others (others is not somehow added on in thought to some thing). *Rather*: others are always already there concretely in our concernful dealings—that is, the world of Dasein is a with-world.

However, granted that the other is always already there, we might still misconstrue the situation: we might suppose that there is a plurality of subjects (I's), so that it would still be necessary to explain how one I gets over to another. *But* in everydayness, this is *not* the sense in which others are present. With others (as with the handy), it is not a matter of escaping from an "inner sphere" to things outside but rather a matter of being already in the midst of what is "outside." "In order to avoid this misunderstanding, we must observe in what sense we are talking about 'others.' 'Others' does not mean everybody else but me—those from whom the I distinguishes itself. Others are, rather, those from whom one mostly does *not* distinguish oneself, those among whom one also is" (BT 118/115). This being among others must be understood existentially, not categorially—that is, it is not a matter of relations between distinct present things (neither already established relations nor to be established relations). That is to say, it is not a matter of "intersubjectivity." Rather, "Being-with-Others" is to be understood *existentially*, which is to say, in terms of existence, which is to further say, in reference to Dasein's comportment to its own Being. Being-with-Others is something in which Dasein is implicated simply in existing; specifically, by virtue of that twofold relation to world that Dasein has simply in existing.

(2) If we designate existence as "Being-in," then "Being-in is Being-with-Others." In this connection, we can see what is at issue in Heidegger's assertion that Being-with concerns the *essence* of Dasein. The point is this: in saying that Being-in is Being-with-Others, Heidegger is *not* merely saying that others of my kind happen factually to occur. "The phenomenological assertion that Dasein is essentially Being-with has an existential-ontological meaning. It does not intend to ascertain ontically that I am factually not presently alone, rather that others of my kind also are [*vorkommen*]" (BT 120/117). However, he is not simply deducing Being-with-Others from some abstractly preconceived essence of Dasein. "Our procedure is therefore not to lay down some concept of man and then maintain, since man presumably has to be a 'social being,' that the structure of Being-with belongs to Dasein. Instead, from the phenomenal state of the everydayness of Dasein itself it becomes evident that not only the others but remarkably 'one oneself' is there in what one attends to everyday" (HCT 241). That is, the essence of Dasein is existence—and in everyday existing, one is always implicated in a world *with others*.

---

1. Maurice Merleau-Ponty, *Phénoménologie de la Perception* (Paris: Gallimard, 1945), 400. In English, *Phenomenology of Perception*, trans. C. Smith (New York: Humanities, 1962), 347.

(3) Heidegger stresses that others are encountered from out of the *world*, in which Dasein dwells. In the first instance, they are encountered in the way already described—in terms of their involvement with equipment (the handy). But they may also, of course, be encountered "more directly"; however, even then, they are not encountered as person-things over against me but rather from out of our world: "We meet them 'at work,' that is, primarily in their Being-in-the-world" (BT 120/117). Others, *as* encountered (in either mode) from out of world, have the character of with-Dasein [*Mit-Dasein*]. That is, "The innerworldly Being-in-itself of others is *with-Dasein* [*Mitdasein*]" (BT 118/116). *Furthermore*, Dasein also encounters *itself* from out of world; that is, it finds itself in its concernful dealings with the handy in the midst of others. "This nearest and elemental worldly way of Dasein encountering the world goes so far that even one's *own* Dasein *initially* becomes 'discoverable' by *looking away* from its 'experiences' and the 'center of its actions,' or by not yet 'seeing' them at all. Dasein initially finds 'itself' in *what* it does, needs, expects, has charge of, in the beings at hand with which it initially *concerns* itself in the surrounding world" (BT 119/116). Here, again, we see how the world is the focal point (anchorage) for everyday Dasein: Dasein encounters itself in the world—*which means*: the character of its self (the *who* of everyday Dasein) is fundamentally bound up with its concernful dealings in the world.

Most of the remainder of section 26 is devoted to consideration of the various specific forms that Being-with can take. Heidegger mentions the mode in which the other remains inconspicuous and one remains indifferent to the other—these are modes, common in everydayness, in which one fails to recognize the other *as* other, as *Mitdasein*, ontologically, the other as present thing. What is most significant in this entire account are those modes that Heidegger designates as the two extreme possibilities. (1) Dasein can take over the cares of the other. It can "*leap in* for him" (BT 122/118): "It can, so to speak, take the other's 'care' away from him and put itself in his place in taking care, it can *leap in* for him. Concern takes over what is to be taken care of for the other. The other is thus displaced, he steps back so that afterwards, when the matter has been attended to, he can take it over as something finished and available or disburden himself of it completely. In this concern, the other can become someone who is dependent and dominated even if this domination is a tacit one and remains hidden from him" (BT 122/118–19).

(2) Dasein can *leap ahead* of the other. "In contrast to this [i.e., leaping in for him], there is the possibility of a concern which does not so much leap in for the other as *leap ahead* of him in his existentiell possibility-for-being, not in order to take 'care' away from him, but rather to first give it properly back to him as such" (BT 122/119). This mode "helps the other to become transparent to himself *in* his care and *free for* it" (BT 122/119). Heidegger says that this mode of concern "pertains to authentic care" (BT 122/119). This is one of the first references to *authenticity*.

Section 27: Everyday Being a Self and the They

We have seen that everyday Dasein is anchored in a world among others (from whom Dasein does not, for the most part, distinguish itself); that is, Dasein is caught up in concernful dealings, among others. Thus the peculiar selfhood, the "who" of everyday Dasein, is determined *from* this focal point. That is, everyday Dasein's way of being anchored (caught up) in the world among others determines the character of everyday Dasein's selfhood, the "who." The "who" thus determined is called the "they" (*das Mann*) in the sense of indefinite others. Heidegger's principal task is to exhibit this determination, which is to show how everyday Dasein's way of being caught up in the world among others prescribes that its "who" have this sense (the "they"). Heidegger does this by exhibiting a series of "characters of being" (ontologically determining factors), which arise from everyday Dasein's anchorage and which together describe how the "they" functions *as* the "who," as "the self of everyday Dasein."

Distantiality (*Abständigkeit*). In everyday being among others, "there is constant care as to the way one differs from them" (BT 126/122). That is to say, there is a constant and engaged assessing of differences (whether one's intent is to eliminate differences or maintain them). Furthermore, one's own self-determination follows the directions indicated by this preoccupation with differences from others. In this sense, Dasein stands "in subjection to others" (BT 126/122). That is, others dictate Dasein's self-determination, dictate "who" Dasein is—that is, become its "who."

Distantiality is related to another character pertaining to the "they": *averageness* (*Durchschnittlichkdeit*). This means that the "they" prescribes what it considers valid (what is standard, average) and enforces it. "We take pleasure and enjoy ourselves the way *they* enjoy themselves. We read, see, and judge literature and art the way *they* see and judge. But we also withdraw from the 'great mass' the way *they* withdraw, we find 'shocking' what *they* find shocking. The they, which is nothing definite and which all are, though not as a sum, prescribes the kind of Being of everydayness" (BT 126–27/123).

This is linked, in turn, to another character: "This averageness, which prescribes what can and may be ventured, watches over every exception which thrusts itself to the fore. Every priority is noiselessly squashed. Overnight, everything that is original is flattened down as something long since known. Everything won through struggle becomes something manageable. Every mystery loses its power. The care of averageness reveals, in turn, an essential tendency of Dasein, which we call the *levelling down* of all possibilities of Being" (BT 127/123). So here emerges a third character: *leveling-down* (*Einebnung*).

Distantiality, averageness, and leveling-down together constitute a fourth character: *publicness* (*Öffentlichkeit*). Publicness involves controlling the way the world and Dasein get interpreted, a controlling that is insensible to every difference of level and genuineness. "Publicness obscures everything, and then claims that what has been thus covered over is what is familiar and accessible to everybody" (BT 127/124).

By this controlling, the "they" takes over from Dasein its responsibility for itself—the "they" is answerable for everything. Thus Dasein is "disburdened"—hence, another character: *disburdening* (*Entlastung*).

Finally, as disburdening Dasein, the "they" accommodates Dasein—that is, accommodates whatever tendency Dasein may have toward making it easy for itself. Thus the final character: *accommodation* (*Entgegenkommen*).

Hence the self of everyday Dasein, the "who" in the form of the "they," is characterized by distantiality, averageness, leveling down, publicness, disburdening, and accommodation.

Authenticity/Inauthenticity. In the modes that Heidegger has described, Dasein is *inauthentic*, which is to say, everyday Dasein is inauthentic (Note: *eigentlich* > *eigen*). In terms of the initial characterization of Dasein as own (*meinen*) (cf. chap. 1), this means that everyday Dasein's comportment to itself (its way of being is ownness) is such as to conceal itself in its proper Being. Heidegger's description is decisive: "The self of everyday Dasein is the *they-self*, which we distinguish from the *authentic self*, that is, the self which has explicitly grasped itself. As the they-self, Dasein is *dispersed* in the they and must first find itself. This dispersion characterizes the 'subject' of the kind of being which we know as concernful absorption in the world encountered as closest" (BT 129/125). This means, then, that any movement toward authenticity (i.e., toward the self-comportment in which Dasein would be disclosed to itself in its proper Being) will always be a *recovery of self*, a recalling *from* dispersion, a wresting from concealment. Regarding such authentic self-disclosure, Heidegger says that it "always comes about by clearing-away concealments and obscurities, by breaking up the disguises with which Dasein cuts itself off from itself" (BT 129/125). It is thus that Heidegger characterizes authenticity as *"an existentiell modification of the they"* (BT 130/126).

Conclusion: we have said repeatedly that everything leads back to (unfolds from) Dasein's comportment to its own Being. Let's trace out this "order."

We begin at the level of Husserl's intentional analysis; for example, an act in which a particular thing (yellow, upholstered couch) is identified as such. Heidegger would say that such an act in which the thing is apprehended as present (merely perceived) is founded on the more intimate, practical involvement with handy things. That is, before the couch is an object having the perceptible properties called "yellow" and "upholstered," it is a piece of furniture in a room, something to sit on, which is to say, something with which we deal concernfully.

But then, in turn, our concernful dealings with what is handy can take place only insofar as those things belong to a world, a world we must somehow have in view in advance—or, more precisely, a world with which we must be implicated.

How are we implicated with world? That is, how is Dasein *in* a world? By virtue of existing—that is, in Dasein's comportment to its own Being, it is implicated in a world (understanding and constituting). And so, in this sense, everything leads back to existence, to Dasein's comportment to its own Being.

We have seen that this is also the case with regard to the encounter with others. Others are encountered from out of world—and, by being implicated in a world, Dasein is always already implicated with others. Since it is *in* existing that Dasein is *in*-the-world, here, too, we are led back to existence, to Dasein's comportment to its own Being.

The question to which all these analyses lead is thus: What precisely is the character of Dasein's comportment to its own Being? So far, Heidegger has only alluded to its character by speaking of Dasein's comportment to (seizing on) *possibilities*. This is the point, then, where chapter 5 begins.

5. Being-in as Such

Introduction

We have reached the threshold of a very significant turn in the development of *Being and Time*. To proceed, we need to briefly recall the major stages through which the preparatory analysis of Dasein has passed.

I. The analysis began by focusing on *existence*. Heidegger says: the essence of Dasein lies in its existence. This means that what Dasein is, is to be understood in terms of its peculiar comportment (relatedness) to its Being. So Dasein's relatedness to its Being will be the focal point of the entire analysis. That is, everything will be "unfolded" from this. Determinations that express various aspects of this comportment Heidegger calls *existentials*.

II. In chapter 2, he introduces *Being-in-the-world*. This names the more articulated structure on which existence is grounded. It involves three constituent moments: world, the "who," and Being-in. As a way of orienting the entire analysis, Heidegger gives a preliminary account of the first moment; namely, Being-in.

III. In chapter 3, Heidegger turns to the analysis of the world of Dasein's *concern*. World is the equipment-totality within which individual items of equipment can show themselves. Worldliness (the structure of the world) is the totality of references (involvements, assignments) by which:

A. each item of equipment is assigned to the work to be done so that all of the equipment is gathered into a unity by this common assignment.

B. the work to be done is, in turn, referred ultimately to a for-the-sake-of-which (*Worumwillen*) that pertains to Dasein—to some possibility of Dasein.

IV. In chapter 4, Heidegger takes up the question of the "who" of Dasein. Here the task is: to resist the seemingly obvious answer (that the "who" is an I, a subject) and instead to determine the "who" in terms of the character of Dasein as *existence*—that is, in terms of Dasein's way of comporting itself to its own Being. As the basis for this, Heidegger takes up first the question of the other in which he shows: Dasein is essentially *Being-with*—that is, Being-with others belongs to Dasein's existential constitution, to Dasein's very comportment to its Being. On this basis, he then shows: the "who" of everyday Dasein is the "they"—the vague, indefinite others among whom Dasein is.

Section 28: The Task of a Thematic Analysis of Being-in

In chapter 5, Heidegger turns to the third moment of Being-in-the-world: Being-in. In fact, this moment has already been dealt with, even if in a preliminary way—namely, in that account (chap. 2) by which Heidegger sought to orient the entire analysis of Being-in-the-world. Being-in was described as an existential, as the basis that makes possible Dasein's dealing with things-in-the-world—also as factual and spatial—each in its own unique way. So, it is a matter now of a certain *return* to Being-in—that is, a certain circling back to it by way of other analyses (namely, of world and the "who").

Chapter 5 is divided into two main parts. The first, and by far most important, is titled: "The Existential Constitution of the There [*Da*]." The second part returns to the sphere of everydayness, and it complements the account of the "they" from chapter 4. Just preceding the first (in section 28), Heidegger explains the sense of the title by introducing two of the most important words in *Being and Time*. "The being which is essentially constituted by Being-in-the-world *is* itself always its 'there' [*Da*]" (BT 132/129). That is, Dasein is itself its "there" (*Da*). This means Dasein has, in some sense, the character of *place*. But in what sense? Not just in a spatial sense. Of course, Dasein has its proper spatiality, its existential spatiality. But its spatiality is not primordial. Rather, this spatiality is founded on Dasein's character as Being-in-the-world and hence is founded on its character of being its "there."

So what is the relevant sense of "place"? It is that sense that we came across in the introduction, that sense intended when we spoke of Dasein as the place where *Being and Time* begins: the *place* (prephilosophical) of the understanding of Being, the place of the disclosure of Being. Thus in the present context, Heidegger says Dasein has the character of "not being closed off" (*Unverschlossenheit*) (BT 132/129). That is, Dasein is not closed up, sealed off within itself in such a way that it would lack openness to other beings and even to itself. In other words, Dasein is not-closed, disclosive—*or rather*: Dasein is open in such a way that beings get disclosed, in such a way that there is *disclosedness*. So what kind of place is Dasein? A place of disclosedness. "This being [*Seiende*] bears in its ownmost Being [*Sein*] the character of not being closed off [*Unverschlossenheit*]. The expression 'there' means this essential disclosedness [*Erschlossenheit*]. Through disclosedness this being (Dasein) is 'there' for itself together with the there-being [Dasein] of the world" (BT 132/129). This is the first of the two key words: disclosedness (*Erschlossenheit*). Heidegger says: "*Dasein is its disclosedness*" (BT 133/129).

This character of Dasein (as disclosedness) Heidegger also thinks in terms of *clearing* (*Lichtung*), which is the second key word. The paradigm here is a clearing in the forest where light can shine down so as to illuminate things. Heidegger introduces the issue by referring to the traditional notion of *lumen naturale*. "When we talk in an ontically figurative way about the *lumen naturale* in human being, we mean nothing other than the existential-ontological structure of this being, the fact it *is* in such a way as to be its there [*sein Da zu sein*]. To say that it is 'illuminated' means that it is cleared in itself *as* Being-in-the-world, not by another being, but in such a way that it *is* itself the clearing [*Lichtung*]" (BT 133/129). This says: when we say that Dasein is illuminated (has a natural light), what this really refers to is Dasein's character as disclosedness, as clearing. Dasein does not receive this character from some other being but has it "by nature"—it brings it along with itself—that is, Dasein is its disclosedness, is the clearing.

Nota bene: at the end of the next-to-last paragraph on page 129 of the translation, Heidegger writes (as we have already noted): "*Dasein is its disclosedness*" (BT 133/129). To this, there is attached an important marginal note: "Dasein exists, and it alone. Thus, existence is standing out, into and enduring, the openness of the there: Ek-sistence" (BT 133/129).

This is a very critical juncture in *Being and Time, for* here we see emerging a distinction that after *Being and Time* will become ever-more important for Heidegger, a distinction by which he will eventually differentiate his thinking from the entire philosophical tradition. What distinction? Between light (*Licht*) and clearing (*Lichtung*). He is saying (though here without emphasis) *not* that Dasein is illuminated (that it is lit or that it lights up) *but rather* that Dasein is *cleared*, that it is the clearing. *And* that, when we talk "in an ontically figurative way of the *lumen naturale*, what we really refer to is *clearing*" (BT 133/129). There is one sentence that makes this distinction unmistakably: "Only for a being thus cleared existentially do present things become accessible in the light or concealed in the darkness" (BT 133/129). This says that the clearing is presupposed by light and darkness. *So* to sum up: to say that "Dasein is itself its 'there'" means that Dasein is a place of disclosedness in the sense of clearing. So, then, to analyze the "Existential Constitution of the There" means to exhibit those constitutive moments *by which* Dasein is disclosedness; that is, the clearing.

Heidegger mentions three fundamental moments.

1. *Befindlichkeit* (disposition or attunement).
2. *Verstehen* (understanding).
3. *Rede* (discourse).

It is not entirely clear at this point whether these three are simply coordinate, simply equiprimordial. We should note how he presents the matter: he refers to attunement and understanding as the *two* equiprimordial ways of being the "there." Then he says: "Attunement and understanding are equiprimordially determined by *discourse*" (BT 133/130).

Section 29: Dasein as Attunement

The first constituent of Dasein's disclosedness is called *Befindlichkeit*. The relevant prephilosophical sense is best seen in the corresponding verb: "*Wie befinden Sie sich?*," which means "How are you (feeling)?" Literally: How do you find yourself (in which kind of mood do you find yourself to be)? So *Befindlichkeit* refers to something very familiar ontically; namely, our moods, our being-attuned. *Stimmung* (mood) connotes attunement (*stimmen* means "to tune," e.g., a musical instrument). Elsewhere, Heidegger himself renders it as *dispositio* (disposition).

Heidegger's task is to indicate how attunement belongs to Being-in, which is to say, how it belongs to the fundamental disclosedness that Dasein is (how it places Dasein in a clearing). He specifies three essential characteristics of attunement. Each of these characteristics consists in a peculiar kind of disclosedness effected by attunement.

(1) Attunement discloses Dasein *in its thrownness* (*Geworfenheit*). It is in this character that the sense of "finding oneself" is especially important. Heidegger expresses the sense of this in the following way: he speaks of "the phenomenal fact that moods bring Dasein before the that [*das Daß*, the "that it is"] of its there, which stares at it with the inexorability of an enigma" (BT 136/132). This peculiar character, this "that" (that it is, the thatness of its there) is Dasein's *thrownness*. We can see more precisely what thrownness is if we consider another description: "We shall call this character of the Being of Dasein which is veiled in its whence and whither, but in itself all the more openly disclosed, this 'that it is,' the *thrownness* [*Geworfenheit*] of this being into its there; it is thrown in such a way that it is the there as Being-in-the-world. The expression thrownness is meant to suggest the *facticity of its being delivered over* [*Überantwortung*]" (BT 135/131–32). Here, the word *facticity* refers to the sheer "thatness": what is disclosed in mood is simply *that* Dasein is as it is—*without* any reason, origin, or goal being disclosed. Dasein's "whence" and "whither" remain veiled. But, further, Dasein's facticity is here a "facticity of its being delivered over." To what is it delivered over? "In being in a mood, Dasein is always already disclosed in accordance with its mood as *that* being to which Dasein was delivered over in its Being as the being which it, existing, has to be. To be disclosed does not, as such, mean to be known. And even in the most indifferent and harmless everydayness the Being of Dasein can burst forth as the naked 'that it is and has to be.' The pure 'that it is' shows itself, the whence and whither remain obscure" (BT 134/131). This is to say that it is delivered over (i.e., disclosed in moods as delivered over) to that being that, in its Being (i.e., as existing) it has to be. In other words, it is delivered over to the "there"—brought before its being—and having to be, its always already being—its "there." So Dasein's thrownness is its thrownness into the "there"; that is, into disclosedness, which is to say, into being a clearing. Thus attunement discloses

Dasein's thrownness into disclosedness. That is to say, attunement is that mode of disclosedness in which is disclosed Dasein's character as disclosedness.

It should be noted that here we touch on the peculiar disclosive power of moods that will prove of decisive importance for the Existential Analytic. Eventually, the Analytic will tap the disclosive potential of one very special mood: anxiety.

(2) The second essential character of attunement is that it discloses Being-in-the-world as a whole. What is important here is that mood is not some merely inner condition, on the basis of which we then see things with a certain "subjective coloring." A mood comes from neither inside nor outside but rather "arises out of Being-in-the-world" (BT 136/133)—*and* as arising from out of Being-in-the-world, moods are disclosive of Being-in-the-world.

(3) The third essential character of attunement is that it discloses *world*. In the analysis of world, Heidegger showed that beings within-the-world can be encountered only if the world is already disclosed. This prior disclosure of world is *partly* constituted by attunement—but *only partly*: understanding will prove to be coconstitutive of the general disclosure of world. However, there is one specific aspect of the disclosure of world that can be regarded primarily as constituted by mood. This aspect is suggested if we speak of a mood as a being-attuned to the world (for example, so that things that appear in that world can *matter* to us). The same is suggested if we speak of an "openness to the world" in the sense of a receptive attunement, submissive disclosure, or discovery. Thus Heidegger says: "The attunedness of attunement constitutes existentially Dasein's openness to world" (BT 137/134). And: "Indeed, we must *ontologically* in principle leave the primary discovery of the world to 'mere mood'" (BT 138/134).

Two additional issues now arise.

(1) Note how in this connection, Heidegger introduces the question of the *senses*. "And only because the 'senses' belong ontologically to a being whose kind of Being is an attuned Being-in-the-world can they be 'touched' and 'have a sense' for something so that what touches them shows itself in an affect. Something like an affect would never come about under the strongest pressure and resistance, resistance would be essentially undiscovered, if attuned Being-in-the-world were not already related to having things in the world matter to it in a way prefigured by moods. *In attunement lies existentially a disclosive submission to world out of which things that matter to us can be encountered*" (BT 137–38/134). What this says is that it is not as though Dasein is first affected by things through the senses and then comes to have a certain attunement to them. Rather, conversely, only because Dasein is always already mooded, already attuned to the world can things affect the senses in some way or other. What does this say, then, about sensibility as such? It says: sensibility is founded on something else that must always already

be in play, which is to say, on an a priori in the phenomenological sense (just as Kant showed sensibility, sensible intuition, to be founded on an a priori; namely, pure intuition). For Heidegger, this a priori is attunement—or, more generally: disclosedness.

(2) Heidegger concludes section 29 with a methodological reflection. As always, the reflection is provoked by what the preceding analysis has brought to light. What has the analysis of moods brought to light that is methodologically provocative? The disclosive power of moods, a disclosive power that, Heidegger insists, goes beyond the range of cognition. The methodological question is, then: How can the Analytic itself make use of this disclosive power since it itself is not a matter of mood but of knowing? The answer is: the Analytic must "listen in" to such primordial disclosure:

> Attunement is an existential, fundamental way in which Dasein is its there. It not only characterizes Dasein ontologically but is at the same time of fundamental methodological significance for the existential analytic because of its disclosure. Like every ontological interpretation in general, the analytic can only listen in, so to speak, on beings already previously disclosed with regard to their Being. And it will keep to the eminent disclosive possibilities of Dasein of the widest scope in order to gain from them information [*Aufschluß*, what is disclosed] about this being. The phenomenological interpretation must give to Dasein itself the possibility of primordial disclosure and let it, so to speak, interpret itself. It goes along with this disclosure only in order to raise the phenomenal content of disclosure to a conceptual level. (BT 139–40/135–36). (Cf. Hegel!)

Section 31: Da-sein as Understanding

The analysis of understanding is one of the most important and most difficult in *Being and Time*. The outcome of this analysis will be taken over by and will permeate the entire remainder of *Being and Time*. So we will need to work through the analysis step by step. Throughout, we must keep in mind: understanding does not designate a certain kind of cognition, alongside others such as, for example, explanation, reason, and so on. More generally, understanding is not some immanent (representational) activity by a subject. Rather, it is to be regarded existentially, which is to mean in connection with Dasein's comportment to its Being, and that is to say, as a way in which Dasein is its disclosedness, its "there."

So understanding is a mode of disclosiveness. More specifically, its structure is such that in and through understanding something gets disclosed. What gets disclosed? (a) Existing Being-in-the-world, which is Dasein. (b) Significance, which is world as structured by worldliness. So, by means of understanding, Dasein and its world get disclosed.

What is understood? That is, to what does understanding relate (comport itself) in order to carry out the disclosure of Dasein and world? Initially, Heidegger identifies this as the "for-the-sake-of-which (*Worumwillen*)."

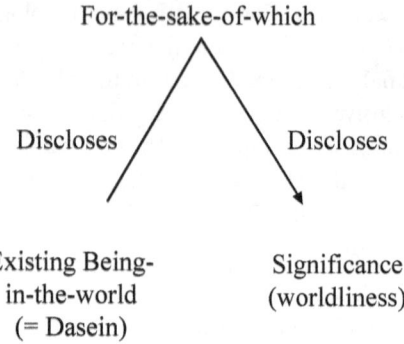

We have seen how the for-the-sake-of-which discloses significance: the for-the-sake-of-which prescribes an in-order-to, which prescribes another in-order-to, so that a whole system of references is traced out, which is to say, disclosed. We should recall the example:

> If it is a matter of providing shelter for-the-sake-of Dasein, then—
> in order to do that: protection against bad weather
> in order to do that: fasten down the shingles
> in order to do that: drive the nails
> for which I need to use a hammer, etc.

So the for-the-sake-of-which unfolds (discloses) an entire system of references, and this is significance. Furthermore, the for-the-sake-of-which refers directly (discloses) Dasein since the system of references culminates in Dasein.

Now for the first major step in the analysis, Heidegger determines the for-the-sake-of-which *as possibility*. The point here is that in taking up (relating to) a for-the-sake-of-which, Dasein relates itself to a possibility—to something that it *can* do. Thus, *understanding* is the mode of disclosedness in which Dasein *relates to possibilities*: "The mode of Being of Dasein as a potentiality-of-Being [*als Seinkönnen*, can be] lies existentially in understanding. Dasein is not something present which then has as a bonus the ability to do something, rather it is primarily Being-possible. Dasein is always what it can be and how it is its possibility" (BT 143/139). The main point is as Dasein's possibility, this possibility discloses Dasein. Dasein is comportment to possibility. "In contrast, possibility as an existential is the most primordial and the ultimate positive ontological determination of

Dasein" (BT 143–44/139). And as it is still a for-the-sake-of-which, this possibility discloses world.

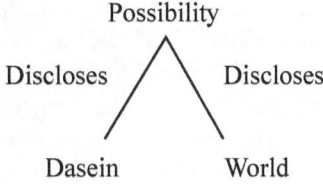

What does possibility mean here? At this point, it cannot be defined positively, only negatively: possibility as an existential is radically different from mere logical possibility and from the contingency of things. Further, it is to be distinguished from a free-floating possibility in the sense of the "liberty of indifference." Rather, possibility is always integrally connected with another existential: "As essentially attuned, Dasein has always already got itself into definite possibilities. As a potentiality for Being which it *is*, it has let some go by; it constantly adopts the possibilities of its Being, grasps them, and goes astray. But this means that Dasein is a Being-possible which is entrusted to itself, it is through and through *thrown possibility*" (BT 144/139). And this points to the connection between understanding and attunement (as well as thrownness).

Now for the second major step in the analysis. Thus far we have seen that Dasein comports itself (relates to) the for-the-sake-of-which, and this, in turn, is determined as possibility. This comportment is what Heidegger calls understanding. But what is the character of this comportment? Heidegger describes it as *projection* (*Entwurf*—NB the connection with *Geworfen*).

Understanding is projecting. But what does it project (throw out before itself)? At first glance, one might say: understanding projects possibilities. **However**, this is not the primary sense, and it is very significant that it is not: possibilities are not just thrown out (invented) by Dasein. So what does Dasein project in the primary sense? It projects *itself* upon its possibilities. "Projecting has nothing to do with being related to a plan thought out, according to which Dasein arranges its Being, as Dasein, it has always already projected itself and is, as long as it is, projecting. As long as it is, Dasein always has understood itself and will understand itself in terms of possibilities [*aus Möglichkeiten*]" (BT 145/141). **So**: Dasein projects itself upon its possibilities—and precisely *from* those possibilities is given back to **itself** (i.e., disclosed to itself, mirrored back to itself). Here we see more specifically how it is that the "direction" of disclosure is from possibility to Dasein.

But this is still not the full structure of projection; it has a certain twosidedness that we need to take into account. Heidegger asks, how is it that understanding, in its way of disclosing, has a twofold structure? And what exactly is this structure? He answers: "Because understanding in itself has the existential structure which we call *projection [Entwurf]*. It projects the Being of Dasein just as primordially upon its for-the-sake-of-which as upon significance as the worldliness of its particular world" (BT 145/140). So Heidegger is saying that Dasein projects itself upon two things: the for-the-sake-of-which (= possibility) *and* significance (= worldliness). Or, rather, he is saying that this two-sidedness belongs to every projection. This is why he keeps repeating: projection always pertains to the full disclosedness of Being-in-the-world. One could further say that projection can have this two-sidedness precisely because of the intrinsic connection between the two things on which it projects: possibility and world. This is the connection that Section 18 had laid out.

Furthermore, corresponding to the two-sidedness of projection, there are also two modes of that existential self-disclosure that are correlative to Dasein's self-projection. That is, Dasein is disclosed to itself not only from possibility but also from significance (worldliness). And so, in the broadest terms, projection can assume two forms: "Understanding *can* turn primarily to the disclosedness of the world; that is, Dasein can understand itself initially and for the most part from [*aus*] the world. Or else understanding throws itself primarily into the for-the-sake-of-which, which means Dasein exists as itself. Understanding is either authentic, originating from its own self as such, or else inauthentic" (BT 146/141). Thus these two forms, authentic and inauthentic understanding, derive from the fact that one or the other moment can be predominant. *But* Heidegger insists that *both* moments belong to the structure of projection and are always (to some degree) present. That is, when one is engaged in one of these moments, "the other is not laid aside" (BT 146/141).

Three final points with regard to understanding.

The first concerns the form that possibilities have when Dasein projects upon them. "Furthermore, the project character of understanding means that understanding does not thematically grasp that upon which it projects, namely, possibilities themselves. Such a grasp precisely takes its character of possibility away from what is projected, it degrades it to the level of a given, intended content, whereas, in projecting, project throws possibility before itself as possibility, and as such lets it *be*. As projecting, understanding is the mode of Being of Dasein in which it *is* its possibilities *as* possibilities" (BT 145/141). This says that Dasein projects possibilities—that is, it projects itself upon possibilities—**as** possibilities. That is, it does not project them as having the character of presence—rather, it lets possibilities *be* as possibilities.

The second fundamental point is that it is not as though Dasein first *is* and *then* engages in the activity of understanding. Rather, understanding is one of the primary ways in which Dasein *is*, which is to say, one of the ways in which there is disclosedness, clearing.

A third, more general point serves to show how revolutionary is Heidegger's concept of understanding. Heidegger says that understanding makes up Dasein's sight (*Sicht*), in the sense in which he spoke earlier of circumspection (*Umsicht*) and considerateness (*Rücksicht*). Then he adds, almost as if in passing: "By showing how all sight is primarily based on understanding—the circumspection of concern [not taking care of things] is understanding as *comprehension* [*Verständigkeit*]—the priority of pure intuition [*Anschauen*] is taken away, which noetically corresponds to the traditional ontological priority of present things [or: of what is present—not: objective presence]. 'Intuition' and 'thought' are both already remote derivatives of understanding" (BT 147/142-43). He goes on to include—as derivative—the "phenomenological 'intuition of essences'" (BT 147/143). He shows that throughout the tradition (from Plato and Aristotle up through Kant and Hegel), knowledge has been regarded as preeminently (essentially) *intuition*—that is, as the sheer beholding of what is present. This priority of intuition (as he indicated here in *Being and Time*) is correlative to the priority accorded in the tradition to the present—that is, to the priority given to the intuition of present things.

Heidegger's concept of understanding is thus intended to constitute a radical break with the tradition. Not only does he show that something else (understanding) is presupposed by intuition (of what is present); he also, most decisively, shows that the underlying structure is such as to render our primary comportment to things something *other than* intuition (of what is present). That is, the concept of understanding (or, more generally, that of Dasein as disclosedness, clearing) serves to displace (deconstruct) intuition as the primary mode of comportment to things. In this break, we have the germ of Heidegger's entire later critique of metaphysics as the metaphysics of presence.

Section 32. Understanding and Interpretation

The next step in exhibiting the constitution of the "there" is to show how understanding can develop itself. Such development Heidegger calls interpretation (*Auslegung*).

In the most general terms, what is interpretation? It is the *appropriation* of what has been understood in understanding. That is, it is the *working-out* of the possibilities projected in understanding. How does such working-out proceed? From the analysis of understanding, we see that it can proceed in two directions. Possibilities are disclosive in two directions, toward Dasein *and* toward world—and "working-out" can proceed in either direction. These two directions correspond to authentic and inauthentic interpretations. In keeping with the character of the entire preparatory analysis (i.e., its link to everydayness), Heidegger limits his consideration to *in*authentic interpretation (i.e., oriented toward world).

So in inauthentic interpretation, there is an appropriation of what has been understood, as an appropriation in the direction of world. What has always been understood in the direction of world? Significance—that is, the referential totality that constitutes the worldliness of world. So the question is: How does this get appropriated, worked-out? What does appropriation involve? It involves letting what is at hand come *explicitly* into view. Heidegger says: "We display in its in-order-to that which is circumspectly at hand" (BT 149/144). That is, we let it stand out explicitly *in* its reference (relevance, in-order-to)—in contrast to the way a piece of equipment can remain in the background, subordinate to our attention to work to be done.

This displaying of what is at hand grants it a peculiar structure: it lets it have the structure of *something as something*. For example, it lets the hammer stand out *as* hammer (rather than remaining "submerged" in an equipment-context polarized toward work to be done). *However*, this "as" is completely determined by the equipmental context—that is to say, it is determined by what the piece of equipment is *for* (by its specific "in-order-to"). For example, for the hammer to stand out *as* hammer means: it stands out *as* something that is *for* hammering, something that we use *in order to* hammer. Furthermore, the process of letting something stand out *as* something (which is equivalent to interpretation in the concrete sense) is prior to the level of judgment or the predicative assertion. Judgment and assertion are based on this level of interpretation. They take over what has already been interpreted and express it at a higher level. However, interpretation at this level is also presupposed by mere seeing, by pure sight. These are constituted by a reduction of what has always already been interpreted. Later, in his analysis of hearing, Heidegger expresses this in graphic terms:

> "Initially" we never hear noises and complexes of sound, but the creaking wagon, the motorcycle. We hear the column on the march, the north wind, the woodpecker tapping, the crackling fire.
> It requires a very artificial and complicated attitude in order to "hear" a "pure noise." (BT 163–64/158)

Here, again, we see how Heidegger is calling into question the priority given by the tradition to sheer intuition and its correlate, presence. Heidegger is saying that seeing is always interpretive—and when we do just behold (stare, intuit), this is a privative modification (a narrowing-down) of our interpretive seeing. Later, he will bring out this contrast by distinguishing between two senses of the "as": (a) the hermeneutical "as" (the "as" of interpretation), which we have when interpretation makes explicit something *as* something *in terms of* involvement in totality; (b) the apophantical "as" (the "as" of the statement or assertion), which is where something present is asserted *as* having some specific determination (e.g., the hammer *as* heavy).

One of Heidegger's primary goals is to dissociate interpretation from the traditional priority of intuition. He says: "Interpretation is never a presuppositionless grasping of something previously given" (BT 150/146). The point is that if something is simply and wholly present, then its apprehension is pure, direct seeing (i.e., intuition). But if something is not simply present, if it is at hand, if it is "submerged" in our dealing with things, *then* its apprehension will require that one get it in view—that is, approach it so as to bring it forward into the light. That is, one must interpret it rather than intuiting it. This approach that brings things to light involves a *Fore-structure*.

This structure involves three moments that pertain only to inauthentic interpretation.

(1) Interpretation of something that has been understood requires that one *have*, in advance, an understanding of significance; that is, of the referential totality (in which things-at-hand are situated). So interpretation is grounded on a *fore-having* (*Vorhabe*) (a having of totality in view).

(2) Interpretation involves appropriating (working-out) what has been understood. *But* it is always an appropriating *in some specific regard*—that is, a working-out (making-explicit) in certain connections rather than others. Heidegger writes of "an act of appropriation that is always done under the guidance of a perspective which fixes that with regard to which what has been understood is to be interpreted. In each instance [*jeweils*], the interpretation is grounded in a *foresight* [*Vorsicht*] that 'approaches' [*anschneidet*] what has been taken in a fore-having with a definite interpretation in view" (BT 150/145). In other words, interpretation involves a certain directive view of what is to be interpreted—a certain sighting in advance. Interpretation is grounded in a *fore-sight* (*Vorsicht*).

(3) In and through the interpretation, what is interpreted becomes conceptualizable. But any conceptualizing already involves a certain conceptuality (*Begrifflichkeit*), a certain conceptual orientation. So Interpretation is grounded on a fore-conception (*Vorgriff*). Thus all interpretation operates in the fore-structure, which involves fore-having, fore-sight, and fore-conception.

The relation between interpretation and its fore-structure constitutes the "hermeneutical circle."

Heidegger adds another moment to the structure of understanding. This additional moment serves to clarify the relation between understanding and interpretation. It also provides a way of introducing the concept of *meaning* into the problematic. Previously, we considered how *Dasein* gets disclosed through the disclosedness of understanding: Dasein projects itself upon possibilities—*and from* these possibilities is disclosed. Heidegger now extends this conception to beings other than Dasein: they, too, get projected upon possibilities, though, of course, they do not simply project themselves. "In the projecting of understanding, beings are disclosed in their possibility. The character of possibility always corresponds to the kind of Being of the beings understood. Innerworldly beings in general are projected upon the world, that is, upon a totality of significance in whose referential relations taking care, as Being-in-the-world, has rooted itself from the beginning. What innerworldly beings are uncovered along with the Being of Dasein, that is, when they become intelligible, we say that they have *meaning [Sinn]*" (BT 151/146). So just as Dasein is projected upon its possibilities (and thus disclosed), so equipment is projected upon significance (and thus disclosed). It is precisely this disclosure that is developed in (inauthentic) interpretation.

When beings have been so disclosed (i.e., understood), we say that they have *meaning (Sinn)*. But here we must be precise: what is understood is not the meaning but the beings. What, then, is the meaning? "Meaning is that wherein the intelligibility [*Verständlichkeit*] of something maintains itself. That which can be articulated in disclosure that understands we call meaning. The *concept of meaning* includes the formal framework of what necessarily belongs to what interpretation that understands articulates. *Meaning, structured by fore-having, fore-sight, and fore-conception, is the upon which of the projection in terms of which something becomes intelligible as something*" (BT 151/146–47). This says: meaning is that upon which something is projected and *from* which it becomes understandable (i.e., disclosed). In the case of Dasein, this "upon-which" is preeminently possibility (properly, in the authentic instance). In the case of equipment, the "upon-which" (which is equivalent to meaning) is significance. We can thus say that the understandability of equipment maintains itself in significance since it is *from* significance that equipment is understandable (can be disclosed). Furthermore, this upon-which (significance) is what gets articulated in that development of understanding that Heidegger calls "interpretation." In that development (as we have seen), the threefold fore-structure comes into play.

This concept of meaning obviously has an important bearing on the project of *Being and Time* itself—whose goal is to work out the question of the *meaning* of Being. Now we can see better what is asked about in the question: it does not ask about what stands behind Being—*but rather*: "And when we ask about the meaning of Being, our inquiry does not become profound and does not brood on anything which stands behind Being, but questions Being itself in so far as it stands within the intelligibility of Dasein" (BT 152/147). That is, it asks about the "upon-which" of an ontological projection—the "upon-which" from which Being would be understandable—*and* it asks about this in order to carry through such a projection. So to question about the meaning of Being is to question about Being itself—but to do so in such a way as to take into account the kind of disclosedness that Dasein, the questioner, is.

The fore-structure (as we have seen) makes explicit how interpretation, as the development of understanding, takes something for granted. This "taking for granted" can be expressed in a more direct way—in terms of the "hermeneutical circle." Heidegger expresses the circularity thus: "Every interpretation which is to contribute some understanding must already have understood what is to be interpreted" (BT 152/147). This says: to understand something (to carry through interpretation, in which understanding is developed, fulfilled), we must already have understood it (with that kind of preunderstanding expressed in the fore-structure). If we look at this circle as a vicious circle, as to be avoided, or as some inevitable imperfection—then we have misunderstood understanding; specifically, we have measured it by an ideal that is inappropriate, an ideal derived from presence. Rather: "What is decisive is not to get out of the circle, but to get in it in the right way" (BT 153/148). The circle is not something to get out of, to avoid—"it is rather the expression of the existential *fore-structure* of Dasein itself" (BT 153/148).

So it is a matter of coming into the circle in the right way. How? "The circle must not be degraded to a *vitiosum*, not even to a tolerated one. A positive possibility of the most primordial knowledge is hidden in it which, however, is only grasped in a genuine way when interpretation has understood that its first, constant, and last task is not to let fore-having, fore-sight, and fore-conception be given to it by chance ideas and popular conceptions, but to guarantee the scientific theme by developing these in terms of the things themselves" (BT 153/148). Here the self-reference is evident: phenomenology is precisely the attempt to come into the circle in the right way—that is, to be genuinely hermeneutical. For example, the hammer *as* heavy (having the property of heaviness).

Let me develop this self-reference. We have, in fact, arrived at a very appropriate point at which to develop it: at the outset (§7), the procedure of phenomenology (of the Existential Analytic) was characterized as interpretation—*and* now, in that Analytic, we have arrived at the analysis of interpretation. So let us apply the results of the analysis to the Analytic itself.

We may say that the Existential Analytic, like interpretation in general, is not a presuppositionless apprehending but rather has itself a *fore-structure* in relation to which it goes about making manifest its matter, which is Dasein in its Being. Although Heidegger has analyzed only *in*authentic interpretation, this still allows us some insight into the character of the *ontological* interpretation going on here. Let me suggest what the operative fore-structure is.

The fore-having is primarily just the preontological understanding that Dasein has of its own Being. The fore-having is what is granted by the fact that Dasein is the *place* of the prephilosophical disclosure of its own Being. Here we see in a more profound way (namely, in terms of the structure of interpretation) why Dasein is the *place* where *Being and Time* begins.

The fore-sight is provided by the concept of *existence*. This is the direction, the regard in which what is understood in advance is to be worked out—in *this* direction (i.e., in terms of Dasein's comportment to its Being) rather than other directions (e.g., in terms of properties or the objectively present things). This is the way Dasein is sighted in advance by the Existential Analytic.

The fore-conception is provided by the concept of Being-in-the-world. This provides the conceptuality (orientation) from which Dasein gets conceptualized.

What is crucial is that the Existential Analytic has attempted to enter into the circle prescribed by this fore-structure. It has not attempted to escape the fore-structure *but rather* to work it out by going to the things themselves. That is, by placing the entire Analytic on a phenomenal basis; that is, by subordinating the Analytic to a self-showing of Dasein; that is, by letting Dasein interpret itself.

But there is much here that still remains enigmatic. And so, let me conclude by quoting a remark Heidegger made during a seminar on Heraclitus in 1966. "*Es gibt einen alten chinesischen Spruch, der lautet: Einmal gezeigt ist besser als hundertmal gesagt. Dagegen ist die Philosophie genötigt, gerade durch das Sagen zu zeigen.*" (There is an old Chinese proverb which says: once shown is better than a hundred times said. But then philosophy is obliged to show precisely by saying.)[1]

Section 33: Statement as a Derivative Mode of Interpretation

Here there are two principal tasks. To determine: what the statement (*Aussage*) is—what the various senses (significations) of the word are; how it is a derivative mode of interpretation—that is, what is involved in the transition from interpretation to statement.

I. What the statement is. There are three significations of statement. They are connected, and in their unity, they encompass the full structure of the statement.

A. The primary signification is *pointing-out* (*Aufzeigen*). This is to be understood in the sense of λόγος as ἀπόφανσις: letting beings be seen from themselves. We should note especially that what the statement makes manifest (and is directed to) is a being—and *not* a meaning or a representation. Heidegger's example: "In the statement, 'the hammer is too heavy,' what is uncovered for sight is not a 'meaning,' but a being in the mode of its being at hand" (BT 154/149).

B. The statement also signifies "predication." A predicate is asserted of a subject, and the subject is thus determined by the predicate (e.g., "the hammer is heavy"). We should especially note that this signification presupposes the first:

---

1. Martin Heidegger, *Heraclitus Seminar 1966/67*, trans. Charles H. Seibert (Tuscaloosa: University of Alabama Press, 1979), 17.

in predication, there is a focus within what is already manifest (what has already been pointed out). That is, there is a narrowing of content (a restricting of view) in order to make a certain determinateness explicit.

C. The statement signifies "communication." "It is letting someone see with us what has been pointed out in its definite character" (BT 155/150). In other words, communication means speaking forth in such a way as to let someone share one's Being-toward what has been pointed out.

II. How the statement is a derivative mode. The way in which the statement is a *derivative* mode of interpretation can best be seen by considering how the operative fore-structure gets transformed in each of its three moments.

A. In the statement as pointing-out, we must *already have* in view what is to be pointed out—just as in interpretation, we must already have in view what is to be interpreted. In both cases, there must be a *fore-having* of the relevant beings. However, the fore-having does not have the same character in the two cases; rather, in the transition to the statement, there is a transformation of the fore-having. "Something *at hand with which* we have to do or perform something, turns into something 'about which' the statement that points it out is made" (BT 158/152). So the "thing" comes to be held differently in our fore-having.

B. For there to be a statement (especially as predication), we must (prior to predication) *view* the thing in such a way that the predicate gets loosened up (detached) from its unexpressed inclusion in the thing itself. This is the kind of fore-sight required by the statement—*and* here again there has been a transformation of the corresponding fore-structure within interpretation—perhaps the most decisive transformation. "Fore-sight aims at something present in what is at hand. Both *by* and *for* the way of looking, what is at hand is veiled as something at hand. Within this uncovering of presence which covers over handiness, what is encountered as present is determined in its being present in such and such a way. Now the access is first available for something like *qualities*" (BT 158/152–53). So the fore-sight of the statement is a sighting of the present thing in what (for interpretation) is handy.

C. In the case of fore-conception, there is also a decisive, but different kind of, transformation. Here the transformation corresponds to the fact that, with the transition to the statement, we are transposed into language and hence into all that can be sedimented within a language. "The fore-conception always also contained in the statement remains mostly inconspicuous because language always already contains a developed conceptuality" (BT 157/152).

This overall transformation of the fore-structure Heidegger expresses also as a transformation of the "as-structure":

> The as-structure of interpretation has undergone a modification. The "as" no longer reaches out into a totality of relevance in its function of approaching

what is understood. It is cut off with regard to its possibilities of the articulation of referential relations of significance which constitute the character of the surrounding world. The "as" gets pushed back to the uniform level of what is merely present. It dwindles to the determination that belongs to the structure of just letting what is present be seen. This leveling down of the primordial "as" of circumspect interpretation to the as of the determination of presence is the specialty of the statement. (BT 158/153)

So, regarded as the transformation of the as-structure, it is a transition *from* the hermeneutical "as"—in which the interpretation makes explicit something *as* something *in terms of* its involvement in an equipment-totality—*to* the apophantical "as"—in which something present is asserted *as* having some specific determination. For example, the hammer *as* for hammering down shingles versus the hammer *as* heavy (as having the property of heaviness).

Section 34: Dasein and Discourse. Language

Heidegger's concern in chapter 5 is to analyze existentially the "there"—disclosedness, clearing—of Dasein. We have followed his account of the two moments of attunement and understanding. We will now turn to his analysis of the third moment: *Discourse* (*Rede*).

Heidegger's discussion of language here is rather brief and, in some respects, undeveloped, especially in comparison with his later writings on language. Nevertheless, this discussion is quite decisive in that it locates the phenomenon of language, sets out the *place* of the question of language.

Heidegger's concern here is primarily not with language (in the usual sense) but with "*the existential-ontological foundation of language*" (BT 160/155)—that is, with that mode of disclosedness (that existential constituent of the "there") in which language is grounded. This foundation he calls: *Rede* (discourse—the translation of λόγος from section 7).

He says that discourse is equiprimordial with attunement and understanding. What, then, is discourse, and how is it a constituent in Dasein's disclosedness? "*Discourse is existentially equiprimordial with attunement and understanding.* Intelligibility is also always already articulated before its appropriative interpretation. Discourse is the articulation of intelligibility." (BT 161/155). We should note that intelligibility is a translation of the German *Verständlichkeit*, and that this has nothing to do with "intellectus." So discourse is the articulation of understanding and that on which understanding projects—and this articulation will already have taken place before understanding is developed in interpretation. So it is a primordial articulation that belongs to understanding as such.

What, then, about language? Heidegger says: "The way in which discourse gets expressed is language" (BT 161/156). Further: "The totality of significations of intelligibility *is put into words [kommt zu Wort]*. Words accrue to significations" (BT 161/156). So there is first (always already) the primal articulation at the level of understanding—and then the signification produced through/in this articulation comes into words. Heidegger later adds the following marginal note: "For language thrownness is essential" (BT 161/156). This says that one finds oneself *thrown* into a language. What is most important here is that language in the usual sense (as the totality of words, as a system of signs) is grounded in Dasein's disclosedness. That is, within Dasein's disclosedness, there is operative at a fundamental level a moment that is (in a primordial sense) linguistic.

There has been considerable controversy over the interpretation of the place of *discourse* in the existential analysis. Otto Pöggeler takes it as the third of three equiprimordial moments of the "there," along with understanding and attunement. But then he calls attention to the fact that discourse seems to drop out when Heidegger comes to regard Dasein's Being as care. He then regards this as a certain failing in the analysis. Over against this, Friedrich-Wilhelm von Herrmann proposes a different interpretation. He points out that not only does Heidegger say that discourse is equiprimordial with attunement and understanding; he also says (at the very beginning of section 34) that the fundamental existentials that constitute the "there" are attunement and understanding. So he proposes that discourse is equiprimordial with attunement and understanding—*without* being, however, a third primordial constituent of the "there." In this regard, he argues that the operation of discourse is "within" that of understanding. This does not really solve the problem, for one can say this of all the moments: they form a whole, and each already involves the others. It is perhaps better to take discourse as the third moment (which the text mostly supports) and then to see whether there is really the problem of discourse somehow (unaccountably) dropping out later.

One additional point regarding discourse and language. Compared to section 34 of *Being and Time*, we find in Heidegger's later writings a radicalizing of the question of language. This is expressed most succinctly in *Letter on Humanism*: "Language is the house of Being." Although, certainly, in a sense, this goes beyond *Being and Time*, its germ is already in *Being and Time*. Language and discourse belong to the constitution of the "there"—of the place, the "house" in which beings can be "disclosed" in their Being. Here one could also point in another direction: what Heidegger carries out is a certain regress from language (as a system of signs) to a prior operation that makes it possible for language (signs) to function. That prior operation is a primal articulation; that is, a certain differencing. So here we have in germ the Derridean move from a system of signs to *différance* as the operation that is presupposed.

We have been dealing with the analysis of Being-in—specifically, with regard to the analysis of the existential constitution of the "there." We have discussed the three primary moments that belong to this constitution (that constitute disclosedness or the clearing): attunement (mood), understanding (projection), and discourse (λόγος). But this is only the first of the two parts into which the analysis of Being-in is divided.

Why is a second part needed? Because in the analysis of the ontological structures (moments) that constitute the "there," the horizon of everydayness has been largely ignored, left out of the analysis. That is, Heidegger has analyzed the general (formal, undifferentiated) structures without attending to the specific (ontic) form they assume in everydayness. Thus the analysis has proceeded without bringing into play the *phenomenal basis*. In the second part of the analysis ("The Everyday Being of the There and the Falling of Dasein"), Heidegger undertakes to regain the phenomenal basis (horizon) provided by everydayness. Specifically, Heidegger analyzes the constitutive moments of the "there" *of everyday Dasein* (of the "they"): idle talk, curiosity, and ambiguity. These correspond to discourse, attunement, and understanding. What is new here and of great importance is Heidegger's introduction of the concept of falling.

Let us note here that the translation of *Verfallen* as *falling prey* is completely wrong. *Verfallen* means to decline, to fall into disrepair. In his 1921/22 *Vorlesung* (*Phenomenological Interpretation of Aristotle*), Heidegger called this *Ruinanz*. Let's say simply: falling or fallingness.

Heidegger refers to idle talk, curiosity, and ambiguity, and then he says: "In them and in the connectedness of their Being, a basic kind of the Being of everydayness reveals itself, which we call the *Verfallen* [*falling*, certainly not *entanglement*!] of Dasein" (BT 175/169). He continues by indicating just what "falling" is: "This term, which does not express any negative value judgment, means that Dasein is initially and for the most part *together with* the 'world' of concern" (BT 175/169).[2] *So*: falling is a falling into the world, into having the "they" as one's self, falling into inauthenticity, into the dispersal of self. Furthermore, as chapter 4 showed, such involvement in the "they" pertains not merely to everyday (inauthentic) Dasein but also to Dasein as such. Even authentic existence is a modification of everyday existence, a recovery of self from dispersal. Thus Heidegger says: "Falling reveals an *essential*, ontological structure of Dasein itself" (BT 179/172).

The outcome of chapter 5 is that Heidegger has given an analysis of Dasein's modes of disclosedness. *However*, through this very analysis, he has also exposed certain structures that are *not* simply modes of disclosedness, though, of course, they relate to disclosedness, as they must in order to be structures of Dasein.

---

2. We must note that this is not "together with the world that it takes care of" (as the translation reads). The German is *bei der besorgten "Welt"*—so, alongside [along with] the world of its concern; the world of its concernful dealings. NB: *Besorgen*: concern, and this is related to *Sorge*: care.

Falling is such a structure. This is not a mode of disclosedness in the sense that understanding and attunement are. Rather, it is an "inclination" (movement) toward being disclosive *in* a certain direction, in the direction of world, whether in moods, understanding, or discourse. That is, it is Dasein's propensity to disclose itself (whether in moods, understanding, or discourse) *from* world and *from* the "they" rather than from its own possibilities. That is to say, it is Dasein's inclination toward a certain "global modification" of its disclosedness. This modification is such as to inject a decisive self-concealment into the heart of Dasein's disclosedness.

Another such structure is *thrownness*. Thrownness is Dasein's peculiar "relatedness" to its disclosedness: Dasein is thrown into its "there" (its "whither" and "whence" remaining veiled)—that is, thrown into (delivered over to) being disclosive. So at the end of chapter 5, a new configuration of the structural moments has emerged:

I. Being-in (existence, disclosedness, the "there")
   A. Attunement
   B. Understanding
   C. Discourse
II. Falling
III. Thrownness

6. Care as the Being of Dasein

When Heidegger summarizes the results at the beginning of chapter 6, he does so primarily in terms of this configuration of structures. And the question that he poses (the basic question of chap. 6) concerns this configuration. The question is: "Can we succeed in grasping this structural whole of the everydayness of Dasein in its wholeness?" (BT 181/176) That is, how can we grasp these moments as a whole, in their unity? Heidegger says what is required: "To put it negatively, it is beyond question that the wholeness of the structural whole is not to be reached phenomenally by means of cobbling together elements. This would require a blueprint. The Being of Dasein, which ontologically supports the structural whole as such, becomes accessible by completely looking *through* this whole *at a* primordially unified phenomenon that already lies in the whole in such a way that it is the ontological basis for every structural moment in its structural possibility" (BT 181/176). That is, we need to grasp the unity that is immanent in these moments and in terms of which they become manifest in their character as moments within the whole. However, this unity must be grasped *phenomenologically—*

> That is, not by merely adding up the parts.
> That is, not by empirical observation.
> That is, not by psychological reflection.
> That is, not by a deduction from some idea of the human being.

Rather, Heidegger sets his sights on what phenomenology requires. He asks: "Can we gather from our previous interpretation of Dasein what ontic-ontological access to itself it requires, *from itself,* as the sole appropriate one?" (BT 182/176). Already, we have seen how, in general, Heidegger must answer this question: the way of access required must be one by which Dasein discloses itself. And so, Heidegger asks: "Is there an understanding attunement" and then specifies what an answer will require:

> If the existential analytic of Dasein is to maintain a fundamental clarity about its basic ontological function, then, in order to accomplish its preliminary task of setting forth the Being of Dasein, it must search for the *most far-reaching* and *most primordial* possibilities of disclosure which lie in Dasein itself. The kind of disclosure in which Dasein brings itself before itself must be such that in it Dasein becomes accessible to itself as *simplified* in a certain way. Together

with what has been disclosed to it, the structural whole of the Being we seek must then come to light in an elemental way. (BT 182/176)

Heidegger proposes that the mode of disclosure that meets these "methodological requirements" is that attunement called *anxiety* (*Angst*). Thus anxiety is to provide the phenomenal basis for grasping theoretically the whole of Dasein's Being. This whole (the Being of Dasein) will reveal itself as *care* (*Sorge*). So the principal task of chapter 6 is to carry through the interpretation of this primordial disclosure of the Being of Dasein as care.

Section 40: The Fundamental Attunement of Anxiety as an Eminent Disclosedness of Dasein

The Analytic is to interpret (grasp) the whole of Dasein's Being by attending to Dasein's self-disclosure in anxiety. Heidegger describes it in the following way: "It only carries out the explication of what Dasein itself discloses ontically" (BT 185/179). Here we see again the methodological issue: Dasein is to disclose itself ontically, and this is taken up in the Analytic. This task is carried out in sections 40–42. Section 40 prepares for the interpretation by thematizing that attunement (anxiety) whose disclosive power is to be exploited. This leads up, then, to the actual interpretation carried out in section 41. Section 42 then adds a preontological confirmation: an ancient fable in which Dasein interprets itself preontologically as care.

The analysis of anxiety, curiously, does not begin with anxiety. Why? Because anxiety, this distinctive self-disclosure, is not immediately manifest; that is, it is initially covered over, concealed. Thus one must first gain access to it. Heidegger proposes to do so by beginning with *falling* (using it as *Ausgang*— a way out of everyday concealment). But how does falling, which is manifestly operative in everydayness, provide theoretical access to anxiety? It does so by the fact that it is *essentially connected* with anxiety—so essentially that it presupposes anxiety. That is, they are connected in such a way that, if we attend to falling, anxiety becomes manifest as an essential moment within it. Look at how Heidegger thematizes the structure: "The absorption of Dasein in the they and in the 'world' of concern reveals something like a *flight* of Dasein from itself as an authentic potentiality for being itself" (BT 184/178). The crucial point is: Dasein can flee from itself *only if* it is already disclosed to itself. And it can flee from itself as authentic potentiality for being *only if* it is somehow disclosed to itself as authentic potentiality for being. "Only because Dasein is ontologically and essentially brought before itself by the disclosedness belonging to it, *can* it flee *from* that from which it flees" (BT 184/179). That is, this fleeing and the self-concealing it accomplishes is merely the *privation* of a fundamental disclosedness of self. That disclosedness is: *anxiety*.

We will now touch on only the main points of this analysis.

Heidegger asks: In anxiety, what is it that one is anxious about? That is, what is that in the face of which (before which, *Wovor*) one has anxiety? Heidegger answers this question by contrasting anxiety with fear: one has fear in the face of some definite thing that poses a threat. *But* that about which one has anxiety is not some particular innerworldly being. It is completely indefinite: it is no thing and no specific region of one's environment—that is, it is nothing and nowhere.

Heidegger stresses that in anxiety things lose their significance, they sink into meaninglessness. This retreat of things into insignificance has the effect of making the world in its worldliness *obtrude*—so that that about which (in the face of which) one had anxiety is just the world as such (and by extension Being-in-the-world). "In what anxiety is about, the 'it is nothing and nowhere' becomes manifest. The recalcitrance of the innerworldly nothing and nowhere means phenomenally that *what anxiety is about is the world as such*. The utter insignificance which makes itself known in the nothing and nowhere does not signify the absence of world but means that innerworldly beings in themselves are so completely unimportant that, on the basis of this *insignificance* of what is innerworldly, the world in its worldliness is all that solely obtrudes" (BT 186–87/181). So in anxiety, innerworldly beings fade into utter insignificance so that what obtrudes is *world as such*—that is, world (as *Wovor*) comes to show itself in a certain "separation" from innerworldly beings; that is to say, world as such, in its worldliness, shows itself in its radical difference from innerworldly beings. One could even say: world shows itself as *nothing*.

So the *Wovor* of anxiety, *which* thus gets disclosed in anxiety, is the world as world, world in its worldliness. But world in *this* sense belongs to the Being of Dasein as Being-in-the-world. One can thus say more generally: the *Wovor* of anxiety is Being-in-the-world. "What anxiety is anxious for is Being-in-the-world itself. In anxiety, the things at hand in the surrounding world sink away, and so do innerworldly beings in general. The 'world' can offer nothing more, nor can the Dasein-with of others. Thus, anxiety takes away from Dasein the possibility of understanding itself, falling, in terms of the 'world' and the public way of being interpreted" (BT 187/181).

Heidegger also thematizes the *Worum* of anxiety (that *about* which one has anxiety). Here there is a similar indefiniteness. That which Dasein is anxious *about* is not some *definite* way of Being, not some *definite* possibility for Dasein. Rather, it is Being-in-the-world as such. But what specific form does such anxiety *about* Being-in-the-world take? More precisely: within anxiety, how is Being-in-the-world disclosed such that there is anxiety *about* it? In general, it is disclosed in precisely the way prepared by the fading of beings within-the-world *into* insignificance.

> In anxiety, the handy things in the surrounding world sink away, and so do innerworldly beings in general. The "world" can offer nothing more, nor can the Dasein-with of others. Thus, anxiety takes away from Dasein the possibility of understanding itself, falling, in terms of the "world" and the public way of being interpreted. It throws Dasein back upon that for which it is anxious, its authentic potentiality-for-Being-in-the-world. Anxiety individuates Dasein to its ownmost Being-in-the-world which, as understanding, projects itself essentially upon possibilities. Thus along with that for which it is anxious, anxiety discloses Dasein as *being-possible*, and indeed as what solely [*einzig*] from itself, can be individualized in individuation [*Vereinzelung*]. (BT 187–88/181–82)

So: in anxiety, the innerworldly beings of everydayness sink into insignificance—and thus Dasein is *deprived* of the way in which, in everydayness, it understands itself, namely, in terms of innerworldly beings and in reference to the "they." Thus, Dasein is thrown back upon itself, individualized—that is, disclosed to itself *as* projection upon possibilities and hence as *not* simply submitted to significance, not bound to take its self-understanding from the world of innerworldly beings. In terms of freedom, anxiety reveals Dasein to itself as "*being free for* the freedom of choosing and grasping itself" (BT 188/182).

The third moment is the attunement itself, being-anxious and in reference to it, Heidegger sums up the entire analysis. In anxiety, Being-in-the-world is disclosed in two fundamental directions: with regard to world and with regard to existing Dasein. Furthermore, since anxiety, as attunement, is a mode of Dasein's disclosedness (i.e., a mode of Being-in-the-world), Heidegger can say: here there is an "*existential sameness of disclosing and what is disclosed*" (BT 188/182). This, he says, is why anxiety is a distinctive attunement—namely because it is preeminently *self-disclosure*.

Section 41: The Being of Dasein as Care

The task is to interpret (show) the way in which, in anxiety, Dasein's Being is disclosed as care (*Sorge*). More specifically, Heidegger considers, in turn, each moment (Being-in or existentiality, thrownness or facticity, and falling, etc.) and shows how each is disclosed in anxiety in unity with the other moments.

The analysis of anxiety has already shown how existentiality gets disclosed: in anxiety, Dasein is torn away from its involvements with innerworldly beings and the "they"—and thrown back upon itself (disclosed) *as* projection upon possibilities; that is, as existentiality. Heidegger introduces a terminological refinement: Dasein's existentiality consists in comporting itself to possibilities—that is, Dasein *is* in terms of those possibilities—that is, it *is* in terms of something "beyond" to which it comports itself. As Heidegger says: "Dasein is always already 'beyond itself' . . . as Being toward the potentiality-for-Being which it itself is"

(BT 192/185). Heidegger expresses this moment (existentiality) as Dasein's being-ahead-of-itself (*das Sich-vorweg-sein des Daseins*).

How is facticity disclosed in anxiety (in unity with existentiality)? Heidegger explains: "But to Being-in-the-world, however, belongs the fact that it is delivered over [*überantwortet*] to itself, that it is already been thrown *into a world*. The abandonment [*überlassenheit*] of Dasein to itself is shown with primordial concreteness in anxiety. More fully grasped, 'Being-ahead-of-itself' means: *being-ahead-of-itself-in-already-Being-in-a-world*' [*Sich-vorweg-im-schon-sein-in-einer-Welt*]" (BT 192/185). This says: facticity refers to two interconnected phenomena. (a) Dasein's being thrown into a world. This is precisely what is disclosed primordially in anxiety by the sinking of innerworldly beings into insignificance and the correlative obtrusion of world. (b) Dasein's being abandoned to itself. This is what is disclosed when, in anxiety, Dasein is deprived of the usual everyday way of understanding itself in terms of things and the "they"—when it is *thrown* back upon itself. Furthermore, Dasein is thrown back upon itself *as* potentiality-for-Being; that is, as projection upon possibility, which is to say as *existence*. So in anxiety, Dasein's facticity (its Being-already-in-a-world) is disclosed *in unity with* existentiality (its being-ahead-of-itself).

How is falling disclosed in anxiety? It is disclosed as the counterphenomenon to anxiety, as its privation—or, rather, as that *from which* Dasein is called back in anxiety. That is, in being thrown back upon itself and thereby disclosed as thrown potentiality-for-Being, Dasein is disclosed as having been lost in the "they" (fallen into the world)—that is to say, in being cast out of "fallenness," that "fallenness" is first really disclosed. Furthermore, in this very movement out of fallenness, Dasein is disclosed (as we have seen) as thrown potentiality-for-Being; that is, as characterized by existentiality and facticity. As such, falling has the character of Being-alongside (*Sein-bei*, together-with) (innerworldly beings encountered within-the-world).

So: Finally, Heidegger presents his precise formulation of that total structure that constitutes care: "The formal existential totality of the ontological structural whole of Dasein must thus be grasped in the following structure: the Being of Dasein means Being-ahead-of-oneself-already-in-(the-world) as Being-together-with (innerworldly beings encountered). This Being fills in the significance of the term *care*" (BT 192/186).

Beyond this working-out of the definition of care, there are two additional points we need to note in section 41. First, care is "a primordial structural totality" on which all special attitudes, situations, and acts of Dasein are founded. In particular, Heidegger goes on to show in some detail how such things as willing and wishing are just derivative modifications of care. The case of "willing" is especially important. From Leibniz to Nietzsche, "will" is regarded as a (or: the) fundamental determination of the subject—and so, here again, we see how

Heidegger, through the Dasein-analytic, is attempting to get beneath the level of the concept of the subject. Second, toward the end of section 41, Heidegger again raises the question of the unity of the constitutive moments of Dasein's Being. He refers to the fact that care is structurally articulated and then asks: "But is that not a phenomenal indication that the ontological question must be pursued still further until we can set forth a *still more primordial* phenomenon which ontologically supports the unity and totality of the structural manifold of care?" (BT 196/189).

So at the end of chapter 5, a threefold configuration of moments emerged: Being-in (existence), falling, and thrownness (facticity). The task in chapter 6, then, is to grasp these moments in their unity, to grasp Dasein's Being as a whole. More precisely, the task is to attach the analysis to some distinctive mode of disclosedness in which Dasein is disclosed to itself as a whole. The analysis will analyze (raise into concepts) the disclosure in such a way as to clarify what gets disclosed in it. Heidegger proposes *anxiety* as such a mode.

We should recall the two most important points from this analysis of anxiety. (1) In anxiety, things are drained of meaning. That is, things and the usual ontic connections lost their significance, and the result is: the world *as such* becomes obtrusive, which is to say, the world shows itself in its radical difference from beings-within-the-world—world shows itself as "nothing." (2) Because in anxiety, things and ontic connections become insignificant, Dasein is deprived of its everyday way of understanding itself (in terms of the world and the "they"), which is to say, it loses its everyday bearings. Thus Dasein is individualized, thrown back upon itself as Being-possible, as projection upon possibility.

Heidegger then goes on to show how in this disclosure Dasein's three moments are disclosed in their unity. That unity he calls *care*. He expresses the structure thus: the Being of Dasein is ahead-of-itself-Being-already-in-(the world) as Being-alongside (beings encountered within-the-world). The question is whether there is not a still more primordial phenomenon that grounds the unity of this articulated structure. This question is the point of departure for Division Two.

However, before moving on to this question, Heidegger "rounds out" the preparatory analysis by consolidating its results and bringing them to bear more directly on the question of the meaning of Being. In section 43, he does this in a negative, critical way: he takes up certain issues related to the concept of reality and to the modern understanding of Being as reality. He here deals with Kant and with his own immediate predecessors and contemporaries (for example, Dilthey, Scheler, and Hartmann). In section 44, he appropriates positively what has been gained in the analysis by bringing its results to bear on the problem of *truth*. This serves to bring these results into connection with the question of Being because, since the beginning of philosophy (Parmenides, Aristotle), Being and truth have always been very closely associated.

Section 44: Dasein, Disclosedness, and Truth

The analysis of truth refers back to the entire existential analytic. It gathers up—from a new perspective—the determination of the Being of Dasein as care. At the same time, it opens the analysis to the still more fundamental task of determining the meaning of Being as such. He will carry this out by interrogating the relation between being and truth—which, since Parmenides and Aristotle has been thought as an identity—best expressed as τὸ γὰρ αὐτὸ νοεῖν ἐστίν τε καὶ εἶναι.

The first step in the investigation of the Being and truth is to give an analysis of truth—that is, a phenomenological analysis that breaks through the traditional concept of truth. This is the task of section 44.

I. General Orientation of the Analysis

In general, the analysis is intended to undercut the traditional conception of the essence of truth—that is, to penetrate beneath this concept to a more primordial one. By this "descent," it can eventually be shown how the traditional concept arises from the more primordial concept. Heidegger launches this analysis by introducing three theses in which the traditional concept is expressed, theses that his own analysis is to call into question.

> Three theses characterize the traditional interpretation of the essence of truth and the way it is supposed to have been defined:
> 1. The "locus" of truth is the statement [*Aussage*] (judgment).
> 2. The essence of truth lies in the "agreement" of the judgment with its object.
> 3. Aristotle, the father of logic, attributed truth to judgment as its primordial locus; he also started the definition of truth as "agreement" [*Übereinstimmung*]. (BT 214/206)

So what is central to the traditional concept is the concept of *agreement*. This follows Aquinas: *adaequatio intellectus et rei*. The question is: What does *adaequatio* mean? What constitutes agreement (*adaequatio*)?

This statement makes it clear that Heidegger's task is both phenomenological *and* historical (in the sense of the *destruction* of the history of ontology). A phenomenological analysis of truth is needed—one capable of undercutting the first two theses—that is, an analysis capable of showing that truth has a more primordial locus than the proposition and that "agreement" (as an abstract relation between knowledge and the object) is grounded in a more primordial phenomenon. The analysis that Heidegger develops draws on Husserl's *Logical Investigations* as interpreted in *History of the Concept of Time*. Historically, through this analysis Heidegger wants, then, to be able to take up the issue of truth at the level at which it was taken up by Heraclitus, Parmenides, and especially Aristotle. That is, he wants to get beneath the sedimented conception of truth *and* beneath the interpretation of Greek thought correlative to this sedimented conception.

In other words, through the analysis, he wants to appropriate more primordially what was at issue in the Greek word ἀλήθεια. It is in this connection that he says that "in the end, it is the business of philosophy to preserve the *force of the most elemental words* in which Dasein expresses itself and to protect them from being levelled off by the common understanding to the point of unintelligibility, which in its turn functions as a source of illusory problems" (BT 220/211). This is Heidegger's task here: to preserve—and that means here to restore, recover—the force of the word ἀλήθεια.

II. The Analysis of Truth

A. Method

We must begin by seeing clearly what the method of the analysis is. It is not an analysis determining the meaning of a word (namely, *agreement*) or the concept it expresses. Rather, it is a phenomenological analysis. This means that the analysis proceeds in terms of the *way truth shows itself.* That is, it attends to the process within which truth comes to show itself *as* truth—*and* it thematizes what truth then shows itself to be. So Heidegger begins by asking: What is this process? "When does truth become phenomenally explicit in knowing itself? When knowing demonstrates itself *as true.* This self-demonstration [*Selbstausweisung*] assures it of its truth. Thus the relation of agreement must become visible in the phenomenal context of demonstration" (BT 217/208-9). What this says is that truth shows itself as truth in the context of demonstration (*Ausweisung*). So the phenomenal context to which the analysis must attend is *demonstration*. We must try to see how truth shows itself.

B. The Analysis

The analysis takes place in four steps. First, Heidegger considers the situation in which a person, with his back to the wall, makes the true statement: "The picture on the wall is hanging crookedly" (BT 217/209). The demonstration occurs when the person turns around and perceives the picture hanging crookedly on the wall. Then the statement proves to be true (is demonstrated)—that is, its truth becomes manifest *as* truth. But what exactly happens in such a demonstration? That is, just how does truth show itself in the demonstration? One could say: it shows itself as a kind of agreement. One could even say: it shows itself as, in some sense, an agreement of knowledge (i.e., of the statement) with the thing known. To this extent, the traditional conception is correct. *However*, the question remains: Just what kind of agreement is this? That is to say, in what sense can knowledge be said to agree with things? Said differently, can there be any significant sense in which items as disparate as knowledge and things can "agree"?

Second, Heidegger asks: When the person makes the statement (without seeing the picture), to what is he related? Prephenomenological theories of judgment would say: the stating relates to a representation *of* the picture, a mental image of the real picture, a picture of the picture. The relevant agreement would then be between this representation *and* the real thing. However (as seen), one of the most decisive accomplishments of Husserl's *Logical Investigations* was to expel all such representations, all such mediating images that would stand between an act that means (intends) something **and** that thing itself. This is the most elementary sense of *intentionality*. So the stating is related not to a "picture" of the picture but to the picture itself, to the thing itself. "Making statements is a Being toward the existent thing itself" (BT 218/209).

Third, what, then, happens when he turns around and perceives the picture? That is, what gets demonstrated? Heidegger answers: "Nothing else than *that this being is the being itself that was meant in the statement*" (BT 218/209). So the "agreement" that gets demonstrated is *not* the agreement of representations (something psychic) with the thing itself (something physical)—*but rather*, an agreement between what is meant *and* the thing itself. That is, it is an agreement between the thing itself *as* meant *and* the thing itself *as* perceived, as it shows itself concretely. As Heidegger says, what occurs is "that what is stated (that is, the being itself) shows itself *as the very same thing. Confirmation* means *the being's showing itself in its self-sameness*" (BT 218/209–10). That is, what occurs is what Husserl calls *intentional fulfillment*.

Fourth, what, then does the demonstration serve to demonstrate about the statement? Heidegger answers: "What comes to be demonstrated is that the expressive being [*aussagende Sein*] toward that which has been spoken about is a pointing-out [*Aufzeigen*] of the being; *that* it *reveals* [*entdeckt*] the being toward which it is. What gets demonstrated is the being-revealing [*Entdeckend-sein*] of the statement" (BT 218/209). This says: what is demonstrated is *that* the statement points out that about which it is made, *that* it *reveals* the thing—that is, it is demonstrated that the stating is a revealing (pointing-out, showing) of the thing itself. *So*: In this demonstration of the truth of the statement, how is that truth manifest? What form does it show itself to have? The truth (of the statement) is its character as *revealing*, its "being-revealing." "To say that a statement *is true* means that it discovers the being in itself. It asserts, it points out, it lets beings 'be seen' (ἀπόφανσις) in their uncoveredness. The *Being-true [Wahrsein]* (*truth*) of the statement must be understood as *being-uncovering [entdeckend-sein]*" (BT 218/210).

III. Primordial Truth

What we have considered thus far is only one level in the problem of truth. There is a second, more primordial level. Heidegger carries out a regress to this second level by "radicalizing" the concept of truth just attained. More specifically, he regresses from the sense of truth as being-uncovering to the ground of its possibility. "Being-true as being-uncovering is a manner of Being of Dasein. What makes this uncovering itself possible must necessarily be called 'true' in a still more primordial sense. *The existential-ontological foundations of uncovering itself first show the most primordial phenomenon of truth*" (BT 220/211).

What is this more primordial phenomenon of truth? We should consider what uncovering presupposes: for things to be uncovered (that is, for Dasein to comport itself to them in an uncovering fashion), *world* must already be **disclosed**, and for two reasons. This is because world provides the context (1) in which things can be intended; for example, in the statement; and (2) from out of which they can show themselves in such a way as to demonstrate the statement. Thus disclosedness is the ground of possibility of Being-uncovering—that is, disclosedness is primordial truth. But, as already seen, disclosedness is not something other than Dasein, not something that "befalls" Dasein—rather, as Heidegger says: Dasein *is* its disclosedness. *And so* Dasein is essentially truth (in the primordial sense), or, more precisely: "*Dasein is 'in the truth'*" (BT 221/212).

Finally, we need to connect this analysis to the concept of falling. We have seen that falling belongs essentially to Dasein. It consists of a certain self-dispersal, covering-over, or disguise—in a word: *concealment*. And so: "*Because Dasein is essentially falling, the constitution of its Being is such that it is in 'untruth'* [*Unwahrheit*]" (BT 222/213). Thus, Dasein is both "in the truth" (as disclosedness) and "in the untruth" (as concealment). That is, Dasein is the contention, strife, πόλεμος of truth and untruth.

IV. Conclusion

There are many other issues in section 44, which we cannot deal with, but we should just mention the two most important.

A. Heidegger brings the analysis back full circle to its starting point; that is, from the phenomenological concept of truth to the traditional concept. That is to say, he traces out the origin of the traditional concept. What is most important in this origination is the capacity of language to preserve a certain disclosure while at the same time emptying it.

B. Heidegger makes explicit the connection that his analysis has established between Dasein and truth. Since truth is disclosedness, and since disclosedness is Dasein's way of Being, there is truth only insofar as Dasein *is*. Thus truth is relative to Dasein, though of course this relativity is not a matter of subjective arbitrariness. Heidegger clarifies the sense of relativity with a scandalous example: "Before Newton's laws were uncovered, they were not 'true'" (BT 226/217). The point is that these laws, *as* expressions in which the uncoveredness of certain beings is preserved, were not true (i.e., uncovering) before that *original uncovering* that Newton accomplished. That is, only through that uncovering were beings brought into an uncoveredness that could then be expressed and preserved in laws. This example, in turn, explains Heidegger's even more scandalous statement: "That there are 'eternal truths' will not be adequately proven until it is successfully demonstrated that Dasein has been and will be for all eternity" (BT 227/217).

Division Two: Dasein and Temporality

Two Epigraphs

Our concern is with *reading* a series of texts by Heidegger. But what is reading? What does reading require? Heidegger addresses this question in a text *"Was heißt Lesen?"* ("What is reading?" or "What does reading mean?"). He writes: "What is reading? That which supports and directs reading is gathering/gatheredness. To what is it gathered? To what is written, to what is said in writing. Authentic reading is a gatheredness to that which, unbeknown to us, has already claimed our essence, regardless of whether we comply with it or withhold from it."[1]

We should underline two things this text says.

(1) Reading essentially involves coming to be gathered to what is *said* in writing, in the text.

(2) Reading, thus understood, is a *response*—that is, the gatheredness of reading is not something that one simply initiates but rather is a response to a certain claim, a demand, already made on us, a prior appeal. This is why he writes: Was *heißt* lesen? That is, what calls for (calls forth) reading? One could say most succinctly: reading is *responsive gatheredness*.

The second epigraph is quite different: "An American Indian warrior once said to an anthropologist the following: You, on the other hand, feel that you are immortal and that decisions of an immortal man can be cancelled or regretted or denied. In the world where death is the hunter, my friend, there is no time for regrets or doubts; there is only time for decisions."

Section 45: The Task of a Primordial Interpretation

Division Two opens with a question, a question that was already alluded to at the end of Division One, a question that displaces the outcome of Division One into a new questioning—a question that thus unleashes the entire development that will constitute Division Two. That question is: "Are we entitled to the claim that in characterizing Dasein ontologically qua care that we have given a *primordial* interpretation of this being?" That is, is the interpretation of Dasein's Being as care a primordial interpretation?

---

1. Martin Heidegger, *Aus der Erfahrung des Denkens: Martin Heidegger Gesamtausgabe* Band 13 (Frankfurt a.M.: Vittorio Klostermann, 1983), 111.

116 | Heidegger's Ontological Project

What is meant by a primordial interpretation? To contextualize this question, we need to recall Heidegger's description of the hermeneutical situation in which all interpretation operates. This situation is constituted by the fore-structure of interpretation, the fore-structure that interpretation presupposes and operates within—and also reflects back upon. That is, what are the criteria by which to assess the primordiality of an interpretation? Clearly, this needs to be determined before one can deal with the question as to whether the previous interpretation is primordial. Heidegger's analysis brings to light two relevant kinds of criteria, and both pertain to that fore-structure that Heidegger has shown to belong to all interpretations. We should recall that this fore-structure involves three moments:

1. Fore-having, by which we *have* a certain whole in view in advance.
2. Fore-sight, which is the specific regard, the directive view, the "sighting" in advance, which directs the interpretation.
3. Fore-conception, which is the conceptual framework (orientation) in which the interpretation is carried through.

The first kind of criterion for primordiality is this fore-structure must be vindicated by reference to the things themselves. That is, what is "presupposed" in the fore-structure, the totality of presuppositions (the "hermeneutical situation") must be clarified and secured by reference to the things themselves, to the phenomenal basis. In the preparatory analysis, Heidegger has attempted to satisfy this criterion by his constant appeal to phenomenal confirmation.

But there is another kind of criterion: to say that an interpretation is primordial, there must be assurance that (a) in its fore-having, it gets in its grasp the *whole* of Dasein, its *totality*, and (b) that in its fore-sight, it gets in view the *unity* of the structural moments of Dasein. He declares that the interpretation of the Being of Dasein as care does not measure up to these criteria. That is, it is not a primordial interpretation.

One might wonder: Why is this further criterion necessary? Why doesn't the referral of the fore-structure to the phenomenal basis suffice?

We should consider the following. Interpretation (in terms of the fore-structure) *and* the exhibiting of the phenomenal basis are not simply independent (so that the exhibiting could vindicate the fore-structure once and for all); *rather*, they are intertwined, reciprocally related. That is, interpretation brings the things to show themselves—*and* the interpretation (its operative fore-structure) is measured in reference to the things *as* showing themselves. This means, then, that if at the outset a certain dimension or level of the thing is left out of account, there is no guarantee that the subsequent reference to the phenomenal basis will serve to remedy the omission (since the accessibility of that phenomenal basis is already conditioned by the omission). That is to say, if our fore-having is partial (i.e., does not grasp the being as a whole), then, when that being is subsequently brought (through the interpretation) to show itself, it may also show itself *only partially*. Likewise, if our fore-sight is superficial (fails to see the fundamental unity), then when that being is brought to show itself, it may show itself *only superficially*. Thus, primordial interpretation is assured only if the hermeneutical situation involves the dual assurance (a) that the being as a *whole* is brought into fore-having and (b) that the Being of this being is viewed (in fore-sight) in its unity. That is, in order to be primordial, an interpretation must have a fore-structure in which is encompassed Dasein in its full "breadth" and "depth."

Heidegger thus asks: Has the interpretation in Division One met this second kind of criterion? His answer: "No." This requisite assurance is lacking with regard to its fore-having and fore-sight. *Furthermore*: there are even *positive* indications that the fore-having and fore-sight that have been operative are inadequate (i.e., partial and superficial). Fore-sight was directed to the idea of existence (i.e., Dasein was "sighted in advance" as essentially existence). *But*, more precisely, fore-sight was directed at Dasein as existence *within* the horizon of everydayness. In other words, interpretation has been oriented to existence *only* in its inauthentic mode or its undifferentiated mode. As such, fore-sight and the interpretation that it directs have left the authentic mode of existence out of account. Thus, fore-sight is inadequate and the interpretation is not primordial.

It should be noted that leaving out authenticity amounts to failing to grasp the *unity* of Dasein's Being. Why? Because it is in authenticity that Dasein recovers itself from self-dispersal (manifoldness, lack of unity with self) and *draws itself into unity*. However, this character of authenticity has still to be really exhibited, and so Heidegger does not really bring out here the connection between authenticity and unity.

Fore-having is also inadequate. It seems not to have gotten the *whole* of Dasein into its grasp. Why? Because the very character of Dasein (as brought to light through the interpretation) seems to preclude ever getting the whole in grasp. The point here is that Dasein is always ahead-of-itself, *is* in terms of something that it is *not yet*, and so, whenever we grasp Dasein, there is always a "not-yet" left out, and so we never grasp Dasein as a whole. Thus Heidegger concludes: "One thing has become unmistakable: *The existential analytic of Dasein up to now cannot lay claim to primordiality*. Its fore-having never included more than the *inauthentic* Being of Dasein, of Dasein as *less than whole* [*unganzes*]. If the interpretation of the Being of Dasein is to become primordial as a foundation for working-out the fundamental question of ontology, then it will have to bring the Being of Dasein in its possible *authenticity* and *wholeness* [*Ganzheit*] existentially to light beforehand" (BT 233/223). It is with this task that Division Two begins.

General Perspective on Division Two

At the outset, we paid special attention to the way in which *Being and Time* begins. In the most obvious sense of beginning, it begins in the middle of a Platonic dialogue—namely, at that point in the *Sophist* where the Stranger says: "For manifestly you have long been aware of what you mean when you use the expression 'being.' We, however, who used to think we understood it, have now become perplexed." As we move into Division Two, let us again bring up a connection that Heidegger draws between *Being and Time* and a Platonic discourse. This connection he draws in *Basic Problems of Phenomenology* (1927) in a highly developed context. We will need to outline that context in order to appreciate the connection.

In these lectures, he develops the conception of understanding as projection (in much the same way as in *Being and Time*, chap. 5). Then he lays out a sequence of interconnected projections: the understanding of beings→projection on Being→the understanding of Being→the projection on time. The sense is that each item is grounded in the next item. It is especially noteworthy that Heidegger insists that the sequence extends no further, which is to say, it is *not* necessary to ask about the understanding of time; that is, it is *not* necessary to ask what it is that time is projected upon. Why? Because temporality is "the primordial self-project as such." That is to say, temporality is the fundamental project, and so it is not necessary to ask about a further (grounding) project on which it would be grounded. This is most comprehensively what Division Two is devoted to showing: that temporality is the primordial self-project as such—that, consequently, the sequence really does end here. To show this, Heidegger will need to investigate numerous other issues: death, conscience, guilt, resoluteness. And, in connection with the central task, Division Two will redetermine in a radical way the concept of history and a series of related concepts such as fate and destiny. The establishment of the projection on time (more precisely: temporality) as the final member of the sequence leads directly into the basic issue of *Being and Time* (as we've previously identified it: the meaning of Being).

Granted that the regress stops with the projection on time, the issue is then: How does this item ground the previous items? Specifically, the issue is: How does time serve as the horizon for the understanding of Being (i.e., as the meaning of Being)? That is, how is it that time illuminates Being in such a way that Being is disclosed? At this point, we get the connection with a Platonic discourse. Heidegger refers to the discussion in the *Republic* in which Socrates tells Glaucon that the good is ἐπέκεινα τῆς οὐσίας—Heidegger interprets this as saying that the Good is something beyond Being which illuminates Being, lets it be disclosed— *just as* for Heidegger, time is that "beyond" Being, which illuminates Being. Heidegger completes the connection with these words: "We too want nothing else but to bring ourselves out of the cave and to the light" (BPP 285).

1. The Possible Being-a-Whole of Dasein and Being-toward-Death

Section 46: The Seeming Impossibility of Ontologically Grasping and Determining Dasein as a Whole

Heidegger begins section 46 with the question as to whether Dasein is accessible *as a whole* and then proceeds to elaborate on the aporia already introduced in section 45. More generally, the problem is that there appears to be a contradiction between care (the Being of Dasein) *and* the possibility of Dasein's Being-a-whole. More specifically, a primary moment in the care-structure is the "ahead-of-itself." This structural moment indicates that in Dasein, there is always something *still outstanding*; that is, some possibility upon which Dasein projects itself, which has *not yet* become actual. That is to say, the constitution of Dasein is such that there is always something still to be settled. Thus, the "ahead-of-itself" indicates a perpetual incompleteness, an intrinsic lack of wholeness, *eine ständige Unabgeschlossenheit*. Furthermore, when Dasein has become such that nothing else remains outstanding (in death), Dasein *is* no longer at all. Heidegger formulates this aporia in the following way: "As long as Dasein *is* as a being, it has never attained its 'wholeness.' But if it does, this attainment becomes the absolute loss of Being-in-the-world. It is then never again to be experienced *as a being*" (BT 236/227–28).

If these conclusions are correct, if there is a genuine contradiction between care and Dasein's possible wholeness, then it is not possible to bring Dasein as a whole into our fore-having—*and then* the Existential Analytic cannot achieve the level of primordial interpretation. *But*, Heidegger asks, are these conclusions correct? *Or* are they merely formal? Do they conceal presuppositions inappropriate to an interpretation of Dasein? Clearly, a further investigation is needed: it must focus on that *end* that limits and determines whatever wholeness Dasein could possibly have—namely, *death*. What is needed is an existential interpretation of death.

Section 47: The Possibility of Experiencing the Death of Others and the Possibility of Grasping Dasein as a Whole

The question is: How can we get access to death and thus to that wholeness of Dasein that would be delimited by this end? Clearly, the problem here is that in attaining the end, one becomes no-longer-Dasein. In other words, one loses the very possibility of experiencing this end and thus the wholeness that it delimits. But, granted that such experience is impossible for any Dasein in relation to itself, is it perhaps possible in relation to the *death of others*? Section 47 is devoted to showing that this is *not* possible: we cannot genuinely gain access to death through the way in which the death of others shows itself to us. Here, Heidegger proceeds by describing how the death of others shows itself. Through these descriptions, he tries to make it *concretely* evident that in our experience of the death of others, "in suffering this loss, the loss of Being as such, which the dying person 'suffers,' does not become accessible. We do not experience the dying of others in a genuine sense; but we are at best always just 'near by' [*dabei*]" (BT 239/230).

However, through these considerations, Heidegger not only reaches this negative result but also gives a first indication of the proper orientation of the inquiry. He discusses the phenomenon of *Vertretbarkeit* (representableness). He points out how in everyday dealings, such "representing" is a common thing—*but that* the possibility of representing breaks down completely in the case of death: "*No one can take the other's dying away from him*" (BT 240/231). In terms of the concepts of the Analytic, death is in every case *mine*—and rather than being an event externally observable, it has instead to do with Dasein's possibility; that is, with existence. "Insofar as it 'is,' death is always essentially mine. And it indeed signifies a peculiar possibility-of-Being in which it is absolutely a matter of the Being of my own Dasein. In dying, it becomes evident that death is ontologically constituted by mineness and existence. Dying is not an event, but a phenomenon to be understood existentially in an eminent sense still to be delimited more closely" (BT 240/231). So what is required is an analysis in which death is interpreted as an *existential* phenomenon, which is to say, a genuinely *existential* analysis of death. And if death is to be regarded existentially, so, likewise, with that wholeness of Dasein that death delimits, it also needs to be regarded existentially.

Section 48: What Is Outstanding, End, and Wholeness

Heidegger here develops the negative side of this analysis. Let me *merely* situate and summarize the outcome. Heidegger raises the question: What is the precise character of the end (ending) of Dasein? Or, more generally, what is the character of that "not-yet" that prevents Dasein from being a whole as long as it exists? He proceeds to delimit the proper sense of this end ("not-yet") from various other senses. Methodologically, it is important to note that this sense-delimitation does not take the form of an analysis of concepts but rather proceeds *concretely* in reference to various phenomenal contexts that exhibit the senses at issue.

I. The "not-yet" may be regarded as meaning what is still outstanding. Heidegger uses the example of a debt. If part of a debt owed to me is not yet paid, I say it is still outstanding. What happens as the debt gets paid off? The money that was outstanding (not yet paid) comes in successively and gets added to the sum already paid. That is, the money that belongs with what has been paid but that is still missing (not yet paid) gets successively added to the paid sum until all that belongs to that sum has been added. As Heidegger expresses it: "The remainder is paid off, so that the not-yet is, as it were, fills up until the sum that is owed is 'all together'" (BT 242/233). Ontologically interpreted, the situation is this: the money still outstanding is un-handy yet belongs together with the paid sum, which is handy. And so the "not-yet" (in the sense of "still outstanding") refers to a lack-of-togetherness between handy things that belong together in the sense that certain of those things are missing, still lacking.

From this analysis, Heidegger draws two conclusions.

A. This sense of "not-yet" is *not* appropriate to Dasein because Dasein is not something handy. The inappropriateness is strikingly evident if we compare Dasein's running its course (toward its end) *with* the paying off of the debt: Dasein's running its course is not a matter of adding to a sum, of continually piecing on something handy. *And*, as Heidegger says: "That Dasein should *be* together only when its not-yet has been filled up is so far from the case that it is precisely then that Dasein is no longer" (BT 243/234).

B. What does this show positively about the character of Dasein's "not-yet"? It cannot have the character of something still outstanding (something missing, to be added on) *but rather* must be such as to *belong* to Dasein. "Dasein always already exists in such a way that its not-yet *belongs* to it" (BT 243/234).

II. So Heidegger considers another sense of "not-yet." This sense is exhibited by the phenomenon of the moon when not yet full. Here it is not a matter of something outstanding (something missing), which is to say, it is not a matter of parts that are not yet together. On the contrary, the moon is already present as a whole—*and* the "not-yet" pertains only to our getting it into our perceptual grasp; that is, it is not-yet perceptible as a whole. Again, two conclusions follow.

A. This sense of "not-yet" is also inappropriate to Dasein because it is a "not-yet" of perceptibility, whereas Dasein's "not-yet" is one of Being (actuality). That is, in the case of the moon, it is a matter of something already actual and merely not-yet perceived, *whereas* in the case of Dasein, it is a matter of an end that is not-yet actual at all.

B. What does this show positively about the character of Dasein's "not-yet"? Since it is a matter of something not-yet being actual, we may say that Dasein's "not-yet" must be something that Dasein *becomes*.

III. So Heidegger considers still another sense of "not-yet," a sense oriented to becoming. This sense is exhibited by the phenomenon of unripe fruit: unripe fruit is not-yet ripe. However, its ripeness is not something missing that just gets added on (like debt), *nor* is it something merely not-yet perceived (as with the moon). Rather, the fruit itself ripens, it becomes ripe—that is, it becomes that which, while unripe, it was not-yet. Furthermore, it becomes ripe *not* through some external agent but of its own accord, *and*, in fact, its ripening belongs to its very Being as fruit. Thus Heidegger says: "The not-yet is already included in its own Being, by no means as an arbitrary determination, but as something constitutive" (BT 244/235). Once again, two conclusions follow.

A. This phenomenon indicates something important about the sense of Dasein's "not-yet." Heidegger continues: "Correspondingly, Dasein, too, *is always already its not-yet* as long as it is" (BT 244/235). This means that just as the ripening of fruit belongs to its very Being as fruit, *so* Dasein's becoming what it not-yet is belongs to its Being. Thus when Heidegger says that Dasein *is* already its "not-yet," he means that Dasein's character as becoming its "not-yet" (Dasein's character as "ripening") is a constituent of Dasein's very Being. It should be noted that Heidegger has brought together the previous indications regarding Dasein's "not-yet": that it *belongs* to Dasein and is something Dasein becomes.

B. However, this sense of "not-yet" (fruit) still does not coincide with the sense of Dasein's "not-yet." What is the difference? When the fruit reaches ripeness, it has *fulfilled* itself (in the sense that its possibilities have come to actualization). But this is not the case with Dasein: Dasein's arrival at its end (death) is *not* a fulfillment. That is, its possibilities are not exhausted (in the sense of being actualized)—*but rather* its possibilities are taken away.

So the question now becomes: What is the precise sense of Dasein's *ending*? Heidegger pursues the question by elaborating (phenomenally) various senses of ending (i.e., being-at-an-end). Ending can mean:

1. stopping, as rain stops
2. stopping, as a road stops (either as finished or as unfinished)
3. being-at-an-end as "bread is at an end"—is used up and no longer available

However, none of these senses of ending are appropriate to Dasein. To regard dying as ending in any of these senses would amount to treating Dasein as present or as something handy. So if the issue is considered existentially, Dasein's ending is *not* a matter of Being-*at*-an-end (in any sense)—but rather of Being-*toward*-the-end. Heidegger says Dasein *is* already its end. This means: Dasein's ending, Dasein's comportment to its end belongs to its very Being. And so: "Death is a way to be that Dasein takes over as soon as it is. 'As soon as man comes to life, he is at once old enough to die'" (BT 245/236).

However, the question remains: Just how is this Being-toward-the-end to be differentiated from the kind of directedness toward the end that a ripening fruit has? That is, how is the sense of this Being-toward-the-end to be *positively* determined? This can be done only by interpreting it in reference to the basic constitution of Dasein, which is to say, in reference to care.

Section 49: How the Existential Analysis of Death Differs from Other Possible Interpretations of This Phenomenon

There is one more preparatory step, which delimits, negatively, the aim of the forthcoming existential analysis of death: Heidegger separates off the various issues to which this analysis will *not* be addressed. We will note only two points here.

I. Heidegger distinguishes between the existential-ontological interpretation of death *and* the biological-ontical investigation (which would be grounded by the ontological investigation). In this connection, what we need to note is the specific distinction that Heidegger draws between three terms, all of which in a sense denote death (*Tod*).

A. Perishing (*Verenden*): this pertains not specifically to Dasein but to living things as such. It designates the ending of a living thing.

B. Demise (*Ableben*): the point here is that Dasein also has a death of the kind appropriate to any living thing. *But* because of its peculiar Being-toward-death, even the character of its "perishing" gets transformed, and so Heidegger says that qua Dasein, it does not simply perish. Its peculiar perishing he calls "demise."

C. Dying (*Sterben*): this designates "that *way of Being* in which Dasein *is toward* its death" (BT 247/238). It is with this that the existential interpretation of death is primarily concerned.

II. Heidegger insists that his analysis of death remains strictly "this-worldly." That is, it interprets death "with respect to the question of how it *enters into* each and every Dasein as its possibility-of-Being" (BT 248/238). This means, then, that the analysis takes no existen*tiell* stand (makes no ontical decision) regarding whether or not Dasein continues on after death. That is, it makes no decision with regard to immortality. However, this ontological interpretation would first provide the basis for even asking properly the question regarding immortality, and even for deciding whether the question of immortality is a possible theoretical question at all.

Through the various differentiations in section 49, Heidegger withdraws the *ontological* problem of death from biology, theology, ethnology, and psychology. We can see this as an attempt to regain the ontological, philosophical problem of death. This is to make death again philosophically problematic, and this includes making problematic the complicity between philosophy and death. We can regard Heidegger's efforts here as an attempt to open up again a dimension of questioning that has been closed off—perhaps ever since Plato's enigmatic dialogue on the death of Socrates.

Section 50: A Preliminary Sketch of the Existential and Ontological Structure of Death

In this section, Heidegger presents the fundamental analysis of death. It is called a "preliminary sketch" (*Vorzeichnung*). *However,* this does not mean that it deals only with preliminaries and leaves the fundamental analysis for later. Rather, this two-and-one-half-page sketch contains the very essence of the death-analysis; it is the basic existential-ontological structure of death, which is to say, the formal, neutral, undifferentiated structure. Everything else is ancillary to this analysis. The sketch is preliminary only in the same way that the discussion of disclosedness in chapter 5 was preliminary: it is a fundamental analysis that must then be exhibited in everydayness and thus concretely filled out.

The task is to interpret death in reference to the basic ontological constitution of Dasein. Dasein's Being (its ontological constitution) has been exhibited as *care*. The constituent moments of care are: existence—"ahead-of-itself"; facticity (thrownness)—"Being-already-in"; falling—"Being-alongside." So death is to be interpreted in terms of these moments.

I. Death and Existence. There are two steps here leading into the main analysis.

First, the previous analysis showed that death (as end, the ultimate "not-yet") cannot be regarded as something outstanding. It also showed that death has the character of something *toward which* Dasein comports itself. Now Heidegger expresses this by saying that death is something that stands before us, something *impending, imminent* (*ein Bevorstand*, in contrast to *Ausstand*).

Second, however, the character of being impending does not suffice to distinguish death. There are many things that can impend for Dasein, and Heidegger proceeds to give some examples.

1. The first set of examples: a storm, the remodeling of the house, the arrival of a friend. Here, what is impending are beings (present things, handy things, Dasein-with). *But* death is not a being, and so its impending must be of a different character from these.

2. The second set of examples are concrete ways of Being: a journey, a disputation with others, the foregoing of something that one could be. Here, we have certain of Dasein's *own possibilities* of Being, and these come somewhat closer to the character of death as impending. In effect, Heidegger proceeds to identify the character of death by differentiating it from this kind of possibility.

The main analysis of death begins with the following: "Death is a possibility-of-Being that Dasein itself has always to take over. With death, Dasein stands before itself in its *ownmost* potentiality-of-Being. In this possibility, what is at issue for Dasein is its Being-in-the-world as such [*schlechthin*]. Its death is the possibility of no-longer-being-able-to-be-there [*die Möglichkeit des Nicht-mehr-dasein-könnens*]" (BT 250/241). We should note two things here.

First, as the earlier analysis indicated, death has the character of *mineness*. ("No one can take the other's dying away from him.") In other words, death is Dasein's *own*—not just in that sense in which other possibilities can be Dasein's own but rather in a more radical sense—hence, *ownmost* (*eigenste*).

Second, death has the character of a possibility. As previous analyses showed, "possibility" has the concrete sense of something that is *at issue* for Dasein. What *specifically* is at issue in this possibility? In fact, nothing specific, nothing definite—but rather Being-in-the-world as such. The issue is: Dasein's no-longer-being-able-to-be-there; that is, its no-longer-being-there (its no longer being Dasein) *and* its no-longer-being-able (its loss of *all* possibilities). *So*: this first passage identifies death as Dasein's *ownmost possibility*.

"When Dasein stands before itself [*seiner selbst sich bevorsteht*] as this possibility, it is *fully* referred to its ownmost potentiality-of-Being. Standing thus before itself, all relations to other Dasein are lost in it" (BT 250/241). This passage brings out the peculiar *impending* character of death—it shows how (as he will say a few lines later) it is "something distinctively impending." It is distinctive in that it delimits three interrelated moments.

a. Death is impending—or, literally, *stands before* Dasein. But death, as we've seen, has the character of *possibility*—and (we recall) possibility is that from which Dasein is disclosed to itself (in understanding). So death, standing before Dasein as possibility, discloses Dasein to itself. That is, in terms of this passage, as this possibility (as projecting upon it) "Dasein stands before itself" (i.e., disclosed to itself). That is to say, death is an impending possibility.

b. But this could be said of any impending possibility: in every case, Dasein is disclosed to itself from that possibility. So the problem is: How is it that death is *distinctively* impending? That is, what is *distinctive* about the self-disclosure that "rebounds" from this possibility? When Dasein projects upon this possibility, then, Heidegger says, it is "fully referred" to it. This means: Dasein does not merely project this possibility along with various others pertaining to relevances in the everyday world; rather, this possibility tears Dasein away from its everyday involvements and relevances. Why? *Because of* its character as possibility of losing all possibilities. It is the possibility that suspends all others. Thus, fully referred, standing before this impending possibility, Dasein is referred exclusively to itself as one's ownmost.

c. Thus referred, thus bound to its ownness, this possibility tears Dasein away from its everyday involvements *and* sets it before its "ownmost"; this possibility also tears Dasein away from its relations with others—undoes those relations. More precisely, when Dasein stands before itself as this possibility, when Dasein is fully assigned to it and disclosed to itself solely from this possibility, then our everyday relations with others become insignificant and, in that sense, fall away, are undone.

So this second passage identifies death as *nonrelational*.

"This ownmost, non-relational possibility is at the same time the most extreme one. As a potentiality-of-Being, Dasein is unable to bypass the possibility of death. Death is the possibility of the absolute impossibility of Dasein" (BT 250/241). This passage makes explicit a character of death that was already in play in the previous passage: death as possibility of losing all possibilities—that is, as most extreme possibility that suspends all others—*and* which thus cannot be surpassed (outstripped) in favor of some further possibility. *So* this passage identifies death as unsurpassable (*unüberholbar*).

Heidegger proceeds next to put together the three determinations of death: "Thus *death* reveals itself as the *ownmost, nonrelational, unsurpassable* possibility. As such, death is something *distinctively* imminent [*Bevorstand*]" (BT 250–51/241). These three determinations distinguish death from all other impending possibilities; for example, from the sort of possibilities Heidegger mentioned earlier: journey, disputation with others, and foregoing something. In fact, we can now see that these three examples allude to merely relative forms that become absolute in the case of death: the journey separates oneself from the familiar environment; the disputation with others separates oneself from the opinion of others; foregoing something separates oneself from some further possibilities.

"The existential possibility of a distinctive impending is grounded in the fact that Dasein is essentially disclosed to itself, and indeed in the manner of Being-ahead-of-itself" (BT 251/241). This passage sets something back upon its ground. What precisely is the grounded and what is the ground? The grounded is death *as* existential possibility. On what is it grounded? On Dasein's character *as* essentially disclosed to itself or, more specifically, on Dasein's character *as* disclosing itself by projecting itself upon possibilities, which is to say, on Dasein's character as "ahead-of-itself," as existence. *So* this passage shows that Dasein's disclosedness is integral to death. That is, it is from death (as impending, ownmost, nonrelational, unsurpassable possibility) that Dasein is most primordially disclosed to itself.

"This structural moment of care has its most primordial concretion in Being-toward-death" (BT 251/241). This says: existence assumes its *most primordial* form in the mode of Being-toward-death. Why most primordial? Because in Being-toward-death, Dasein is torn away from its involvement with the everyday world and with others and possibilities in that world—*and thus* brought back from understanding itself in terms of those involvements; that is, brought back before itself (its ownmost). This means, then, that Being-toward-death comes into a certain unity with itself, into a certain wholeness. This is why Heidegger uses here the word *primordial*: unity and wholeness are, as we saw, precisely what is required for primordiality.

And now, the final passage: "Being-toward-the-end becomes phenomenally clearer as Being toward that distinctive possibility of Dasein that we have characterized" (BT 251/241). This is precisely what was required at the end of the earlier analysis: to clarify existentially the sense of Dasein's ending. The clarification that has now been given shows once and for all how Dasein's Being-toward-the-end differs from the ripening of a fruit: the difference lies in the fact that Dasein is disclosedness and that, consequently, Dasein's end has the character of possibility *from* which Dasein is disclosed to itself. That is, Dasein's Being-toward-its-end (unlike that of fruit) is a mode of disclosedness.

However, to say that Being-toward-death is preeminently a mode of existence is *not* to deny its relation to the other moments of the care-structure. Thus Heidegger proceeds to interpret death in relation to thrownness and falling.

II. Death and Thrownness

In its relation to existence, death has been characterized as Dasein's ownmost, nonrelational, unsurpassable possibility. Now Heidegger asks, in effect: How does Dasein come to "have" this possibility? That is, how does Dasein come to project upon it and hence disclose itself from it? He answers: Dasein is always already *thrown* into this possibility. In his own words, this possibility "is not created by Dasein subsequently and occasionally in the course of its Being. Rather, when Dasein exists, it is already *thrown* into this possibility" (BT 251/241).

One might ask: How does this thrownness into death get disclosed? That is, how does death get brought before Dasein as a possibility to which it is delivered over, to which it is thrown? Heidegger answers: this happens especially in that disposition called *anxiety*. How are we to understand this connection between anxiety and Being-toward-death? We can only make some tentative connections.

1. Both anxiety and Being-toward-death are modes of disclosedness—preeminently, of self-disclosure.

2. In both cases, the disclosure pertains not to any specific everyday possibilities *but rather* to Being-in-the-world as such.

3. In both cases, Dasein is torn away from its everyday involvements and the kind of self-disclosure that goes with such involvements—*and thus* is individualized, brought back to its ownmost.

So in anxiety and Being-toward-death, we have to do with two moments of Dasein's primordial self-disclosure. The difference is that anxiety is on the side of attunement, whereas Being-toward-death is on the side of projective understanding. Because anxiety is the attunement moment, it is what discloses thrownness.

III. Death and Falling

Being-toward-death, as a mode of self-disclosure, is something in which Dasein can "hold" itself in different ways; that is, can maintain itself, comport itself. In particular, Dasein can hold itself in this self-disclosure in such a way that what is disclosed gets evaded or covered up. Heidegger says: "That factically many people initially and for the most part do not know about death must not be used to prove that Being-toward-death does not 'universally' belong to Dasein; rather, it only proves that Dasein, fleeing *from* it, initially and for the most part covers over its ownmost Being-toward-death. Dasein dies factically as long as it exists, initially and for the most part in the mode of *falling*" (BT 251–52/242). Thus the structure of Being-toward-death is determined not only by existence and thrownness but also by falling, which is to say, by all three moments of care. Thus Heidegger concludes: "*With regard to its ontological possibility, dying is grounded in care*" (BT 252/242).

At this point, the *formal* analysis of Being-toward-death is complete—that is, the analysis of the undifferentiated structure, without regard to its differentiated, concrete modes (inauthentic, authentic). The remainder of the chapter is then devoted to analyzing these modes in which the formal structure is concretized: sections 51–52 concern inauthentic (everyday) Being-toward-death; section 53 concerns authentic Being-toward-death.

Section 51: Being-toward-Death and the Everydayness of Dasein

There is a certain *methodological* need to move from the formal structure *to* its everyday concretion: the everyday concretion supplies at a certain level a phenomenal confirmation of the formal analysis. So Heidegger wants to show what guise Being-toward-death assumes in everydayness.

He takes as his clue the idle talk of the "they." By considering how everyday Dasein expresses itself about death in idle talk, he tries to discern the "shape" of everyday Being-toward-death; that is, how everyday Dasein comports itself toward death. This issue was already touched on at the end of the formal analysis in the connection established between death and falling. There we saw that everyday Dasein flees in the face of death and in doing so evades the disclosure. What Heidegger now shows (following the clue of idle talk) is that the evasion takes the form of a covering-up of precisely those characteristics that are distinctive of death. Thus in everydayness, death's character as *possibility* gets leveled down: death gets taken as just an event occurring within-the-world, as something actual. This is manifest in idle talk: we speak of death as a "mishap," a familiar and constantly occurring event within-the-world. We say: "One of these days, one will die too, in the end, but right now, it has nothing to do with us."

Also, death's character as *ownmost* gets covered over (leveled down). "The public interpretation of Dasein says that 'one dies,' because in this way everyone can convince him/herself that in no case is it I myself, for this one is *no one*. 'Dying' is leveled down to an event which does concern Dasein, but which belongs to no one in particular. . . . Dying, which is essentially and irreplaceably mine, is distorted into a publicly occurring event which the they encounters" (BT 253/243).

Likewise with the nonrelational and unsurpassable characters of death—they, too, get leveled down and covered over.

Section 52: Everyday Being-toward-Death and the Complete Existential Concept of Death

Here Heidegger extends his analysis of everyday Being-toward-death, then connects the result to the formal analysis (from section 50) so as to arrive at the full existential concept of death.

The evasions and covering up that belong to falling become accentuated in the way the "they" comport themselves to death; that is, in the relation to death characteristic of everydayness. Heidegger focuses on the way the "they" concedes the *certainty* of death *and yet* distorts, covers over, evades, this certainty. "They" say: "Death certainly comes, but not right away." In this way, "they" evade the certainty of death, defer death to some later time. Heidegger continues: "Thus the they covers over the peculiar certainty of death *that is possible at every moment*. Together with the certainty of death goes the *indefiniteness* of its when. Everyday Being-toward-death evades this indefiniteness by conferring definiteness upon it. . . . Everyday concern makes definite for itself the indefiniteness of certain death by interposing before it those manageable urgencies and possibilities of the everyday matters nearest to us" (BT 258/247–48).

On the other hand, the authentic mode of Being-toward-death must be such that the evasions and concealment fall away, such that Dasein can hold itself in its disclosedness without letting **what** is disclosed get covered over. This certainty and indefiniteness of death, which makes manifest the "evasions of the 'they,'" Heidegger now incorporates into the concept of death yielded by the formal analysis. The result of this incorporation is the full existential concept of death: "The full existential-ontological concept of death may now be defined as follows: *Death, as the end of Dasein, is the ownmost, non-relational, certain and, as such, indefinite, unsurpassable possibility of Dasein*" (BT 258–59/248).

Finally, Heidegger refers again to the question of Dasein's Being-a-whole (the question from which the entire interpretation of death has arisen). The point is that death has turned out not to be some outstanding event to which Dasein would come only in its demise. Rather, through the existential analysis, it has been seen that death, in its character as possibility, is already *included in* Dasein. That is, the ultimate "not-yet," which would delimit whatever wholeness Dasein can have, is itself included in Dasein rather than being something perpetually missing. Clearly, some progress has been made with this problem, *but* Heidegger does not yet try to resolve it. Instead, he moves on to consider the other issue that arose in connection with the question of the primordiality of the interpretation: the question of authenticity.

Section 53: Existential Project of an Authentic Being-toward-death

The problem now is: How is authentic Being-toward-death possible? Here, we must recall: "authentic" and "inauthentic" denote existentiell (ontic) modifications of Dasein's basic structure. So authentic Being-toward-death would be an existentiell possibility. The question then is: What are the existential (ontological) conditions of this existentiell possibility? That is, how is this existentiell possibility existentially possible? In other words, what is the existential structure that would underlie and make possible an authentic Being-toward-death?

The previous analyses, in effect, determine this existential structure up to a certain point: (1) It must have that general character already worked out in the formal analysis and summed up in the "full existential concept of death." Regardless of its existentiell modification, Being-toward-death is Dasein's disclosive comportment toward its ownmost, nonrelational, certain (and indefinite), unsurpassable possibility. (2) Furthermore, the analysis of inauthentic Being-toward-death prescribes in a negative way the character that must be had by authentic Being-toward-death. That is, it must be such that Dasein can hold itself in the relevant disclosedness without letting what is disclosed get covered over.

Heidegger begins his positive analysis by focusing on the character of death as possibility: Being-toward-death is a Being-toward-a-possibility. Heidegger proceeds to more precisely determine just what Being-toward-a-possibility can mean here; that is, in the case where that possibility is death. Specifically, he considers several senses and excludes them—yet in such a way as gradually to focus on the proper sense.

(1) "Being-toward-a-possibility" may mean "Being out for" something possible in the sense of concerning ourselves with actualizing it (as, for example, we actualize equipment by producing it, getting it ready, etc.). Clearly, this is not the sense in which Dasein is toward death since to actualize death would destroy the very possibility of Being-toward-death.

(2) "Being-toward-death as possibility" may mean "dwelling upon the end in its possibility." That is to say, brooding over death and pondering over when and how this possibility will be actualized. But this, too, is inappropriate *because* in such brooding, in such calculative pondering, in pondering over how and when death may be actualized, we weaken its character *as* possibility. In other words, in such comportment its character as possibility gets covered over. Yet precisely what is required for *authentic* Being-toward-death is the exclusion of such covering over within the disclosive comportment. As Heidegger says: "In such Being-toward-death this possibility must not be weakened, it must be understood *as possibility*, cultivated *as possibility*, and *endured as possibility* in our relation to it" (BT 261/250).

(3) Still another way in which to comport oneself toward possibility is by *expecting*. However, even in expecting, the possibility-character of death gets leveled down *since* expecting is essentially a waiting for the actualization. So this sense, too, is inappropriate for characterizing Dasein's authentic way of Being-toward-death.

All of these inappropriate senses serve to point up the appropriate sense of Being-toward-death (as possibility): it must be such as to grant to death its *full* character *as* possibility: such a way of Being-toward-death Heidegger designates: *anticipation* (*Vorlaufen*, literally, running ahead).

What is the positive (general) character of anticipation? It is a *running-ahead* (forward, out in front) toward this possibility (death)—a coming close to it— **yet** in a way that, rather than diverting it (transforming it) into some actuality, adheres to its character as *sheer possibility*.

But what is the character of death as sheer possibility? Heidegger says: death is "*the possibility of the impossibility of existence [Existenz] in general*" (BT 262/251). Heidegger already touched on this issue in characterizing death as unsurpassable, but now he develops it further. He says: "The more clearly this possibility is understood, the more purely does understanding penetrate to it *as the possibility of the impossibility of existence [Existenz] in general*. As possibility death gives Dasein nothing to 'be actualized' and nothing which it itself could *be* as something real" (BT 262/251). That is, in distinction from all other possibilities, death is *not* something that Dasein can *be*—it is such *sheer* possibility that there is nothing to be actualized. Heidegger continues: "Essentially, this possibility offers no support for becoming intent on something, for 'picturing' for oneself the actuality that is possible and so forgetting its possibility. As anticipation of possibility, Being-toward-death first *makes* this possibility *possible* and sets it free as such" (BT 262/251). Death as sheer possibility absolutely cannot be diverted into actuality. As sheer possibility, it is detached from everything actual—and in this sense is "nothing."

In anticipation, as we have said, Dasein comports itself toward this possibility in an appropriate way; that is, in a way that adheres to its character as sheer possibility, that does *not* cover up this character. In other words, anticipation lets it be *as* sheer possibility, projects this possibility *as* sheer possibility—"first *makes* this possibility *possible* and sets it free as such." We should recall here that anticipation, as a mode of Being-toward-death, is a mode of disclosedness; specifically, of understanding. It belongs to the structure of understanding to project possibilities in such a way as to project them (let them be) *as* possibilities. Thus we see here how this moment of understanding is exemplified (indeed paradigmatically) in authentic Being-toward-death.

But understanding, and hence anticipation, has another side: it is not only a projecting of possibility as possibility; it is also *self-disclosure* from the possibility projected. So in anticipation Dasein understands itself *from* death *as* possibility—that is, from its *ownmost* possibility. This is authentic self-understanding.

The remainder of section 53 is devoted to working out the specific character of anticipation and especially to showing just what kind of self-disclosure it yields, which is to say, just how Dasein is disclosed to itself when it understands itself *purely* from death as sheer possibility. Heidegger proceeds by considering the various characters that death has been shown to have (ownmost, nonrelational, unsurpassable, certain but indefinite) and identifies with regard to each character the corresponding disclosure of Dasein. That is, he shows *how* Dasein is disclosed to itself *from* each of these characters of death as possibility. Many of the issues he develops here have already come up in our consideration of the character of death from section 50, so I will just touch on the main points of the analysis.

In anticipation Dasein understands itself *from* death as *ownmost*. Here Dasein stands before its *ownmost* possibility, before what is radically its *own* and so "encounters" its radical mineness. In coming face-to-face with its radical mineness, Dasein must have been wrenched away from the "they" and from that absorption in the "they" that conceals mineness—*and thus*: from this character, Dasein is disclosed as having been lost, as proximally and for the most part suffering lostness in the they-self.

In anticipation Dasein understands itself *from* death as *nonrelational*. From this character of death, Dasein is *individualized*; that is, disclosed to itself *as* individual. "Death [*er*] *lays claim* on it as something *individual*. The nonrelational character of death, as understood in anticipation, individualizes Dasein down to itself" (BT 263/252). Here Heidegger makes an important clarification: to say that in anticipation (in authentic existence) Dasein is individualized *does not mean* that authentic Dasein simply cuts itself off from concernful dealings in the world with others. "But if concern and caring for fail us, this in no way means, however, that these modes of Dasein have been cut off from its authentic Being-itself. As essential structures of the constitution of Dasein, they also belong to the condition of the possibility of existence in general" (BT 263/252). Thus authentic existence is *not simply* a withdrawal from concernful dealings with things and from others *into oneself*. He continues: "Dasein is authentically itself only to the extent that, *as* concernful Being-with and Being-alongside things cared for, it projects itself upon its ownmost potentiality-of-Being rather than upon the possibility of the they-self" (BT 263/252). We could say, then, that what Dasein withdraws from concernful dealings and Being-with-others is its self-understanding: that is, rather than understanding itself from the world and the "they," it comes to understand itself from its ownmost (nonrelational) possibility. *And*: thereby, a more genuine comportment to the everyday world and to others first becomes possible.

Heidegger alludes to such a genuine comportment toward the everyday world in his discussion of how Dasein is disclosed *from* the character of death as unsurpassable. From this character, Dasein is disclosed to itself as *bound* by this end. Or, as Heidegger expresses it, Dasein is (in anticipation) *freed for* its own death, given to itself as "freedom toward death," in contrast to the evasions by which inauthentic Dasein conceals its being bound by this end. Heidegger continues then: "Becoming free *for* one's own death in anticipation liberates one from one's lostness in chance possibilities urging themselves upon us, so that the factical possibilities lying before the unsurpassable possibility can first be authentically understood and chosen" (BT 264/253). Thus from out of its self-disclosure as bound by the unsurpassable end, Dasein understands its possibilities *as finite*.

We should also note: this disclosure bears on the question of Dasein's wholeness; it is, in effect, a disclosure of Dasein in its peculiar wholeness. So in anticipation, Dasein is "given" to itself *as a whole—and hence* the possibility is provided for taking Dasein as a whole into the fore-having of an interpretation.

In anticipation Dasein understand itself *from* the character of death as certain but *indefinite*. Here Dasein is disclosed to itself as exposed to a *constant threat*, and in anticipation, it holds itself open to this threat. This dimension of the self-disclosure is especially important because, in relation to it, the *connection* between *anticipation and anxiety* becomes evident. "*But the attunement which is able to hold open the constant and absolute threat to itself arising from the ownmost individualized Being of Dasein is anxiety*. In anxiety, Dasein finds itself *faced* with the nothingness of the possible impossibility of its existence" (BT 265–66/254). So anxiety is the attunement that accompanies that understanding that has been described as anticipation—anxiety and anticipation constitute the two sides of one and the same basic mode of disclosedness.

At this point, we know that in anticipation, Dasein is disclosed to itself as a whole, that it is bounded by an end that belongs to it. To this extent, anticipation *can* provide the basis for getting Dasein as a whole (and its authenticity) into the fore-structure of an interpretation, and hence it *can* provide such a basis. More precisely, anticipation *can* provide such a basis *if* anticipation is not merely an ontological possibility *but also* is *ontically possible*. The problem is now this: the analysis thus far has shown *only* that anticipation (which is equivalent to Dasein's authentic Being-a-whole) is ontologically possible. Heidegger explains: "The ontological possibility of an authentic potentiality-for-Being-a-whole of Dasein means nothing as long as the corresponding ontic potentiality-of-Being has not been shown in terms of Dasein itself. Does Dasein ever project itself factically into such a Being-toward-death?" (BT 266/255) This is what remains to be shown. Specifically, it needs to be shown how an authentic Being-a-whole at the ontic (existentiell) level is *attested* by Dasein. That is, the question is: How does Dasein testify to the *ontic* possibility of its authentic Being-a-whole? This is the question from which chapter 2 proceeds.

Let us now take some distance from Heidegger's analysis. More specifically, the suggestion arises that there are at least two other moments (phenomena) that are essentially related to death—to "the situation of death."

While death is indeed Dasein's ownmost possibility, it is a possibility that—in relation to the deceased—may be owned by certain others, that may even be ownmost for them. They are the ones who bring back the deceased in memory, especially if the deceased is one for whom there was respect or love. He can be brought back in the form of memorials (events or objects). So the full structure of death includes mourning and remembrance.

The other phenomenon is *birth*. This is essentially linked to thrownness: into a language, society, and possibilities harbored by these. Yet one might wonder whether this is appropriately called thrownness. For one has no experience of being thrown but rather of unaccountably finding oneself in a predetermined milieu. More generally: Can one fully understand death without also understanding birth? Is mortality not intrinsically bound to natality?

2. The Attestation of Dasein of an Authentic Potentiality-of-Being and Resoluteness

Section 54: The Problem of the Attestation of an Authentic Existentiell Possibility

Let us provide a context for section 54.

In its authentic Being-toward-death, Dasein projects itself upon death as its ownmost possibility, and it does so in such a way as to let this possibility be as sheer possibility. This authentic Being-toward-death Heidegger calls anticipation (*Vorlaufen*, running ahead). In anticipation, Dasein is, in turn, disclosed to itself as a whole, as bounded by an end (death as possibility) that belongs to it. Thus anticipation can provide a basis for getting Dasein as a whole (and in its authenticity) into the fore-structure of the interpretation—hence it can provide the basis for a primordial interpretation. And yet if anticipation is actually to provide such a basis, it must be shown to be not merely an ontological possibility but also something that factically, ontically occurs. That is, the question, as Heidegger puts it, is: "Does Dasein ever throw itself factically into such a Being-toward-death?" (BT 266/255) To confirm that this is so (that anticipation can and does happen ontically), Heidegger will show that Dasein itself attests to such a happening. That is, he will exhibit in Dasein itself an attesting to the ontic (existentiell) possibility of its being authentic.

We need to have in view, in advance, the general structure of the analysis by which this attestation is to be exhibited.

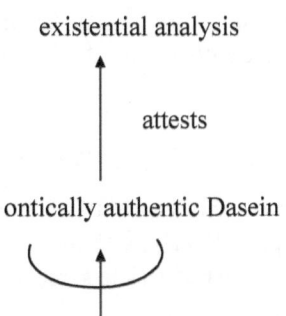

Heidegger develops the task in terms of the issue of attestation. To show that authenticity is ontically possible, he will simply let Dasein attest to this possibility. That is to say, he will simply exhibit an attestation (*by* Dasein, *that* it can be authentic). In other words, he will circumscribe a certain attestation by Dasein and show it is an attestation of Dasein's possible authenticity. Of course, to do this, more is required than merely pointing—namely, an existential analysis through which the phenomenon in question can be circumscribed and shown to be an attestation of authenticity. So even the question of existentiell possibility requires for its development an existential analysis.

We must distinguish (as often before) between two levels:

1. that of the existential analysis
2. that of the Dasein being analyzed

In the present case, this distinction is, specifically, between:

1. Dasein that attests to its ontically possible authenticity
2. the existential analysis to which Dasein attests that it can be authentic

Yet the structure is still more complex because this attesting (Dasein→ analysis) must be rooted in a more primordial attestation *within Dasein itself*. That is, there will be a primordial attestation in which Dasein attests its possible authenticity *to itself*. The existential analysis will proceed by "listening in" on this primordial attestation.

How does such primordial attestation occur in Dasein? The attestation has to do with (i.e., attest to) the possibility of authenticity. Authenticity is possible only through self-recovery (withdrawal), the recovery of oneself from dispersal in the "they." This recovery is a recovery of *choice* (which inauthentic Dasein had relinquished to the "they"). It is a choosing to choose from out of one's *own* self. Heidegger continues: "But because Dasein is lost in the 'they,' it must first *find* itself. In order to find *itself* at all, it must be 'shown' to itself in its possible authenticity. In terms of its *possibility*, Dasein *is* already a potentiality-for-Being-its-self, but it needs to have this potentiality attested" (BT 268/258). So in the primordial attestation, Dasein has its possible authenticity *shown* to itself: Dasein is *disclosed* to itself as regards its possible authenticity. And thus the primordial attestation is a mode of *disclosedness*.

Section 55: The Existential-Ontological Foundations of Conscience

This primordial attestation coincides with the phenomenon of *conscience*. What is thus required is an existential analysis of conscience. In this analysis, it will not be a matter of tracing conscience back to some power or faculty of the psyche (for example, cognition, will, or feeling). Rather, conscience is to be analyzed as a mode of existence, of disclosedness, which is to say in terms of the constitution of the "there." More specifically, Heidegger begins (§55) by focusing on the form that Dasein's disclosedness takes when Dasein is absorbed in the "they." He thematizes especially one particular character of disclosedness: it involves a *listening* to the they-self (in such a way that the "they" dictates its possibilities)—and correlatively, a *failing to hear* its own self. The possibility of authenticity requires that this listening to the "they" get broken off, that it be interrupted by another kind of hearing (radically opposed to it). The call that can arouse this other kind of hearing is the call of conscience. So conscience has the character of a *call*—**and**, as such, it is a mode of *discourse*.

Section 56: The Character of Conscience as a Call

Heidegger proceeds (§56) to interpret the character of conscience as call (i.e., as a mode of discourse). He refers to the main constitutive moments that discourse was shown (cf. chap. 5) to have—and then shows what specific form each such moment takes in the case of conscience.

There are three primary moments of discourse.

1. What the discourse is about (what is talked about in it) (*das Beredete*).
2. What is said in the discourse (*das Geredete*).
3. The making-known (*die Bekundung*), which usually takes the form of communication, which, in turn, usually takes the form of verbal utterance.

Heidegger goes on, then, to indicate what specific form each of these moments takes in the case of conscience.

(1) In the call of conscience, what is the discourse about?—Dasein. But also, the call is a call *to Dasein*—a call to it; specifically, in its everyday lostness in the "they." Thus conscience is a call to Dasein about Dasein.

Let us look at this more closely. Conscience is a calling to Dasein in its everydayness in such a way that Dasein is *called to something* (*angerufen*, summoned)—namely, to its own self. Heidegger expresses it thus: it is a calling directed only to the *self* of the they-self, which is a calling that passes over the "they" and makes the "they" collapse for the self thus called. Thus the call serves to push the "they" into insignificance. And "Because only the *self* of the they-self is summoned and made to hear, the *they* collapses. The fact that the call *passes over* both the they and the public interpretedness of Dasein by no means signifies that it has not been *reached too*. Precisely in *passing over* the they, the call pushed it (adamant as it is about public recognition) into insignificance. But, robbed of its refuge and this subterfuge by the summons, the self is brought to itself by the call" (BT 273/263).

We should note here that Heidegger insists that being thus brought to oneself is *not* simply a matter of turning away from the world into oneself, it is not a matter of being brought to the "self that unrestrainedly dissects its 'inner life' with excited curiosity" (BT 273/263). He then continues:

> The they-self is summoned to the self. However, this is not the self that can become an "object" for itself on which to pass judgment, not the self that unrestrainedly dissects an "inner life" with excited curiosity, and not the self that stares "analytically" at states of the soul and their backgrounds. The summons of the self in the they-self does not force it inwards upon itself so that it can close itself off from the "external world." The call passes over all this and disperses it, so as to summon solely the self which is in no other way than Being-in-the-world. (BT 273/263)

(2) In the call of conscience, what is said in the discourse? *Nothing!* The call asserts nothing, conveys no information. "But how are we to define *what is talked about* in this discourse? *What* does conscience call to the one summoned? Strictly speaking—nothing. The call does not say anything, does not give any information about events of the world, has nothing to tell. Least of all does it strive to open a 'conversation with itself' in the self which has been summoned. 'Nothing' is called *to* the self which is summoned, but it is *summoned* to itself, that is, to its ownmost potentiality-of-Being" (BT 273/263).

(3) In the call of conscience, the making-known does *not* take the form of communication and does not involve verbal utterance. Rather: "*Conscience speaks solely and constantly in the mode of silence* [keeping silent, *Schweigen*]" (BT 273/263).

Section 57: Conscience as the Call of Care

Up to this point, we have seen that conscience is a silent calling in which nothing is said. As such, it is a calling to Dasein that calls Dasein to its ownmost potentiality-for-Being. But now Heidegger asks: Who does the calling? Who is the caller? Or, in precise phenomenological terms, how does the caller show itself? What is its phenomenal character?

Again, however, the caller is *indefinite*. It belongs to the phenomenal character to hold itself aloof from all ways of becoming familiar. It "uniquely coincides with summoning to . . . that it wants to be *heard only as such*" (BT 275/264).

But Heidegger asks: Isn't it obvious who the caller is—namely, Dasein? Can't we say that in conscience Dasein simply calls itself?—that Dasein is both caller and called? In a sense, this is so—*and yet* Heidegger does not merely identify the caller and the called (the one summoned). Rather, the point is that the phenomenal evidence is against this mere identification: the calling is not something that everyday Dasein (which is called) plans, prepares for, or voluntarily performs. The call comes upon me—perhaps even against my will. And yet, at the same time, it does not show itself as coming from someone else. As Heidegger says:

> However, ontologically it is not enough to answer that Dasein is the caller and the one summoned *at the same time*. When Dasein is summoned, *is* it not "there" in another way from that in which it does the calling? Is it perhaps the ownmost potentiality-of-being that functions as the caller?
>
> The call is precisely something that *we ourselves* have neither planned, nor prepared for, nor willfully brought about. "It" calls, against our expectations and even against our will. On the other hand, the call without doubt does not come from someone else who is with me in the world. The call comes *from* me, and yet *over* me. (BT 275/264–65)

The point is that the calling is not planned, prepared, or carried out by everyday Dasein. Though the call does not appear as coming from someone else, it is something that comes over (overcomes) me, perhaps even against my (everyday) will. It is simply not under my control.

Heidegger attempts to do justice to this phenomenal evidence regarding the caller by developing the issue in terms of Dasein's existential constitution. The upshot of the development is this: the caller is Dasein *in* that primordial self-disclosure (attunement) which Heidegger calls *anxiety*, and which he now characterizes in terms of Dasein's finding itself "*in the ground of its uncanniness*" (BT 276/266). *But* a question remains: How can anxious Dasein serve as the one who calls Dasein to its own self? That is, if Dasein is in anxiety, hasn't it thereby already been thrown back upon its own self? The point is this: even when Dasein is lost in the "they," even when falling is in command, still that self-disclosure in anxiety remains in force—*but* it is covered over, evaded. In fact, the evasive character of falling, its character as fleeing in the face of something, betrays that the self-disclosure remains. *Thus* what calls Dasein is the primordial self-disclosure of anxiety *as* it remains within everyday Dasein. If the caller is thus identified, then the phenomenal evidence (namely, indefiniteness; the character of the call as coming from me and yet from over me) is respected. "In its who, the caller is definable by *nothing* [*nichts*] 'worldly.' It is Dasein in its uncanniness, primordially thrown Being-in-the-world, as not-at-home, the naked 'that' in the nothingness [*Nichts*] of the world. The caller is unfamiliar to the everyday they-self, it is something like an *alien* voice. What could be more alien to the they, lost in the manifold 'world' of its heedfulness, than the self individualized to itself in uncanniness thrown into nothingness?" (BT 276–77/266)

Heidegger concludes this part of the existential analysis of conscience by identifying how conscience is grounded in the care-structure; that is, how conscience is the "call of care."

1. The caller is Dasein in its *thrownness* (Being-already-in) as disclosed in anxiety.
2. The one to whom the call is addressed is Dasein as *falling*, in its lostness in the "they" (in Being already alongside the world of its concern).
3. And Dasein is called to its ownmost potentiality-of-Being (its authentic Being-ahead-of-itself, authentic existence).

Section 58: Understanding the Summons and Guilt

At the end of section 57, Heidegger indicates a major gap that still remains in the treatment of conscience: he has not considered the character of the *hearing* that would genuinely correspond to the call—or, more precisely, what one would be given to understand in genuinely hearing the call. This must be considered in order to grasp the full structure of conscience.

Section 58 begins by giving two important moments regarding this hearing-understanding.

(1) Such hearing is more authentic the more *nonrelational* it remains—the less what is understood gets perverted in the direction of the "they."

(2) A second, additional moment in the call of conscience needs to be identified: the *hearing* that would genuinely correspond to the call—or, more precisely, what one would be given to understand in genuinely hearing the call. We have seen that the calling comes *from* Dasein's uncanniness, and this means that what calls is Dasein's primordial self-disclosure in anxiety. *But* what is it that gets understood in hearing the call? Heidegger refers again to the character of the caller: the calling comes *from* Dasein's uncanniness. This means that what calls is Dasein's primordial self-disclosure in anxiety. Then Heidegger makes the following crucial point: "The call directs Dasein *forward toward* its potentiality-of-Being, as a call *out of* uncanniness. The caller is indeed indefinite, but where it calls from is not indifferent for the calling. Where it comes from is not indifferent for the calling. Where it comes from—the uncanniness of thrown individuation—is also called in the calling, that is, is also disclosed. Where the call comes from in calling forth to . . . is that to which it is called back" (BT 280/269). This says that in the calling of conscience, Dasein's primordial self-disclosure in anxiety gets disclosed. This is what (at the deepest level) is given us to understand in the call—this primordial self-disclosure. In other words, this primordial self-disclosure, which remains operative in everydayness but which is evaded or covered over, gets freed of such concealment. That is, in the call of conscience, the self-disclosure of anxiety is allowed to become positively effective.

In being given, through the call, this primordial self-disclosure, Dasein is "given" (disclosed) to itself. This is what (in a secondary sense) Dasein is given to understand in the call—namely, *itself*. In such self-disclosure, Dasein is disclosed to itself as individualized, in its ownness, mineness—*and not* in terms of some ideal or universal. Thus Heidegger says: "The call does not give us to understand an ideal, universal potentiality-of-Being; it discloses it as what is actually individualized in that particular Dasein" (BT 280/269). So the calling forth of Dasein to its ownmost potentiality-of-Being is *not* a matter of presenting it with some kind of universal ideal that it is to actualize.

In slightly different terms, Heidegger says the call is "a calling back that calls forth." That is, Dasein is *called back* to its primordial self-disclosure (in anxiety, in uncanniness). Thereby, it is *called forth* beyond the covering up and evasion of everydayness—called forth *to itself* (in its authenticity)[1]—that is, called forth as individualized in distinction from being lost in the they.

It is at this point that Heidegger turns to the question of guilt. This is because it is generally agreed that what one hears in the experience of conscience pertains to guilt—either that one is guilty, or (in warning conscience) that one is exposed to possible guilt, or (in good conscience) that one is not guilty. So if the hearing (of the call of conscience) is to be fully clarified, the sense of "guilty" must be determined.

Heidegger discusses various senses of being-guilty, following the way in which everyday Dasein talks about guilt.

(1) Being-guilty (*Schuldigsein*) can mean "owing" (*schulden*), in the sense of having a debt. The connection is clearer in German, but we do speak, for example, of a person guilty of crimes as *owing* a debt to society (to be paid by undergoing punishment).

(2) Being-guilty can mean "being responsible for" (*schuld sein an*) in the sense of being the cause or author of something.

(3) These come together in a richer, third sense: making oneself responsible in such a way as to come to owe something to others; that is, in having responsibility (e.g., through crime) for the Other's becoming endangered in his existence, led astray, or ruined.

This signification provides Heidegger's point of departure, and so now he refines it in a more precise definition: Being-guilty in this sense means: "*Being-the-ground* for a lack in the Dasein of an other, in such a way that this Being-the-ground itself is determined as 'lacking' in terms of that for which it is the ground" (BT 282/271).

All these senses of "guilty" remain oriented to our Being-with-others. What Heidegger now proposes, in order to get a more primordial concept, is to *formalize* the concept in such a way that this specific orientation falls away. In this connection, he notes that it is also important to detach the concept of guilt from all relationship to law or to an "ought" (which equals relationships→one would become guilty by failing to comply). This is because if guilt were regarded in terms of such relationships, then it would, in effect, be defined as a *lack* or, stated

---

1. *Eigentlichkeit* = "ownness."

differently, as the not-being-present (*Nicht-vorhandensein*) of something that ought to be present. In other words, if we defined guilt in this way, we would remain completely oriented to the understanding of Being as *presence*. Nevertheless, the idea of guilt does include a certain negative character ("the character of the *not* [*Nicht*]" [BT 283/272]). Also, it includes the sense of "having responsibility for" in the sense of "Being-the-ground-for." Here, then, is Heidegger's formal concept (existential concept) of Being-guilty: "Thus we define the formal existential idea of 'guilty' as Being-the-ground for a being [*Sein*] which is determined by a not—that is, *Being-the-ground of a negativity* [*Grundsein einer Nichtigkeit*, negativity]" (BT 283/272).

Let us finally recall that the whole issue of guilt arose in an attempt to thematize Dasein's hearing-understanding of the call of conscience. What Dasein hears in the call is that it *is* guilty (or at least *can be* guilty). So the question is, then: How does Being-guilty belong to Dasein? That is, in what way does Dasein's Being involve the character of Being-the-ground of a negativity? In other words, how does care ground negativity and hence guilt? To answer this question, Heidegger must show how the character of "Being-the-ground of a negativity" belongs to Dasein, that is, he must show that Dasein is such as to have this character. We can see this if we expand the expression of this character into Being-the-(negative) ground of a negativity. We must, then, consider: 1. How Dasein is a ground; 2. How Dasein is a negative ground; 3. How Dasein is the ground of a negativity.

(1) How is Dasein a ground? Dasein is a ground *as thrown*. That is, it is in its character as thrown that Dasein serves as a ground. A ground of what? It is the ground of Dasein's potentiality-for-Being (= *Seinkönnen* = can-be = projection upon possibilities). That is to say, Dasein's character as thrown into the "there" forms the ground on which is based Dasein's character as potentiality-for-Being (which is equivalent to Dasein's character as comportment toward possibilities).

But how is this more specifically the case? That is, how is Dasein's projection upon possibilities grounded on Dasein's throwness into its "there"? Heidegger answers: "And how *is* Dasein this thrown ground? Only by projecting itself upon the possibilities into which it is thrown [*Einzig so, daß es sich auf Möglichkeiten entwirft, in die es geworfen ist*]" (BT 284/273). This says that Dasein (as thrown) is the ground for projection by the fact that, *as thrown*, Dasein is already delivered over to certain possibilities, upon which it can then project. Said differently, the possibilities upon which Dasein can project are first handed over (brought before it) by virtue of Dasein's thrownness. Said in yet another way, Dasein is first of all thrown amid a certain range of possibilities, so that it can then project on certain of them.

(2) How is Dasein a negative ground? That is, what is the negativity intrinsic to thrownness? It lies in the very sense of thrownness: as thrown, Dasein does *not* bring itself into its "there." More precisely: "Dasein exists as thrown, brought

into its there *not* of its own accord. It exists as a potentiality-for-Being which belongs to itself, and yet has *not* given itself to itself. Existing, it never gets back behind its thrownness so that it could ever release this 'that it is and has to be' from *its Being*-its-self and lead it into the there" (BT 284/272–73). This is to say that Dasein cannot free itself from its "there" so as to be able to situate itself in its "there" by its own power (from out of its own resources). Said differently, Dasein can never get power over its Being "from the ground up." That is, Dasein has not given itself to itself! This *not* being capable of giving itself to itself, to set itself into its "there"—*this* is the *negativity* (of the ground of thrownness). Heidegger expresses this conception also with a specific, slightly different reference to ground: "Even though it [Dasein] has *not* laid the ground *itself*, it rests in the weight of it, which mood reveals to it as a burden" (BT 284/273). That is, Dasein does not lay the ground, does not establish it or constitute it—but is thrown onto (upon) the ground. This is the negativity of the ground.

(3) How is Dasein the ground of a negativity? In general, Dasein is the ground of projection, and thus the question is: What is the negativity intrinsic to projection? Heidegger answers: "Dasein is its ground by existing, that is, in such a way that it understands itself in terms of possibilities and, thus understanding itself, is thrown being. But this means that, as a potentiality-of-Being, it [Dasein] always stands in one possibility or another; it is constantly *not* other possibilities and has relinquished them in its existentiell project. As thrown, the projection is not only determined by the negativity [*Nichtigkeit*] of Being-the-ground, but is itself *as projection* essentially *negative* [*nichtig*]" (BT 285/273). Thus what is the negativity intrinsic to projection? It is the negativity involved in the fact that to project upon a possibility is *not* to project upon other possibilities—it is to forfeit other possibilities. **So**: Dasein (as thrown projection) is the (negative) ground of a negativity. *And thus*: Dasein as such is guilty.

Following the analysis, there are some more general considerations. Though related to the analysis, they point beyond the entire Dasein-analytic.

First, Heidegger stresses that the negativity treated in the analysis does *not* have the character of privation or lack. In contrast to such concepts, which remain completely determined by the concept of Being as presence, the negativity of guilt is an existential negativity. Nevertheless, despite the analysis, Heidegger insists that the ontological meaning of this negativity (of Dasein) still remains obscure and likewise with regard to "the *ontological essence of the not in general*" (BT 285/274). This could be genuinely clarified only in terms of the meaning of Being as such, only within the fully developed context of fundamental ontology (cf. "What Is Metaphysics?").

Second, Heidegger refers to the problem of morality. First, he sets the existential concept of guilt completely apart from the idea of evil (understood as the privation of the good). He does this *because* these ideas—"privation," "good," and also the more abstract idea of "value"—are based on the ontology of presence. *But this does* not *mean that the analysis of guilt (and conscience) has no bearing on the problem of morality.* Rather: "This essential Being-guilty is, equiprimordially, the existential condition of the possibility of the 'morally' good and evil, that is, for morality in general and its possible factical forms. Primordial Being-guilty cannot be defined by morality because morality already presupposed it for itself" (BT 286/274). This says that the analysis of guilt lays the foundation for *ethics*; that is, for elaborating a concept of morality based not on the ontology of presence *but* on an understanding of the Being of Dasein as *existence*, as care.

Heidegger brings the analysis of guilt back into connection with the problem of conscience. The point of departure for the analysis of guilt was the general agreement that *what* Dasein hears in the call of conscience (what the call gives to Dasein to understand) is its Being-guilty. The analysis of guilt allows us to trace out the connection explicitly: in the call of conscience, Dasein's primordial self-disclosure in anxiety (i.e., uncanniness) is released from the concealments of everydayness, which is to say that this primordial self-disclosure becomes positively effective. But anxiety is an attunement, and an attunement is especially disclosive of thrownness. Thus the primordial attunement (uncanniness) discloses thrownness in its primordial character (most unconcealedly). That is, it discloses Dasein as that *negative ground*, which it is *as* thrown, as the negative ground of a negativity. "Uncanniness brings this being [Dasein] face to face with its undisguised negativity" (BT 287/275). But this negativity (which is equivalent to being the negative ground of a negativity) is precisely Dasein's Being-guilty, *and thus* we see how it is that what the call gives Dasein to understand is its Being-guilty.

Furthermore, in giving this to Dasein to understand, the call of conscience calls Dasein forth to itself as thus disclosed. "The summons calls back by calling forth: *forth* to the possibility of taking over in existence the thrown being that it is, *back* to thrownness in order to understand it as the negative ground that it has to take up into existence" (BT 287/275). In other words, conscience calls Dasein forth (summons it) to its Being-guilty; that is, summons it to assume its Being-guilty, summons it to be guilty authentically.

Heidegger expresses this more precisely by bringing up again the question of the hearing. What is the character of the hearing in which Dasein would hear responsibly (understandingly) what it is given to hear in the call of conscience? What is given to hear is also given as something *to understand*. So: Dasein *hears* the call when it *understands* what the call gives it to understand; that is, when it understands its Being-guilty. But granted the projective structure of understanding, this means that Dasein hears the call when it projects itself upon its Being-guilty as its possibility. "Then the correct hearing of the summons is tantamount to understanding oneself in one's ownmost potentiality-of-Being, that is, in projecting oneself upon one's *ownmost* authentic potentiality-for-becoming-guilty.

When Dasein understandingly lets itself be called forth to this possibility, this includes its *becoming-free* for the call: the readiness for being able to be summoned. Understanding the call, *Dasein listens to its ownmost possibility of existence. It has chosen itself*" (BT 287/275–76).

Finally, Heidegger says that in thus projecting, Dasein chooses itself. Or, in different terms: "What is chosen is *having* a conscience as being free for one's ownmost Being-guilty. *Understanding the summons* means: *wanting-to-have-a-conscience* [*Anrufverstehen besagt: Gewissen-haben-wollen*]" (BT 288/276).

At the end of section 58, Heidegger brings up again the character of conscience as an attestation, as an attestation in which Dasein attests to its possible authenticity. He immediately voices the demand that the existential interpretation of conscience (now completed) come to terms with the ordinary interpretation (rather than just ignoring it). This demand he then tries to satisfy in section 59 by showing how conscience (as disclosed in the existential interpretation) is also disclosed in ordinary interpretation (how they correspond)—*though* only within limits since, as he shows, the ordinary interpretation also misses (conceals) the primordial phenomenon of conscience. We need, then, to consider: Why is it necessary to make this connection?

Recall how the entire analysis of conscience was launched; that is, the theoretical situation from which it began. What was required was an appeal to Dasein's own attestation that it *can* be authentic—that this is an existentiell (ontic) possibility. However, we saw at the outset that more is needed than merely pointing to this attestation. It must at least be delimited and shown to be the kind of attestation required (an attestation regarding authenticity). For this, the existential analysis of conscience was needed. In fact, we can now see even better why this analysis was needed—because as it is ordinarily interpreted, the character of conscience *as* attesting to authenticity is *covered up*. Nevertheless, all the analysis is for the sake of exhibiting the *ontic* attestation. For this reason, the existential analysis (delimiting, exhibiting) must be brought into connection with the actual, ontic attestation (conscience as ordinarily interpreted), *so that* this actual attestation is exhibited (certified) *as* the kind of attestation required.

Section 60: The Existential Structure of the Authentic Potentiality-of-Being Attested to in Conscience

What has been shown thus far is that authentic understanding (genuine hearing) of the call takes the form of "wanting-to-have-a-conscience." Heidegger undertakes to unfold the full existential structure that is attached to this. Wanting-to-have-a-conscience is a projective *understanding* of oneself in reference to one's ownmost Being-guilty. But understanding is a matter of disclosedness, and to disclosedness there always belongs not only understanding but also attunement and discourse. So the question is: What are the attunement and discourse that accompany "wanting-to-have-a-conscience"? It is a matter of a response to a readiness for that self-disclosure from which the call comes and which becomes effective in the calling. But that self-disclosure is just anxiety. So the attunement that accompanies "wanting-to-have-a-conscience" is: readiness for anxiety (*Bereitschaft zur Angst*). What is decisive with regard to the discourse is that "in hearing the call understandingly, one denies oneself any counter-discourse . . . because this hearing appropriates the content of the call in an unconcealed way" (BT 296/283). So the mode of discourse is: *reticence* (*Verschwiegenheit*).

The mode of disclosedness constituted by these particular forms of understanding, attunement, and discourse Heidegger calls *resoluteness* (*Entschlossenheit*). "The eminent, authentic disclosedness attested in Dasein itself by its conscience—*the reticent projecting oneself upon one's ownmost Being-guilty which is ready for* anxiety—we call *resoluteness* [*Entschlossenheit*]" (BT 296-97/284).

A note on "*Entschlossenheit*." It is related to "*Erschlossenheit*." It is also related to "*verschlossen*," meaning closed, shut up, or sealed off. Heidegger is shifting the ordinary sense—taking *ent*—as privative rather than as the establishment of a condition. So: *Ent-schlossen* has the sense of keeping unclosed; not "resolve" in the sense of making up one's mind in such a way as to close off stubbornly all other possibilities. In conversation with Heidegger: (a) *Entschlossenheit* has nothing to do with the will, and (b) he approved *Geöffnetsein*, meaning being opened, openedness.

Resoluteness is authentic disclosedness and hence primordial truth. With any disclosedness, there is always disclosed the whole of Being-in-the-world—not only Being-in and the self, *but also* world. Thus in resoluteness, world gets disclosed—*and* it gets disclosed in a way radically different from the everyday disclosure that is dominated by the "they." Resoluteness, thus, does not detach Dasein from its world but lets the world be more primordially disclosed. But if world gets disclosed in a radically different way, then the way in which others and beings-within-the-world are uncovered undergoes a radical modification. Thus resoluteness does not isolate Dasein from others and from things of concern but lets them be uncovered more primordially. Note especially how Heidegger expresses this with regard to others: "The resoluteness toward itself first brings Dasein to the possibility of letting others who are with it 'be' in their ownmost potentiality-of-Being, and also discloses that potentiality in concern which leaps ahead and frees. Resolute Dasein can become the 'conscience' of others. It is from the authentic Being-it-self of resoluteness that authentic Being-with-one-another first arises" (BT 298/285).

As the earlier analysis of truth showed, Dasein is always both in the truth and in the untruth. So, then, even in resoluteness; that is, in being most primordially in the truth, Dasein is still in the untruth. *However*, in resoluteness, it is in the untruth in a *different* way. As Heidegger puts it: "Resoluteness appropriates untruth authentically" (BT 299/286). But what does this mean? Heidegger explains this in terms of the relation of resoluteness to the "they." Resoluteness involves letting oneself be summoned out of one's lostness in the "they." Nevertheless, even in resoluteness, Dasein remains *dependent* on the "they" and on the world maintained by the "they." What is the character of this dependence? Heidegger says that Dasein "as thrown, can project itself only upon definite, factual possibilities" (BT 299/286). This refers to something we've already considered: as thrown, Dasein is delivered over to possibilities, upon which it can project—that is, Dasein is thrown into certain factual possibilities, into "circumstances" that delimit the range of possibilities. *And*: these factual possibilities come out of a world determined largely by the "they." In resoluteness, Dasein does not deny this "dependence" but rather gains a certain transparency regarding it. *But* most importantly, resolute Dasein brings a more primordial disclosedness to bear upon the factual circumstances and the possibilities that are offered. These circumstances and the attendant possibilities *as* thus disclosed—more generally, the "there" as disclosed in resoluteness—Heidegger calls *"situation."*

So, he insists, in conclusion, that conscience does not call Dasein to some empty ideal or to some withdrawal from all involvement. On the contrary, "the call of conscience does not dangle an empty ideal of existence before us when it summons us to our potentiality-of-Being, but *calls forth into the situation*" (BT 300/287).

We need to prepare ourselves for seeing just how Heidegger concludes the preparatory phase. So let us begin by recalling the course followed since the opening of Division Two, trying now to grasp its coherence (unity).

Division Two began with the question of the primordial interpretation. The question was asked: What is required for an interpretation to be primordial? The question was answered: What is to be interpreted (namely, Dasein) must be included in the fore-structure in a certain way. How? As a *whole* and in its *unity* (which, for Dasein, is equivalent to authenticity). So the question now becomes: Can Dasein be (and be disclosed to itself as) *whole* and *authentic*? The entire preparatory phase is devoted to answering this question; that is, to showing how Dasein can be whole and authentic.

Chapter 1 took up the question of Dasein's wholeness. This led back to the problem of death, the limit that delimits Dasein as a whole. Heidegger developed the existential analysis of Being-toward-death, which culminated in the analysis of anticipation (*Vorlaufen*): anticipation was exhibited as authentic Being-toward-death. *Thus*: chapter 1 showed how Dasein can be whole and authentic. *However*, it showed this *only* at the existential-ontological level and *not* at the existentiell-ontic level. So the task remained at that point: to show that authentic Being-toward-death is ontically possible—that is, to provide an *existentiell attestation* regarding authentic Being-toward-death.

Chapter 2 took up this task—*or*, more precisely, took up *one* side of it: it undertook to show how Dasein attests ontically to its possible authenticity (temporarily putting aside the question of the existentiell attestation regarding Being-toward-death). Through the analysis of conscience and guilt, Heidegger provided:

1. the existentiell attestation of authenticity
2. a more precise existential delimitation of authenticity

The analysis culminated in an exhibition of Dasein's authentic disclosedness as *resoluteness*.

We should recall the three main points in the analysis leading to "resoluteness." (1) The structure of the full phenomenon of conscience.

Caller:	anxiety (primordial self-disclosure)
Call:	conscience
Response: called forth	resoluteness (authentic disclosedness)

{
- Understanding: wanting to have a conscience, i.e., projection upon Being-guilty
- Disposition: readiness for anxiety
- Discourse: reticence
}

(2) Since it is authentic disclosedness, resoluteness brings a more primordial disclosure of world and hence provides the basis for a more primordial discovery of others and of things of concern. That is, it opens up the possibility of authentic Being-with-others.

(3) So resoluteness is *not* a matter of turning away from world, of cutting oneself off—it is not a retreat into oneself. On the contrary, even resolute Dasein remains linked to (dependent on) the factical possibilities arising from world, which are largely determined by the "they." Heidegger expresses it thus: in resolution as such, there is complete *indefiniteness* regarding the particular possibilities upon which Dasein is to project—*and so*, resolute Dasein is bound to take up factical possibilities handed over, already delineated in "circumstances." However, in resoluteness, Dasein does *not* merely take these up passively but rather brings a more primordial disclosure into them. These "circumstances" *as* thus disclosed in resoluteness is what is called situation.

So how do matters stand at the end of chapter 2 with regard to the general task of showing how Dasein can be whole and authentic? Chapter 1 has exhibited authentic Being-toward-death (wholeness) at the existential level, which is formulated as anticipation. Chapter 2 has exhibited authenticity at both the existential and existentiell levels, which is formulated as resoluteness.

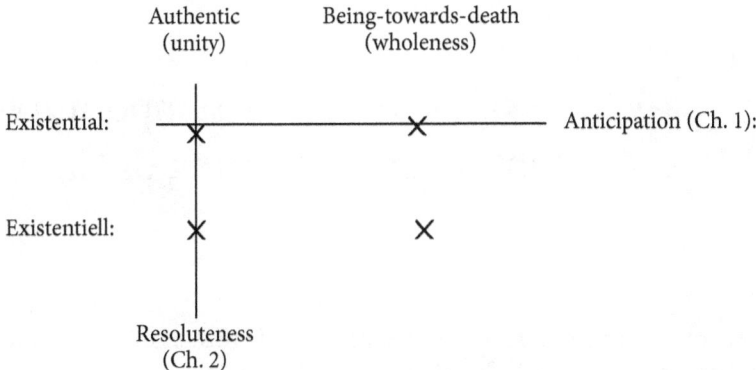

The task now is to bring the two analyses together; that is, to bring resoluteness and anticipation together. This will serve to supply what is lacking (theoretically) in each:

1. It will relate an existentiell attestation to anticipation.
2. It will bring the issue of Being-toward-death into the sphere of resoluteness.

Thereby, Dasein will be gotten in view both as a whole and in its authenticity (unity), at both the existential and existentiell levels. Thus the basis will be established for a primordial interpretation.

3. The Authentic Potentiality-for-Being-a-Whole of Dasein, and Temporality as the Ontological Meaning of Care

HEIDEGGER BEGINS CHAPTER 3 by posing precisely this task: "How are we to bring these phenomena of anticipation and resoluteness together?" (BT 302/289) Heidegger answers that there is only one possible method: resolution will be taken as the point of departure, and it will be asked: "*Does resoluteness, in its ownmost existentiell tendency of Being [Seinstendenz], itself point ahead to anticipatory resoluteness as its ownmost authentic possibility?*" (BT 302/289) This means: Heidegger will exhibit within resoluteness a *tendency* toward a certain specific *mode*. This mode will thus constitute the "ownmost authentic possibility of resoluteness." That is, it will be the mode in which resoluteness becomes most fully and most transparently what it essentially is. *And* he will show that this mode is constituted precisely by the unity (coincidence) of resoluteness with anticipation; that is, that the mode is: anticipatory resoluteness (*vorlaufende Entschlossenheit*). In other words, he will show that resoluteness becomes fully authentic (is fulfilled) only when the projection that belongs to it becomes a projection upon death (i.e., anticipation). So the task, as Heidegger expresses it, is to think resoluteness through to the end, to the point where it becomes anticipatory resoluteness. Section 62 is devoted to this task.

Section 62: The Existentielly Authentic Potentiality-for-Being-Whole of Dasein as Anticipatory Resoluteness

The analysis involves two main phases. We will deal only with the first, more general phase.

One can see in general what the convergence involves if we recall the structure of resoluteness and of anticipation:

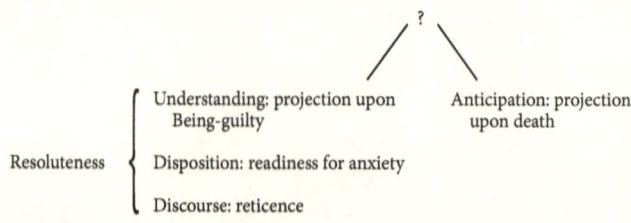

The problem is: How does projection upon Being-guilty converge with (comes to fulfillment in) projection upon death? The connection lies in the relation that both terms have to negativity.

Being-guilty means: Being the (negative) ground of a *negativity*. What is the negativity here? We have seen that it is the negativity involved in the fact that, in projecting upon certain possibilities, other possibilities must be forfeited, excluded—that is, the negativity is one of "possibility-exclusion." In projecting upon Being-guilty, Dasein takes this negativity upon itself, understands itself *from* it.

Death (regarded existentially) is the possibility of the impossibility of existence. Death is the possibility that negates all possibilities. Death is the utter, absolute exclusion of possibilities. Death is absolute negativity. Specifically, one can say that death is an absolute form of that negativity (of possibility-exclusion) that also defines "Being-guilty." That is, in its "Being-guilty" and in its being delimited by death, Dasein is subjected to the *same* kind of negativity (that of possibility-exclusion). The difference is that this negativity is absolute in death: all further possibilities are excluded, whereas in Being-guilty, only *some* further possibilities are excluded.

So Dasein's authentic projection upon death is simply an absolute (radical) form of its projection upon Being-guilty. Authentic projection upon death (which is equivalent to anticipation) is the *fulfillment* of projection upon Being-guilty (which is equivalent to the projective moment of resoluteness). Said differently, resoluteness is fulfilled when it converges with anticipation, when it becomes anticipatory resoluteness.

The second stage of Heidegger's treatment of the convergence of resoluteness with anticipation moves at a more specific level.

I. *The Procedure*

Heidegger takes up the five constituent moments that belong to the existential concept of death. These are expressed in the definition of death as: Dasein's ownmost, nonrelational, unsurpassable, certain, indefinite possibility. We recall that at the end of chapter 1, Heidegger showed how in anticipation (authentic Being-toward-death) Dasein is disclosed to itself *from* each of these constituent moments—that is, he exhibited the specific kind of self-disclosure correlative to each of these moments. He now shows how, for each of these specific kinds of self-disclosure (corresponding, in turn, to moments of death), there is a corresponding self-disclosure in resoluteness, *and* how each specific kind of self-disclosure in resoluteness *tends* to converge with the corresponding kind of self-disclosure in anticipation. Specifically, in each case, he begins with a kind of self-disclosure in resoluteness and shows how it converges with (is fulfilled in) one of the kinds of self-disclosedness in anticipation.

II. *The Analysis*

A. *Ownmost*

The call of conscience reveals lostness in the "they"—and so in resoluteness (which appropriates the call), Dasein is disclosed to itself as having been lost in the "they." The self-disclosure converges immediately with that of anticipation: as Heidegger showed, in anticipation, Dasein projects itself upon death as *ownmost* and from this character is disclosed precisely as having been lost in the "they."

B. *Nonrelational*

Likewise with the second moment: the call of conscience calls Dasein back from self-dispersal in the "they" so that in resoluteness, Dasein is individualized, disclosed to itself as individual. This converges immediately with self-disclosure in anticipation. From the character of death as nonrelational, Dasein is disclosed to itself as individual.

C. *Unsurpassable*

In the call of conscience, what is heard is Dasein's Being-guilty, and in resoluteness, Dasein appropriates this self-disclosure. However, as we've seen, this Being-guilty is *prior* to an indebtedness—it is a negativity that permeates Dasein and is prior to any specific concrete comportment by Dasein. Heidegger then says: "This prior and constant Being-guilty, which is constantly with us, does not show itself without being covered over in its character as prior until that priority is placed in the possibility which is for Dasein *unsurpassable [unüberholbar]*" (BT 307/294). This is the same issue we touched on at the general level of the analysis: Dasein's negativity (Being-guilty) (and the corresponding self-disclosure) is *fulfilled* in projection upon death (and the corresponding self-disclosure). That is, projection upon Being-guilty (and the corresponding self-disclosure).

D. *Certain*

Resoluteness is authentic disclosedness; that is, truth. To any truth (Heidegger now adds), there corresponds a holding-for-true, an appropriating of what has been disclosed. Heidegger calls this a "Being-certain" (*Gewißsein*). In the case of the primordial disclosure of resoluteness, the corresponding Being-certain must be equally primordial: it must be a maintaining of oneself *in* what is disclosed; that is, in the *situation*. Heidegger describes the appropriate Being-certain: "It simply cannot become *rigid* about the situation but must understand that the resolution must be *held* free and *open* for the actual factical possibility in accordance with its own meaning as a disclosure. The certainty of the resolution means *holding oneself free for* the possibility of *taking it back*, a possibility that is always factically necessary" (BT 307–8/294). So in resoluteness, Being-certain takes the form of an openness to current factical possibilities—*and* this requires: being open to the possible withdrawal of these possibilities. This Being-certain amounts to being able to seize upon current factical possibilities—but also being able to release them when they are withdrawn from Dasein's factical situation. This character Heidegger expresses by the word *Wiederholung* (repetition). In resoluteness, Dasein's Being-certain has this character of repetition.

Heidegger only alludes to the convergence of this Being-certain with the certainty involved in anticipation. One can perhaps say: in authentic Being-toward-death, there is this same peculiar relation to possibility—*but* in such a form as to encompass the *whole* of Dasein. In other words, in anticipation, Dasein is most primordially established in an openness to possibility, which at the same time is an openness to the possible withdrawal of possibility (since death is precisely the possibility that withdraws all possibilities).

E. *Indefinite*

In resoluteness, Dasein is also in the untruth, which is to say dependent on the "they." One can express this thus: Dasein's potentiality-for-Being (even in resoluteness) can become definite only insofar as Dasein seizes upon possibilities offered by the situation. This means, then: Dasein's potentiality-for-Being as such is *indefinite*. That is, in resoluteness as such, there is a complete *indefiniteness* regarding particular possibilities. How does this indefiniteness get disclosed (so that resoluteness becomes transparent to itself)? Heidegger answers: "The *indefiniteness* of one's own potentiality-of-Being, however, reveals itself *completely* only in Being-toward-death. Anticipation brings Dasein face to face with a possibility that is constantly certain and yet remains indefinite at every moment as to when possibility becomes impossibility" (BT 308/295). So in anticipation, there is a primordial disclosure of the radical *indefiniteness* that permeates Dasein's Being.

At the end of the analysis (§62), Heidegger notes that the problem of the existentiell attestation of authentic Being-toward-death (i.e., anticipation) has now been fully settled. Already in chapter 2, he showed how authenticity is attested in the phenomena of conscience and resoluteness. Now he has shown how anticipation is precisely that with which resoluteness converges in its fulfillment. *Thus* the previously exhibited attestation is, in effect, extended to cover the case of anticipation. In other words, that attestation proves to have been already an attestation regarding anticipation. *So*: anticipatory resoluteness has now been rigorously exhibited as a mode of disclosedness in which Dasein is disclosed authentically and wholly. *Thus*: anticipatory resoluteness—capable of bringing authentic Dasein as a whole into the fore-structure of interpretation—is capable of providing the basis for a primordial interpretation. That primordial interpretation is now ready to begin.

Section 65: Temporality as the Ontological Meaning of Care

I. The Question of Meaning (*Sinn*)

A. What is the *meaning* of care? And so the first task is to determine what is being asked in asking about meaning; that is to say, to determine what meaning is. Actually, the concept of meaning has already been determined in chapter 5, which Heidegger now recalls. "Meaning is that in which the intelligibility of something keeps itself" (BT 324/309). Or meaning is "that upon which the primary project is projected, that in terms of which something can be conceived in its possibility as what it is" (BT 324/309).

Recall the analysis of projective understanding. This was worked out in relation to the analysis of equipment. Heidegger showed that wherein an item of equipment becomes understandable is the referential totality; that is, the significance, which is to say, world. And to understand such an item means to project it *upon* significance (world). Furthermore, significance (world) is what *makes it possible* for equipment to be what it is. For example, the referential context is what makes it possible for the hammer to be the kind of equipment it is. So meaning (as upon-which) also has the character of that which makes possible. "To expose that upon which a project is projected, means to disclose what makes what is projected possible" (BT 324/309). More generally (disregarding specific cases of equipment), we may say meaning is (a) the upon-which of a projection and (b) that which makes possible what is projected.

Now apply this to the Existential Analytic itself: the Existential Analytic is an interpretation, and so there underlies it a projection. On the basis of that projection, Dasein has been interpreted ontologically as care (and now, more primordially, as anticipatory resoluteness). So to ask about the meaning of care is to ask about the "upon-which" of this projection; that is, to ask about that which makes care possible. "With the question of the meaning of care, we are asking *what makes possible the wholeness of the articulated structural whole of care in the unity of its unfolded articulation?*" (BT 324/309–10).

B. How, then, is the meaning of care to be uncovered? Heidegger answers: "To set forth the meaning of care, then, means to pursue the project underlying and guiding the primordial existential interpretation of Dasein in such a way that its upon-which becomes visible in what is projected" (BT 324/309). This says: it is a matter of following up the projection implicit in the primordial interpretation of Dasein as care, which is to say, of following it up in such a way that care is grasped with regard to its "upon-which"—that is, in such a way that authentic care (which is equivalent to anticipatory resoluteness) brings to light its meaning (which is equivalent to the "upon-which," which is equivalent to that which makes it possible).

Before proceeding, Heidegger corrects a possible misconception. The *meaning* of care is not something "free-floating" outside Dasein; it is not something other than Dasein. Rather, it is what Dasein most primordially *is* ontologically, which is to say, what constitutes its Being.

II. Temporality as the Meaning of Anticipatory Resoluteness

Since Dasein's primordial self-disclosure occurs in anticipatory resoluteness, it is in anticipatory resoluteness that care as the Being of Dasein can be brought into view more fundamentally. According to Heidegger's concept of meaning, to ask about the meaning of care—that is, to ask about anticipatory resoluteness in which care comes into view—amounts to asking how anticipatory resoluteness is *possible*. Heidegger focuses primarily on the moment of anticipation (which is equivalent to authentic Being-toward-death) and asks: What makes this moment possible? His answer:

Authentic Potentiality-for-Being-a-Whole of Dasein

What is projected in the primordial existential project of existence revealed itself as anticipatory resoluteness. What makes possible this authentic Being-whole of Dasein with regard to the unity of its articulated structural whole? Expressed formally and existentially, without constantly naming the complete structural content, anticipatory resoluteness is the *Being toward* one's own-most, eminent potentiality-of-Being. Something like this is possible only in that Dasein *can* come toward itself *at all* in its ownmost possibility and hold itself in this possibility as possibility in this letting-itself-come-toward-itself; in other words, in that it exists. This letting-*come-toward-itself* of the eminent possibility that it endures is the primordial phenomenon of the *future*. If authentic or inauthentic *Being-toward-death* belongs to the Being of Dasein, this is only possible as *futural*. (BT 325/310–11)

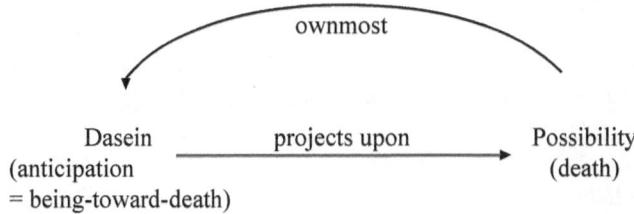

Look at just what Heidegger is saying. Anticipation is Dasein's Being toward its ownmost possibility (death). Here we must recall the character of anticipation (*Vorlaufen*): it is a "running-ahead" toward death as possibility, a coming close to it, which, at the same time, sustains the character of death as sheer possibility. But this possibility can be Dasein's *ownmost* only if it bears on (reflects back on) Dasein. This "reflection back" can happen only if—having projected on this possibility—Dasein can bring this possibility back to itself (that is, to bear on itself). That is, it must be brought back to Dasein, for Dasein is the one whose possibility it is—*and so* this running-ahead toward death is a coming toward itself in its ownmost possibility.

Heidegger is simply saying that this specific coming-toward-itself in its ownmost possibility (i.e., anticipation) is possible *only insofar as* Dasein as such (in general) can come toward itself in its ownmost possibility (and in such a way as to sustain this possibility). That is to say, what makes anticipation possible is the fact that Dasein *can* come toward itself thusly—*that is*, that such kind of "movement toward self" belongs in general to Dasein. This coming-toward (*Zukommen*) is the primordial phenomenon of the *future* (*Zukunft*).[1] *Thus* anticipation is made possible by the future—that is, it "is" possible only as something futural. But, of course, "future" does *not* mean here a "now" that has not yet become actual.

---

1. *Zukommen*: coming back toward
Zukommenlassen: letting come back toward
Zukunft: future

Anticipatory resoluteness involves taking over one's Being-guilty. This, in turn, involves taking over being the *thrown* ground of a negativity—that is, taking over thrownness. But we should recall the character of thrownness: to say that Dasein is thrown means Dasein does *not* bring itself into its "there"—that is, Dasein is always already in its "there." This means that Dasein always already *has been*. So for Dasein to take over thrownness means: to be always already *having been*. Here we have the second primordial phenomenon: the character of having-been (*die Gewesenheit*). However, Dasein is futural (as already shown). And so if Dasein is to take over Being-guilty (which is to be as always already having-been), it must do this **as** futural. In other words, Dasein must come toward itself futurally *in such a way* that it comes back to its having-been. Heidegger thus says: "Authentically futural, Dasein is authentically *having-been*. Anticipation of the most extreme and ownmost possibility comes back understandingly to one's ownmost *having-been*. Dasein can *be* authentically having-been only because it is futural. In a certain sense, having-been arises from the future" (BT 326/311).

Anticipatory resoluteness involves a disclosing of the Situation such that Dasein comes to be circumspectly concerned with what is factically handy—that is, with what is *present* within-the-world. But this is possible only through a *making-present* (*Gegenwärtigen*) of these beings; its possibility requires that these beings be made present, presented. This "making-present" is the primordial phenomenon of the Present (*Gegewart*). These three phenomena (the future, having-been, and the present) in their unity constitute temporality. Heidegger describes this unity: "Futurally coming back to itself, resoluteness brings itself into the situation in making-present. Having-been arises from the future in such a way that the future that has-been (or better, as having-been) releases the present from out of itself. This unified phenomenon of the future, which in such a way has been as presencing, we call *temporality* [*Zeitlichkeit*]" (BT 326/311). We should note here that within this unity, the future has a certain *priority*—in some sense, the having-been and the present arise from the future—but this sense remains largely undetermined here. **So**: temporality has been shown as what makes anticipatory resoluteness possible, or, as Heidegger puts it: "*Temporality reveals itself as the meaning of authentic care*" (BT 326/311).

III. Temporality as the Meaning of Care

Heidegger proceeds to extend this result: temporality is the meaning not only of *authentic* care but of care in general. According to the earlier analysis, care involves three moments:

1. existence—"ahead-of-itself"
2. facticity—"Being-already-in"
3. falling—"Being-alongside"

Now Heidegger follows up the indications already provided by reference of authentic care to temporality *and so* shows that the meaning of these moments (that which makes them possible) lies in the future, having-been, and present. He then concludes: "Temporality makes possible the unity of existence, facticity, and falling and thus constitutes primordially the wholeness of the structure of care" (BT 328/313). Thus he has answered the question that was left open at the end of the analysis of care in Division One—the question of whether there is a more primordial phenomenon in which the structural manifoldness finds its unity. Temporality has now been shown to be that more primordial phenomenon.

IV. The Character of Temporality (three points)

A. "Temporality 'is' not a *being* [*Seindes*] at all. It is not, but rather *temporalizes* itself" (BT 328/314). Heidegger has described this temporalizing in its most general character: a coming toward itself that comes back to its having-been so as to make present. We should note that the future, having-been, and the present do not designate sequences of "nows" but rather a complex of "movements" (or directionalities). Heidegger indicates that there are different modes of temporalizing and that this variety is what founds the multiplicity of Dasein's modes of Being. But this is what is *most important*: temporality is what Dasein primordially *is*. This means that it is not as though Dasein first *is* and then temporalizes, which is to say, engages in such "movements" as coming toward itself; rather, primordially considered, Dasein is nothing other than this complex of "movements" designated by the word *temporality*. That is, it is nothing but temporalizing. Or, as he says, it is *not*. Thus the most primordial phenomenon *is not*—negativity.

B. Each of the phenomena of temporality has a certain "directedness":

1. Future has the character of "toward oneself."
2. Having-been has the character of "back to."
3. The Present has the character of letting-oneself-encounter or of "alongside."

Each of these has the phenomenal sense of movement in a direction, of standing-out in a certain direction. So, Heidegger says: these phenomenal characters make temporality manifest as the ἐκστατικόν (that which moves outward, stands out). This leads to a very important statement: "*Temporality is the primordial 'outside-its-self' in and for itself*" (BT 329/314). In accord with this, the phenomena of future, having-been, and present are to be called the "ecstases" of temporality. Heidegger emphasizes that the character of temporality as "outside of itself" must not be misconstrued in such a way that we end up regarding temporality as a being. Specifically, temporality is not, first, a being, which then moves out from itself; rather, "its essence is temporalizing in the unity of the ecstases" (BT 329/314).

C. Heidegger now draws the contrast between temporality and time as ordinarily understood: time as ordinarily understood is regarded as a pure sequence of "nows"—that is, the ecstatical character of temporality has been leveled off. In contrast to this derivative phenomenon, temporality may be designated as: primordial time.

In more general terms: even in Dasein's authentic disclosedness (*Erschlossenheit*) there is a radical self-concealment—that is, even in authentic ἀλήθεια, there is a radical λήθη.

V. Further Tasks (§66)

Section 66: The Temporality of Dasein and the Task of a More Primordial Repetition of the Existential Analysis Arising from It

In section 66, Heidegger sketches the three principal tasks that arise from the uncovering of temporality as the meaning of care. Heidegger's accomplishments of these three tasks constitute the remainder of Division Two. In each of the next three chapters one of these tasks will be taken up.

(1) Temporality has been uncovered as the meaning of authentic care (which is the equivalent of anticipatory resoluteness) and of care in general (as undifferentiated). The next task is then to show how temporality is the meaning of *inauthentic* care, which is the uncovering of the specific temporality of Dasein's inauthenticity. To do this, Heidegger will *repeat*, at the more primordial level now achieved, the existential analysis that was carried out in Division One: he will lay out the temporality of Dasein's modes of disclosedness (understanding, attunement, falling, and discourse) *and* the temporality of Being-in-the-world (i.e., the temporality underlying world, concern, spatiality, and even everydayness). This repetition will serve to appropriate the entire analysis of Division One to the *primordial* interpretation of Division Two—that is, to lift that analysis above the merely preparatory character that it originally had.

(2) Heidegger has insisted (cf. especially his criticism of Kant in §64) that the *self* can be understood neither as substance nor as subject. Rather, selfhood is to be understood in terms of care—or, more precisely, in terms of the modes of *self-constancy* possible on the basis of care. That is, inauthentic selfhood lies precisely in that non-self-constancy that Heidegger describes as irresoluteness or dispersal in the "they," *and* authentic selfhood lies in the self-constancy of anticipatory resoluteness. At the level of temporal interpretation, this notion of self-constancy points to the question of "the connectedness of life"; that is, of Dasein's way of "stretching-along" between birth and death. This stretching-along constitutes Dasein's *historicity*. Thus there is the task of analyzing Dasein's historicity—*and* on that basis, of taking up the question of the nature and possibilities of *historical* understanding. With this question, Heidegger renews the efforts of Dilthey to

ground the *Geisteswissenschaften*—and he prepares the basis for that destruction of the history of ontology that was to have constituted part 2 of *Being and Time*.

(3) Finally, there is the task of showing how, on the basis of primordial temporality, there arises the kind of time in which beings occur (i.e., within-time-ness) and how, from this, there arises the ordinary conception of time as a sequence of "nows." Heidegger concludes this sketch: "The elaboration of the temporality of Dasein as everydayness, historicity, and within-time-ness first gives uncluttered insight into the *complexities* of a primordial ontology of Dasein" (BT 333/318).

Conclusion

The decisive transition has now been made: temporality has been exhibited as the meaning of the Being of Dasein. That is, the transition has been made, with regard to Dasein, from Being to time (as the meaning of Being). At this point, it is appropriate to recall a connection mentioned earlier, which was taken from *Basic Problems of Phenomenology*. The connection is one that Heidegger draws between his own project and the discussion in the *Republic* in which Socrates tells Glaucon that the Good is ἐπέκεινα τῆς οὐσίας. Specifically, the connection is just as the Good is something beyond Being, which lets it be understood, *so*, for Heidegger, time is something beyond Being, which lets it be understood. He completes the connection with these words: "We too want nothing else but to bring ourselves out of the cave and to the light" (BPP 285). If we now follow up this connection and regard the course of *Being and Time* as analogous to the Platonic ascent out of the cave, we may say that:

1. Everydayness corresponds to the level of those chained within the cave.
2. The preparation leading to anticipatory resoluteness corresponds to that painful turning-around from the wall of the cave toward the mouth of the cave.
3. The transition from the Being (of Dasein) to time as the meaning of the Being of Dasein corresponds to the step out of the cave into the light and to getting a glimpse of the sun.

It is not surprising, then, that much of the remainder of Division Two will be devoted to a "repetition" of the analyses of everydayness. The Existential Analytic, like the escaped prisoner, must turn back to its beginning, back into the cave.

4. Temporality and Everydayness

ONCE AGAIN, THERE arise three final tasks with regard to time for Heidegger: everydayness, historicality, and within-time-ness. We will now deal with the first task.

The task is to *repeat*, at the level of the temporal interpretation, the main stages of the preparatory analysis done in Division One, which is to uncover the modes of temporality (temporalizing) that underlie the various constituents of Dasein's Being. This amounts to working out explicitly the projection of Dasein's Being upon temporality and that is giving the temporal interpretation of Dasein. Through this interpretation, Heidegger will also lay out the distinction between the authentic and inauthentic modes of temporalizing, and this will indicate how the distinction between the authentic and inauthentic is founded on the distinction between two modes of temporalizing. Specifically, there will be three topics: (I) Temporality of Disclosedness, (II) World and Temporality, and (III) Existential Concept of Science.

Section 68: The Temporality of Disclosedness in General

Heidegger's repetition begins with the temporal interpretation of disclosedness. That is, he uncovers the temporality underlying understanding, attunement, falling, and discourse.

I. Temporality of Understanding
A. Primary Ecstasis: Future

Why is this primary? Consider the character of understanding, which has the structure of projection. Specifically, its structure is this: Dasein projects itself upon a possibility in such a way that it is disclosed to itself *from* that possibility. In this structure, there is the movement of coming-toward-oneself: Dasein comes toward itself in the sense of running-ahead to that possibility *as* which it exists, *and* Dasein comes toward itself *from* that possibility, which is to say, it is given back to itself disclosively. But such coming-toward-oneself is simply the future. Thus Heidegger says: "When one understands oneself projectively in an existentiell possibility, the future underlies this understanding, and it does so as a coming-toward-oneself from the actual possibility as which Dasein in each instance exists" (BT 336/321). So the future is primary in the temporalizing of understanding, which is to say, understanding is primarily futural.

This "coming-toward-oneself" expresses merely the formal, undifferentiated character of the future (now designated ahead-of-itself). However, the temporalizing of the future can take different forms; specifically, it can be an authentic future or an inauthentic future. The authentic future has already been uncovered in the regress from authentic care: it is the coming-toward-oneself from one's ownmost possibility; that is, death. Said differently, it is authentic Being-toward-death, anticipation.

But what about the inauthentic future? This must proceed by means of a regress from: inauthentic care—specifically, from the inauthentic understanding that belongs to everyday concern. To: its temporal meaning.

Here is the regress. In everyday concern, Dasein understands itself in terms of those things with which it is concerned. That is, it projects itself upon its particular world (significance) and is disclosed to itself from that world. But, in turn, world (significance) is linked up with certain possibilities. So, in projecting upon world, Dasein in effect projects upon possibilities *but* through the mediation of world (and things) of concern. And so, in such everyday (inauthentic) understanding, Dasein *comes toward itself* but in a way that is mediated by the world of concern. Dasein is futural but in terms of things of concern. In other words, Dasein's future becomes a matter of whether the things of concern are yielded or denied—whether things "work out" or not. The character of such a "coming-toward-itself" (future) Heidegger designates as: *awaiting* (*Gegenwärtigen*). This expresses the inauthentic future.

B. Present

Although understanding is primarily futural, any ecstasis temporalizes *only* in unity the other two ecstasies. Hence the temporality of understanding must also involve the having-been and the present. Heidegger proceeds to uncover these—again, by a regress from care. Here, too, there are both authentic and inauthentic modes.

The authentic present (that is, the authentic way of making-present) has already been more or less identified in the analysis of resoluteness: it involves Dasein's coming into its situation (taking up its factical possibilities) but does so in such a way as to bring a more primordial disclosure into the situation. This way of making-present (the authentic present) Heidegger calls the "moment of vision" (*Augenblick*). Heidegger stresses that this is not to be taken in the sense of a "now" (which belongs rather to within-time-ness).

The term *making-present* (*Gegenwärtigen*), which up to now has designated the present in its formal, undifferentiated character, Heidegger now restricts to the inauthentic present. What is the inauthentic present? We will note two points.

1. Heidegger says that it can be really clarified only in the analysis of the temporality of falling. If we glance ahead to that analysis, we see that Heidegger

determines the character of the inauthentic present by means of an analysis of "curiosity." It is related to a "distracted not-tarrying" in the sense of leaping after constantly new possibilities—*and* is specifically identified as *Aufenthaltlosigkeit* (lack of abode, "homelessness," translated as "never dwelling anywhere").

2. Another feature (coming back to the analysis of the temporality of understanding): we have seen that inauthentic understanding is a projection primarily upon the world of concern (such that its possibilities are in terms of things of concern in this world), but the things of concern are precisely what get made-present in Dasein's making-present (i.e., the present). Thus there is a peculiar divergence or shift in inauthentic understanding toward the present. "But since inauthentic understanding projects its potentiality-of-Being in terms of what can be taken care of, this means that it temporalizes itself in terms of making-present" (BT 338/323). This divergence does *not* negate Heidegger's previous assertion that understanding is primarily futural; rather, this is a peculiar divergence or modification of understanding *as* futural. Heidegger is explicit about this at the very end of the analysis of understanding: "Although inauthentic concernful understanding is determined in the light of making-present what is taken care of, the temporalizing of understanding comes about primarily in the future [*vollzieht sich doch die Zeitigung des Verstehens primär in der Zukunft*, emphasis added]" (BT 339/324).

C. Having-Been

Authentic having-been has also been virtually identified in the analysis of authentic care: it is a coming back to one's already having-been, which is a coming back to oneself or a taking over of what one already is—a resuming of self. In other words, it is a getting (taking on, *holen*) of oneself again (*wieder*)—a *Wiederholung* (repetition). So Heidegger designates authentic having-been as "repetition."

By contrast, inauthentic having-been is a matter not of taking on one's self but of a decisively closing off of one's thrownness (one's already having-been), of closing it off in such a decisive way that the very closing off gets closed off. Heidegger designates this as forgetting or having-forgotten (*Vergessenheit*). We should note here that Heidegger has circled back to the beginning of *Being and Time*: *Being and Time* began by announcing the forgottenness of the question of Being and proposing a "repetition" of it.

In conclusion, Heidegger's analysis has accomplished two things:

1. He has provided a *temporal interpretation* of understanding.

2. He has effectively distinguished between authentic temporalizing (already uncovered earlier) and inauthentic temporalizing (awaiting that forgets and makes present).

Heidegger's analyses of the other modes of disclosedness follow the same general lines. In each case, he questions back from the mode at issue to its temporality.

Section 68: Temporality of Disclosedness

Temporality of Disclosedness (¶ 68)

(1) Temporality of Understanding

Primary ecstasis: Future (but in inauthentic mode: shift toward present)

	Future	Present	Having-been
Authentic:	anticipation	moment of vision (*Augenblick*)	repetition
Undifferentiated:	ahead-of-itself	making-present	
Inauthentic:	awaiting		having-forgotten

(2) Temporality of Disposition

Primary ecstasis: Having-been (but in authentic mode: springs from nature)

	Having-been	Present	Future
Inauthentic: (fear)	having-forgotten	making-present	awaiting
Authentic: (anxiety)	being brought back to one's thrownness as repeatable	holding ready the moment of vision	possible resoluteness

(3) Temporality of Falling

Primary ecstasis: Present

	Present	Future	Having-been
Curiosity:	making-present (never-dwelling-anywhere)	awaiting which leaps away (distraction)	having-forgotten

(4) Temporality of Discourse

No primary ecstasis: Factually, making present has privilege

One point we should especially note is that in each mode, a different ecstasis is primary.

The subsequent sections of chapter 4 continue the temporal interpretation. Section 69 uncovers the temporality of Being-in-the-world. Section 70 takes up the issue of the temporality of Dasein's spatiality. Section 71 takes up the issue of the temporal meaning of everydayness. We will not deal with sections 70–71. Section 71 is devoted primarily to indicating *that* the meaning of everydayness is not self-evident and that it is bound up with the issue of temporality. *However*, the real working out of the meaning of everydayness is deferred until later. Section 70 is unique. It is the one section in *Being and Time* that Heidegger later retracts. The retraction is in "Time and Being" (1969): "The attempt in *Being and Time* Section 70 to trace Dasein's spatiality back to temporality is untenable."[1]

Section 69c: World and Temporality (§69c)

The task here is to give a temporal interpretation of Being-in-the-world with special reference to world. In other words, to appropriate to the primordial (temporal) interpretation the preparatory analysis carried out in chapter 3 of Division One. The specific question is: How is world in its unity with Dasein possible? What makes it possible? What is its meaning? Or, since temporality has been exhibited as constituting in general the meaning of the Being of Dasein: How does temporality make world possible?

Heidegger answers directly: "*The existential and temporal condition of possibility of the world lies in the fact that temporality, as an ecstatical unity, has something like a horizon*" (BT 365/347). What does this mean? What constitutes the "horizon" of time? He calls its constituents "horizonal schemata." This language is Kantian: just as Kant's schemata mediate between time and understanding, so here "horizonal schemata" mediate between temporality and Being-in-the-world (to which understanding belongs).

But what are these horizonal schemata? He explains them by referring to the ecstases. To each ecstasis there belongs a "whither"—that is, something by which the specific directionality involved in each ecstasis is determined (marked out). This "whither" is the horizonal schema. Heidegger identifies the horizonal schema for each ecstasis.

The schema of the future is "whither" of Dasein's coming toward itself—that is, that *to* which Dasein is carried away (stands out) in coming toward itself. Heidegger identifies this as the "for-the-sake-of-itself." Concretely, this can be filled in in different ways, corresponding to various forms that possibilities can assume.

The schema of having-been is the "whither" that is involved in that disclosedness in which having-been is the primary ecstasis—that is, in attunement. Heidegger identifies this as that in the face of which (*das Wovor*) Dasein is thrown, that to which Dasein has been abandoned.

The schema of the present is the "in-order-to."

---

1. Martin Heidegger, "Zeit und Sein," in *Gesamtausgabe*, vol. 14, ed. Friedrich-Wilhelm von Hermann (Frankfurt am Main: Vittorio Klostermann, 2007), 29. In English, "Time and Being," in *On Time and Being*, trans. Joan Stambaugh (New York: Harper & Row, 1972), 23.

The crucial point is this: because of the unity of the ecstases (that is, of temporality itself), there is a unity of the horizontal schemata, which is to say they form a *unitary* horizon. *And thus*: they serve to hold together:

1. The possibilities upon which Dasein projects itself.
2. The equipmental context into which Dasein is always already thrown.
3. The actual involvements ("in-order-to") with which Dasein (in a given instance) is concerned.

This is to say that the horizon that belongs to temporality holds possibility and significance (*that is*, Dasein and world) together in primordial unity, which is in turn linked up (unified) with Dasein's specific circumspective concern. "The horizontal unity of the schemata of the ecstases makes possible the primordial connection of the relations of the in-order-to with the for-the-sake-of-which. This means that on the basis of the horizontal constitution of the ecstatic unity of temporality, something like a disclosed world belongs to the being that is always its There" (BT 365/348). Now it is clear how Dasein is essentially Being-in-the-world—that is, why it is not the case that there is first of all Dasein, which then takes up a relation to the world. The reason is: insofar as Dasein temporalizes itself (insofar as Dasein *is* at all) the unity of Dasein and world is established. The world is neither "handiness" nor "present" but temporalizes itself in Dasein's temporality.

Section 69b: The Existential Concept of Science (§69b)

In section 69 a–b, Heidegger develops the temporal interpretation of circumspective concern and of that interpretation that operates within the framework of the hermeneutical "as." I want to focus not on these analyses but on Heidegger's development of a problem that he relates to these analyses, but that goes far beyond them. The problem is that of the "*ontological genesis* of the theoretical attitude" (BT 357/340). As Heidegger explains, the question is: "Which of those conditions of possibility in the constitution of the Being of Dasein are existentially necessary for Dasein to be able to exist in the mode of scientific investigation?" (BT 357/340) So the general problem is that of an "*existential concept of science*" (BT 357/340), which is to say, of an interpretation of science as a way of existence (as a mode of Being-in-the-world) in which Dasein uncovers beings (in their Being) in a certain distinctive way. This is to be contrasted with the "logical concept" of science, which considers science in terms of results, as a system of propositions. Heidegger stresses that a full existential interpretation of science cannot be carried out at this point in his analysis. That could be done only in the context of considering the meaning of Being as such and its relation to truth. He notes that within such a full existential interpretation, the idea of phenomenology (as distinguished from a preliminary concept) would also be developed since phenomenology itself is a matter of the theoretical attitude. But, for now, he gives only a preparatory treatment of the problem, centering on the question of how concern with the handy changes over into an exploration of the present thing.

We should note three points.

1. Heidegger is careful to dismiss a possible misunderstanding of the transformation: it would be easy to suppose that what it involves is merely *holding back* from the manipulation of things. That is, that what the emergence of the theoretical attitude involves is the disappearance of praxis—*so that* the theoretical attitude would be determined by privation, by the absence of praxis. But Heidegger insists that this is *not* so and for two reasons.

a. Because holding back from the use of equipment can be itself just a kind of praxis. For example, when, instead of using equipment, we inspect it or count up what has been produced.

b. Because, far from being an absence of praxis, theoretical research has its own kind of praxis. For example, reading off measurements, observing with a microscope, or writing.

2. What, then, is the character of the transformation, granted that it is not a matter of the mere privation of praxis? It is a matter of looking at things in a new way: "*The understanding of Being* guiding the concernful dealings with innerworldly beings *has been transformed*" (BT 361/344). For example, when I say, "The hammer is heavy" (in the sense of having a property), the hammer gets regarded not simply as a tool to be used but as a material thing subject to certain physical laws *and* as something whose *place* has become a matter of indifference, so that it has merely a spatiotemporal position. Heidegger is careful to indicate that this specific type of transition does *not* suffice to explain the emergence of the theoretical attitude in general. For example, in economics, it is precisely such things as equipment-contexts that are studied. However, this specific transition (handy→present thing) is decisive in at least one crucial instance: the theoretical attitude of mathematical physics.

3. Heidegger describes what constitutes this theoretical attitude. What distinguishes modern physics is neither its respect for facts nor its application of mathematics to natural things. Rather, it is distinguished by "the *mathematical projection of nature itself*" (BT 362/345). This means: nature is projected in advance of any scientific research. That is, the constitution of its Being (of Being natural things) gets understood a priori *in such a way* that one is then directed to seek out certain items (those that are quantitatively determinable). *And* it is only in light of this project that facts are found and experiments devised. In other terms, nature gets *thematized* in advance. That is:

a. Its Being gets understood in a certain way.

b. The subject-matter of the science of nature gets delimited.

c. The ways of conceiving proper to such beings get sketched out.

For example, nature gets projected as a three-dimensional manifold of masses in motion, and then this, in turn, prescribes what belongs to nature and what ways of conceiving are appropriate. So: what defines the theoretical attitude of mathematical physics is that way it understands (projects in advance) the Being of those beings to which it is directed. *Thus* what occurs in the transition from circumspective concern to the scientific attitude is a *change* in the understanding of Being. Here we see more fundamentally how the problem of modern science belongs to fundamental ontology.

5. Temporality and Historicity

CHAPTER 5 IS titled "Temporality and Historicity." Heidegger begins by developing the problem named in this title; that is, by showing how the problem arises.

Section 72: The Existential-Ontological Exposition of the Problem of History

Heidegger goes all the way back to the problem of the meaning of Being. He here sketches out the way in which there arises from this problem the need for a primordial interpretation of Dasein. Then he raises again the question of whether the level of a primordial interpretation has been genuinely reached by the disclosure of anticipatory resoluteness and the corresponding uncovering of temporality as the meaning of care. Specifically, he asks: Has Dasein *as a whole* been brought into the fore-having of the interpretation (as is required for primordiality)?

Why does he raise this question again? Has it not been settled by the elaborate analyses developed in chapters 1–3 of Division Two? What is behind the question? What provokes it? Two problems provoke it.

First, in the previous analysis, Dasein's Being-a-whole has been exhibited only in terms of Being-toward-the-end. Here there is an assumption that the end (death) is what determines Dasein's wholeness, delimits Dasein as a whole. But is this so? Isn't death just *one* of the ends that delimit Dasein's wholeness? Must we not also ask about the other end, which is a beginning—namely, *birth*?

Second, but is it sufficient *merely* to ask about the beginning and the end? Must we not also ask about Dasein's way of extending (stretching along, *Erstreckung*) from birth to death? Is it not just such an extending (such a "connectedness of life") that really constitutes the whole delimited by beginning and end? Must this not be brought into the analysis if there is to be the assurance of primordiality? So the issue is: Do these unresolved problems undercut the claim that the interpretation based on anticipatory resoluteness is primordial—the claim that the meaning of care is temporality? *Or*, on the contrary, does temporality (as exhibited) provide the basis for genuinely taking up these problems? He wants to show that the latter is the case.

Heidegger refers to the ordinary understanding of the connectedness of life; namely, the view that it consists of a sequence of experiences, running from birth to death. The immediate problem for such an understanding is that in such a sequence, the only experience that is actual is the one that is present *now*. So the sequence of experiences gets replaced by a sequence of "nows," and Dasein is regarded as hopping through the series while somehow preserving its identity throughout this perpetual change of experience. But clearly, this approach is inadequate, for it turns Dasein into something present in time. So, over against this, Heidegger poses an existential concept of this connectedness, this extending.

Dasein does not successively fill up a stretch of life "between" birth and death. Rather, Dasein extends itself in such a way that the "between" "lies *in the Being* of Dasein" (BT 374/357). That is, Dasein *is* in such a way as to be the "between," in such a way as to be the "extending" from birth to death.

Furthermore, birth (understood existentially) is not something past (no longer present), just as death is not something outstanding (not yet present). Rather, birth is "within" the extending, instead of being some event that befalls Dasein and is then "left behind."

Heidegger expresses the character of birth more precisely: "*Das faktische Dasein existiert gebürtig* [as born, bornedly]" (BT 374/357).[1] The stress here is on "factical," which is to say, facticity, thrownness. Heidegger is saying that as thrown existence, Dasein is born existence. For Dasein to exist on the basis of its thrownness (as thrown basis) is the same as its existing on the basis of its bornedness (as born basis). That is, birth (existentially understood) coincides with thrownness. What both concepts express is Dasein's not having brought itself into its "there."

Both birth and death fall "within" the Being of Dasein, and so their connection (the connectedness, the extending) must be understood in terms of the unity of the Being of Dasein—specifically, in terms of the unity of thrownness and Being-toward-death. *But* this amounts to saying that the connectedness (extending) is to be understood in terms of *temporality* since temporality is precisely what grounds the unity of care.

Heidegger proceeds to formulate the task thus indicated with terminological precision. "The specific movement of the *stretched out stretching itself along*, we call the *happening* [Geschehen] of Dasein [*Die spezifische Bewegtheit des erstreckten Sicherstreckens nenne wir das Geschehen des Daseins*]" (BT 375/358). So the question of Dasein's connectedness is that of Dasein's "happening." More precisely, the task is to exhibit the *structure* of happening. This structure Heidegger calls historicity (*Geschichtlichkeit*).

The task, then, is to exhibit Dasein's historicity. More specifically, to understand it on the basis of temporality. "*The analysis of the historicity of Dasein attempted to show that this being is not 'temporal' because it 'stands in history,' but that, on the contrary, it exists and can exist historically only because it is temporal*

---

1. This passage is in German in Sallis's original manuscript. The SUNY translation reads as follows: "Factical Dasein exists as born [*existiert gebürtig*]."

in the ground of its Being" (BT 376/359). Heidegger says that the analysis of historicity is, in fact, simply a matter of revealing something that already lies enveloped in temporality.

Section 73: The Vulgar Understanding of History and the Happening of Dasein

Heidegger refers now to the problem of history and asks: What is the "entry point" (*Einsatzstelle*) into this problem? In a sense, this is already evident: the problem of history needs to be "entered into" through an analysis of Dasein's historicity. Only on this basis can we understand history (*Geschichte*) considered as an object of the science of history (*Historie*). However, this "entry point" has been made evident (determined) *only* at the level of the existential project, only by drawing out certain issues from the preceding interpretation, and *not* in reference to what we ordinarily regard as the historical and speak of as such. Heidegger wants to bring this phenomenal horizon into the determination of the "entry point." So in section 73, he undertakes to regain this "entry point" by moving through the ordinary way of interpreting and speaking about history. This movement involves two stages.

1. Heidegger asks: What does one ordinarily have in view in using the words *history* and *historical*? He sketches out four senses.

a. History = what is past. Here the "past" refers to what belongs to an earlier time, even though it may still be present-now (e.g., the Greek temple).

b. History = a context of becoming (development, derivation). Here the "past" has no special privilege.

c. History = the realm of those beings that are determined by spirit and culture (human beings, human groups), the realm that we distinguish from nature.

d. Historical = whatever has been handed down to us (whether known historiographically or not).

Heidegger then puts these four senses together: "History is the specific happening of existing Dasein happening in time, in such a way that the happening—which in Being-with-one-another is 'past' and, at the same time, 'handed down' [*überlieferte*] and still having an effect—is taken to be history in the sense emphasized" (BT 379/361). So all four significations come together by referring (in different ways) to the human being as the subject of events—as the subject of history.

2. To clarify this, Heidegger considers some other sorts of things that are also considered historical (focusing, at the same time, on the privileged position that the past has in the concept of history). He begins with certain things that are "historical" in the sense of being somehow "past"; namely, the antiquities preserved in museums (artifacts). Such things belong to a time that is past, *yet* they are still present, that is to say, not themselves past. He asks: How is it that

such things are called "historical" when they are not yet past? Do they have in themselves something past even though they are still present? What is past in such artifacts? Heidegger answers: "Nothing other than the *world* within which they were encountered as handy things belonging to a context of useful things and used by concernful Dasein existing-in-the-world. That *world* is no longer. But what was previously *innerworldly* in that world is still present" (BT 380/362). So they are past in the sense of belonging to a world that is no longer.

But world belongs to Dasein (as Being-in-the-world). Thus Heidegger continues: "The historical character of antiquities that have been preserved is grounded in the 'past' of that Dasein to whose world that past belongs" (BT 380/362–63). More precisely, they are historical by their relation (through world) to a Dasein that no longer exists, a Dasein that has the character not of past (in the sense of no-longer-present) but of having-been-there (*da-gewesen*).

Thus Dasein is what is *primarily historical*, and Heidegger adds (by way of anticipation) that Dasein is historical not only as "no longer there" but simply insofar as it factically exists. What is *secondarily historical* is handy beings in the widest sense and also surrounding nature. These things are historical because they belong to world, and so such beings are called "world-historical." Heidegger adds (without developing it) that the ordinary concept of world-history arises from our orientation to what is secondarily historical. *But* a genuine concept of history must be developed on the basis of what is *primarily* historical—namely, Dasein. It must be developed through an analysis of the *historicity* of Dasein as the subject of history.

Section 74: The Essential Constitution of Historicity

This section provides a primordial interpretation of Dasein's historicity in five stages.

I. The Basis of the Interpretation

How is historicity to be disclosed? That is, what mode of self-disclosure by Dasein is to serve as the basis for the disclosure of historicity? This question is settled by the fact that a *primordial* interpretation is sought. The *primordial* interpretation requires as its basis authentic self-disclosure, and that is anticipatory resoluteness. So anticipatory resoluteness provides the basis for the analysis. More specifically, the analysis will proceed in terms of the structure of anticipatory resoluteness *as* worked out in the analysis of temporality, which takes place in three moments.

1. Anticipation, which is authentic Being-toward-death, and from which the future was uncovered.

2. Coming back to oneself in the sense of taking over one's thrownness, from which having-been was uncovered.

3. Becoming disclosively engaged in a situation, from which the present was uncovered.

II. The Source of Possibilities

We have seen that in anticipatory resoluteness there is an *indefiniteness*—that is, it does not as such prescribe the factical possibilities on which Dasein would project in any actual instance. So through the analysis of anticipatory resoluteness, the existential analytic can decide nothing regarding what these factical possibilities are.

However, there is one question that it does need to raise about such possibilities in general: Whence does Dasein draw those possibilities upon which it factically projects itself? Heidegger observes, in particular, that these possibilities are *not* gotten through projection in death. Although anticipation is what makes resoluteness authentic, no factical possibilities are to be gathered from death (as ownmost possibility). So Heidegger asks whether such possibilities are provided by the second moment (which is equivalent to taking over one's thrownness). He answers yes. It must be considered that Dasein's thrownness is a thrownness into world—that is, Dasein's thrownness does not bring itself into its world (and so, into its "there") but rather is always already in a world. Within the world (into which Dasein is thrown) possibilities are already delineated—*and so*, in being thrown into world, Dasein is already submitted to certain factical possibilities, which is to say, it has a heritage. Thus in taking over thrownness (in anticipatory resoluteness), Dasein takes over these possibilities, takes over its heritage. "The resoluteness in which Dasein comes back to itself discloses the actual factical possibilities of authentic existing *in terms of the heritage* which that resoluteness *takes over* as thrown. Resolute coming back to thrownness involves *handing oneself over* to traditional possibilities, although not necessarily *as* traditional ones" (BT 383/365).

III. Anticipation and Freedom

The fact that Dasein gets to its possibilities by taking over thrownness does *not* mean, however, that anticipation has no bearing on this issue. What role does anticipation play? Already, Heidegger has shown: anticipation serves to bring Dasein back to the lostness in the "they," to individualize Dasein. The result is that rather than merely going along with the possibilities prescribed by the "they," Dasein comes to choose its possibilities—that is, in anticipation, Dasein chooses to choose. Through this choosing to choose, Dasein gains its freedom. Thus anticipation brings Dasein into its freedom.

In the present context, Heidegger expresses this same issue *but* in terms of *finitude*. Anticipation pushes existence into its finitude. That is, in running toward death, Dasein gets cast back upon its finitude. What is the effect of this disclosure of finitude? It liberates one from merely going along with whatever possibilities accidentally thrust themselves upon one. In other words, again, it brings Dasein into its freedom.

But how does it have this effect? Consider: anticipation dispels the inauthentic covering-over of death—that is, it dispels that indefinite postponement of death (in which death is removed to an indefinite "someday"). Thereby, it dispels that boundlessness of life (that "illusion" of indefinite extension) that robs choice of its decisiveness. Instead, it gives life its properly *indefinite bound*, which is that bound (death) that is indefinite in the sense that Dasein lies under *constant threat* of death. This indefinite bound restores the decisiveness of choice—so that Dasein chooses to choose. So: anticipation brings Dasein into its *finite* freedom (cf, the Indian warrior).

IV. Fate

Now bring the role played by anticipation together with Dasein's taking over its heritage (corresponding to the second moment of anticipatory resoluteness): the effect is to introduce into this "taking over" an element of choosing. That is, Dasein does not just take over whatever possibilities happen to be handed down *but rather* hands possibilities down to itself. This handing down to itself Heidegger calls fate (*Schicksal*). This is Dasein's primordial *happening*. "This is how we designate the primordial happening of Dasein that lies in authentic resoluteness in which it *hands itself down* to itself, free for death, in a possibility that it inherited and yet has chosen" (BT 384/365–66). It is clear that such happening; that is, fate, is *founded on temporality*.

V. Destiny

Heidegger proceeds to bring in the dimension of Being-with-others: Dasein is essentially Being-with-others—*and so*, its happening is always a cohappening—that is, a *destiny* (*Geschick*). This designates the happening of a community, a people. However, it is not simply a sum of individual fates.

VI. Repetition

In general, it is not necessary that, in resoluteness, one know *explicitly* the origin of the possibilities that one hands down to oneself. But, of course, one *can* hand down a possibility in a way that relates explicitly to its origin. Such a way of handing down Heidegger calls repetition (*Wiederholung*). Especially important here is that in repetition, Dasein does *not* disclose the origin (its "hero") *in order merely* to actualize it again—that is, *Wiederholung* is not *mere* repetition but rather is a *response* to this possibility—a response that, made in the moment of vision, neither binds itself to the past nor simply abandons the past. Again recall: *Being and Time* is itself a *Wiederholung* of the question of the meaning of Being—explicitly related to the origin of that question in Greek thought. Heidegger's "heroes" are, of course, Plato and Aristotle.

6. Temporality and Within-Timeness as the Origin of the Ordinary Concept of Time

We come to the last of those three tasks that arose from the disclosure of temporality as the meaning of care.[1] The task is to show how the everyday experience of time and the ordinary conception of time arise on the basis of Dasein's temporality. This amounts to accounting for the fact that everyday Dasein takes both history and nature as happening *in time*—*and*, even more importantly, that Dasein reckons with time and regulates itself according to time. (This fact is expressed in ordinary ways of speaking about time: we "have the time," we "take the time," we "lose time," we "waste time.")

This time Heidegger calls "*die besorgte Zeit*," the time of concern. It is the time "of concern" in two senses.

1. It is the time that belongs to the sphere of (circumspective) concern, the time that is "constituted" within this sphere.
2. It is the time *with which* Dasein can be concerned, can reckon—the time to which Dasein's concern can be, in a sense, directed.

So the task is to exhibit the structure of this time of concern and to show how it arises from Dasein's primordial temporality. Beyond this, there is the further task of determining how the time of concern leads over to the ordinary concept of time. Thus there are two general topics: (I) the structure and origin of the time of concern and (II) the genesis of the ordinary concept of time.

I. Structure and Origin of the Time of Concern

A. The first structural moment Heidegger calls "datability" (*Datierbarkeit*).

To see what this is and how it belongs to the time of concern, we must see how such time originates, how there comes to be such time, which is to say, how it arises from Dasein's primordial temporality.

We can express this relation in a general way by saying: the time of concern is self-interpreted temporality. Let us try to see precisely how there is the self-interpretation of temporality and how this gives rise to the time of concern.

---

[1] Ed. note: the previous two tasks correspond to "Temporality and Everydayness" (chap. 4 of Division Two) and "Temporality and Historicity" (chap. 5 of Division Two).

In circumspective concern, Dasein is involved with what is handy within-the-world. It understands these things—that is, it projects them upon world (significance). It interprets them—that is, exhibits them *as* something (in terms of significance, in terms of their meaning). It discourses about them—that is, it articulates the meaning-context. It expresses this discourse in language—that is, addresses itself to these things.

What is crucial is that handy beings are not objects over against Dasein such that, in addressing them, Dasein could leave out of account its own comportment toward them. Rather, in interpreting and addressing what is handy, Dasein *also* interprets and expresses its Being-alongside the handy. That is, in Dasein's comportment to the handy, in circumspective concern, there is a self-interpretation and self-expression. (For example, I say: "I need that tool over there"—"over there" expresses Dasein's Being-alongside, its existential spatiality.)

The fact that there is this self-interpretation and self-expression is based on the character of Dasein as self-disclosive: in every kind of comportment, Dasein is always also disclosed to itself with some degree of self-transparency. But Dasein *is* fundamentally temporality. Thus temporality is always disclosed to Dasein. More specifically, Dasein always understands, interprets, and expresses temporality. Note, however, that Dasein can do this in various ways, with different degrees of transparency. And so: temporality *as* expressed and interpreted is not necessarily manifest as *primordial* temporality. So we may say: in Dasein, there is a self-interpretation of temporality through which temporality can become manifest in various forms.

The time of concern is temporality as interpreted and expressed within the sphere of circumspective concern. That is, the time of concern is the self-interpreted temporality manifest in the sphere of concern. Said differently, it is the form that self-interpreted temporality takes in the sphere of concern.

What is this form? To determine it, we need to answer two questions: What is the character of the temporality that interprets itself here, and how does it interpret itself?

(1) The temporality that interprets itself here is that mode of primordial temporality that Heidegger previously (Division Two, chap. 4) identified as the temporality of circumspective concern: it is a *making-present* that *retains* and *awaits*. Without going into details, the general sense is this: it is an *awaiting*—which is *toward* the system of involvements. A *retaining*—namely, of what is thus involved, the equipment. And a *making-present*—in such a way that Dasein is absorbed in its equipmental world, engaged with the handy.

(2) But how does this temporality get interpreted? That is, what is the horizon, the context of meaning, within which it gets interpreted and expressed? It is that horizon that serves for all interpretation in everyday concern—namely, the world. So Dasein interprets its temporality in terms of the world, in connection with the handy things and events within-the-world.

Present (making-present)→now, that . . .
Future (awaiting)→then, when . . .
Having-been (retaining)→formerly, when . . .

For example:
Now that I reach for the hammer—so that shoes will be finished *then when* someone comes for them—I find it as it was *formerly when* I used it (for some definite purpose).

This interpretation Heidegger calls an assigning of time (*Zeitangabe*). The sense is that Dasein assigns its primordial time (temporality) *to* its factical Being-in-the-world. *And*, by bringing it into the world, Dasein gives time to itself, gives it to itself as something with which it can be concerned (can reckon).

The interpretation he also calls a *dating*: "interpreted time too always already has a date-stamp [*Datiereung-dating*] on the basis of the beings encountered in the disclosedness of the there; now that . . . the door slams; now that . . . my book is missing, etc." (BT 408/389). Therefore, the time of concern has the structure of *datability*: "But every 'then' is, *as such*, a 'then, when . . .'; every 'on that former occasion' is an 'on that former occasion when . . .' every 'now' is a 'now that.' . . . We shall call this seemingly self-evident relational structure of the 'now,' 'on that former occasion,' and 'then' *datability*" (BT 407/388).

This is the first of the four structural moments of the time of concern.

B. The second structural moment: time is spanned.

We need to see what this involves and how it arises.

The crucial statement is this: "If awaiting, understanding itself in the 'then,' interprets itself and in so doing, as a making-present, understands what it is awaiting in terms of its 'now,' then the 'and now net yet' already lies in the 'assigning' of the 'then'" (BT 409/389). What does this mean? It must be seen in terms of the self-interpretation of temporality (within concern). In this self-interpretation, awaiting (future ecstasis) interprets itself as "then, when . . ." Making-present (present ecstasis) interprets itself as "now, that . . ." But in the temporalizing of temporality, there is always a *unity* among the ecstases. And so, in the self-interpretation, the unity (connection) between the ecstases *also* gets interpreted. So in Dasein's assigning time, this connection is *also* assigned: "the 'and now not yet' already lies in the 'assigning' of the 'then.'" That is, there is an assigning of an "until then," an "in-between," a "during"—and this can, in turn, be articulated through the assignment of additional "thens." This "in-between," this "duration," which belongs to time *as* interpreted, constitutes its character as *spanned*. "This duration [*Dauern*] is again the time revealed in the *self*-interpretation of temporality, a time that is thus actually, but unthematically, understood in concern as a 'span'" (BT 409/390).

This is the second of the four structural moments of the time of concern.

Heidegger adds several observations related to this second moment.

1. Its spanned character belongs to time *as interpreted* in the sphere of concern. This means that it corresponds to something within primordial temporality. That is, there is something in primordial temporality that gets interpreted *as* spanning. What? The *connectedness* of primordial temporality, which is Dasein's *extending itself along* from birth to death—that is, what Heidegger calls *Geschehen* (happening) or, structurally regarded, historicity (*Geschichtlichkeit*). This is the condition of possibility of history, and so we begin to see that history gets taken as being "in time."

2. In the assigning of time in the sphere of concern, the character of spanning is not limited to the "during" (the "in-between" that stretches between "now" and "then"). It is carried over to the "now," "then," "formerly"—they are spans, not points. This is clear if we keep in mind their datability-structure: "Now" is a "now while I am eating"; "then" is a "then when I am going home."

3. As long as Dasein is engaged concernfully with things, it is not directed explicitly to the time that it assigns, that it covers up. Or, better: it is directed to it *only* indirectly through its engagement with things. "In the everyday concernful 'just passing through life,' Dasein never understands itself as running along in a continuously enduring succession of pure 'nows'" (BT 409/390).

C. The Third Structural Moment: time is *public*.

This character is already somewhat evident from the description of how time is assigned: time is assigned in terms of the world. But Dasein's world is not merely its own; it is also a world in which it is *with* others—it is a "public world." Clearly, this public character is carried over to time.

But the full public character of time can be seen only if we consider something further: that there is a privileged way of dating within the horizon of which all other dating occurs. This privileged dating originates in response to Dasein's thrownness. Specifically, in response to Dasein's having been delivered over to the need for sight and light *and* to changes of day (which gives the possibility of sight) *and* night (which takes it away). The point here is this: Dasein assigns time in terms of the possibility of sight, which is to say, in terms of what grants it and withdraws it; that is, in terms of the rising and the setting of the sun. Thus arises the "most natural" measure of time—*the day*. In turn, the day gets divided up (as can any span), but even the dividing up is done in a framework of this privileged dating, that is, in terms of the journeying sun. Such a way of dating is distinctively *public*. It introduces a publicly available *measure*—the sun. In other words, it introduces a "natural clock," which then subsequently motivates the production of clocks in the usual sense.

So through this privileged dating (and on the basis of Dasein's thrownness), time has its character as *public*. This is the third structural moment of the time of concern.

D. Fourth Structural Moment: time is *worldly*.

We have seen: time is dated in terms of things within-the-world. Now Heidegger brings out another character linked up with this dating. It is evident in the "concernful" statement: "then—when it dawns—it is *time for* one's daily work." The point is that the time of concern (whether "then," "now," "formerly") is a time *for* something. That is, time has a reference to a "for-which"—something for which it is either appropriate or not appropriate. But any such "for-which" occurs within a context of involvements linked up finally with a "for-the-sake-of-which." In other words, time is bound up with significance, with world. Heidegger calls it "world-time."

This worldly character is the fourth structural moment of the time of concern.

II. The Genesis of the Ordinary Concept of Time

It is clear that the time of concern is quite different from time as ordinarily conceived, which is to say, from time conceived as an endless sequence of "nows." Heidegger's final task is to show how this transition occurs and what it involves; that is, to exhibit the genesis of the ordinary concept of time.

Within the sphere of circumspective concern, Dasein is not explicitly directed to time. Rather, it reckons with time only in reckoning with its own concernful dealings. Now Heidegger asks: How does time itself become explicitly accessible? That is, in what kind of comportment does Dasein explicitly relate itself to time? *And* how does time then show itself?

The relevant comportment lies in the use of clocks. Specifically, it is a matter of making-present the moving hands of the clock, which is following the positions of the hands in such a way as to *count* them up. Time is what shows itself in such a making-present. Heidegger delimits this explicitly accessible time: "*This time is what is counted, showing itself in following, making-present, and **counting** the moving pointer in such a way that making-present temporalizes itself in ecstatic unity with retaining and awaiting horizontally open according to the earlier and later*" (BT 421/400).

But, as Heidegger immediately adds, this is merely an existential-ontological interpretation of Aristotle's definition of time: "This, namely, is time: that which is counted in the motion encountered in the horizon of the earlier and the later" (BT 421/400).[2] And, Heidegger says: all later discussions of the concept of time have remained within the framework of Aristotle's definition. This is especially remarkable if we observe how far the domain of this definition is removed from the domain of primordial temporality—that is, how far this definition falls short of being primordial.

---

2. Ed. note: This is a citation from Aristotle, *Physics*, IV 11, 219b1 et seq, and it is preceded in the text of Heidegger by the Greek.

Heidegger proceeds to show how the Aristotelian concept leads into the ordinary concept of time: time is what is counted as one makes-present the positions of the hands of the clock. Phenomenally speaking, in this making-present, one says something like: "now here," "now here," and so on. And so what gets counted are the "nows." So the time that gets explicitly sighted in the use of clocks is: *now-time (jetzt-Zeit)*. Thus we get the ordinary concept of time: "And thus time shows itself for the ordinary understanding as a sequence of constantly 'present' [*vorhanden*] nows that pass away and arrive at the same time. Time is understood as a sequence, as the 'flux' of nows, as the 'course of time'" (BT 422/401).

What has really happened in this transition from "world-time" to the ordinary concept of time? The pure "nows" result from severing the "nows" of world-time *from* their essential reference to the world. There are two such kinds of reference: these are expressed in two of the structural moments of this time, datability and the worldly character of time. So what happens in the transition is that the datability and worldly character of world-time get covered over: "The ordinary interpretation of time *covers* them *over*. The ecstatic and horizonal constitution of temporality, in which the datability and significance of the now are grounded, is *leveled down* by this covering over. The nows are cut off from these relations, so to speak, and, as thus cut off, they simply range themselves along after one another so as to constitute the succession" (BT 422/401).

Also, however, time gets torn away from its bond to Dasein. This is most striking in what Heidegger calls "the principal thesis of the ordinary interpretation of time—namely, that time is 'infinite'" (BT 424/403). In this thesis, Heidegger sees a remote but decisive result of that fleeing in the face of death, that concealment of the authentic future, of *finite* temporality into which Dasein falls. *So*: time (in the ordinary concept) is torn loose from both Dasein and things within-the-world. In traditional terms, it is torn loose from both the subject and object. *And*, as a result, philosophical thought has (ever since Aristotle) vacillated between locating time in the object and locating it in the subject. *Also*: since time is torn loose specifically from the subject, there arises the problem of how the subject can be in time—that is, of how, in Hegel's terms, spirit can fall into time.

Conclusion

So we come to the end of the published part of *Being and Time*. This part ends with a long series of questions, concluding with these: "Is there a way leading from primordial *time* to the meaning of *Being*? Does *time* itself reveal itself as the horizon of *Being*?" (BT 437/415)

These questions, and the others that precede them, are not merely rhetorical. They express a questioning—and, indeed, Heidegger's engagement in this questioning led him to hold back the remainder of the work—namely, the division in which the matter would have been "turned around" from "Being and time" to "time and Being." That is, in which the movement from the Being of Dasein (care) to temporality (Division Two) would have been followed by a movement from temporality to Being. As he later explains in "Letter on Humanism," the questionable division was held back because an adequate saying of the turning did not succeed with the help of the language of metaphysics.

But this does not mean that he abandoned the thinking of *Being and Time*—rather that he found himself compelled to persevere in the *questioning* that *Being and Time* had initiated.

In a text first published in 1966 under the title "The End of Philosophy and the Task of Thinking," Heidegger writes of his "attempt, undertaken again and again since 1930, to give the questioning in *Being and Time* a more originary form. This means: to submit the beginning of the question in *Being and Time* to an immanent critique."[1]

Here we may appropriately recall again the question with which we began our attempt to interpret *Being and Time*—the question: Where does *Being and Time* begin?

And in this connection, we may then say: Heidegger's thought does not move away from *Being and Time* but rather back to its beginning—in order to attempt a more originary beginning, a beginning more accordant with the beginning of the *Sache* itself.

---

1. Martin Heidegger, "Das Ende der Philosophie und die Aufgabe des Denkens," in *Gesamtausgabe*, vol. 14 (Frankfurt am Main: Vittorio Klostermann, 2007), 69). In English, "The End of Philosophy and the Task of Thinking," in *On Time and Being*, trans. Joan Stambaugh (New York: Harper & Row, Inc. 1972), 55.

Appendix

An Abbreviated Version of Lectures 11–13

These lectures dealt with the decisive transition that is at the heart of Division Two: the transition to the proper task of Division Two, which is the primordial interpretation of the *meaning* of the Being of Dasein. That is, the transition from the Being of Dasein (care) to the meaning of the Being of Dasein (temporality).

We should recall how Heidegger proceeded in the transition: for each of the moments of care, he uncovered the temporal phenomenon that makes it possible (and thus its meaning):

1. Existence: coming toward oneself in one's possibility = future.
2. Facticity: coming back to one's already having-been = the character of having-been (*Gewesenheit*).
3. Falling: making-present = present.

These three phenomena in their unity constitute temporality (primordial time). He calls them: ecstases.

We saw, finally: there arise three further tasks—namely, everydayness, historicity, and within time-ness. We can hardly begin to deal with the vast analyses that Heidegger undertakes in connection with these tasks. Instead, we simply try to indicate what kind of problem he addresses in each chapter and take up one specific analysis from each.

I. Temporality and Everydayness

Here the task is to *repeat*, at the level of the temporal interpretation, the main steps of the preparatory analysis done in Division One. That is, the task is to uncover the modes of temporality (temporalizing) that underlie the various constituents of Dasein's Being. This amounts to working out explicitly the projection of Dasein's Being upon temporality, which is to give the temporal interpretation of Dasein.

From the various analyses, I want to select for consideration the analysis of *world and temporality* in section 69c. The task: to give the temporal interpretation of Being-in-the-world (with special reference to world)—that is, to appropriate to the primordial (temporal) interpretation the preparatory analysis carried out in chapter 3 of Division One. The specific question is: How is world in its unity with Dasein possible? That is to say, what makes it possible? Said differently, what is its meaning? Or, since temporality has been exhibited as constituting in general the meaning of the Being of Dasein, the question is: How does temporality make world possible?

Heidegger answers directly: "*The existential-temporal condition of possibility of the world lies in the fact that temporality, as an ecstatical unity, has something like a horizon*" (BT 365/347). What does this mean? What constitutes the "horizon" of time? Heidegger calls its constituents "horizonal schemata." This language is Kantian: just as Kant's schemata mediate between time and understanding, so here "horizonal schemata" mediate between temporality and Being-in-the-world (to which it belongs).

But what are these horizonal schemata? Heidegger explains by referring to the ecstases: to each ecstasis there belongs a "whither" (*wohin*), which is something by which the specific directionality involved in each ecstasis is determined (marked out). This "whither" is the horizonal schema. Heidegger identifies the horizonal schema for each ecstasis.

A. The schema of the future is "whither" of Dasein's coming toward itself—that is, that *to* which Dasein is carried away (stands out) in coming toward itself. He identifies this as: the "for-the-sake-of-itself." Concretely, this can be filled out in different ways corresponding to the various forms that possibilities can assume.

B. The schema of having-been is the "whither" involved in attunement (which is equivalent to that disclosedness in which having-been has been shown to be the primary ecstasis). Heidegger identifies this as: that in the face of which (*das Wovor*) Dasein is thrown, that to which Dasein has been abandoned.

C. The schema of the present is the "in-order-to." The crucial point here is: because of the unity of the ecstases (that is, of temporality itself), there is a unity of these horizonal schemata—that is, they form a *unitary* horizon. *And thus* they serve to hold together:

1. The possibilities upon which Dasein projects itself.
2. The equipment-context into which Dasein is always already thrown.
3. The actual involvements ("in-order-to") with which Dasein (in a given instance) is concerned.

That is to say, the horizon that belongs to temporality holds possibility and significance (that is, Dasein and world) together in primordial unity, which is in turn linked up (unified) with Dasein's specific circumspective concern. "The horizonal unity of the schemata of the ecstases makes possible the primordial connection [*Zusammenhang*] of the relations of the in-order-to with the for-the-sake-of-which. This means that on the basis of the horizonal constitution of the ecstatic unity of temporality, something like a disclosed world belongs to the being that is always its There" (BT 365/348).

Now it is clear how Dasein is essentially Being-in-the-world—that is, why it is not the case that there is first of all Dasein, which then takes up a relation to the world. The reason is: insofar as Dasein temporalizes itself (insofar as Dasein *is* at all) the unity of Dasein and world is established. The world is neither "handy" nor "present" but temporalizes itself in Dasein's temporality.

II. Temporality and Historicity

Here I want especially to show how Heidegger raises the problem.

Near the beginning of chapter 5, Heidegger takes up again the question of the primordiality of interpretation. Heidegger asks whether the level of a primordial interpretation has been genuinely reached by the disclosure of anticipatory resoluteness and the corresponding uncovering of temporality as the meaning of care.

Specifically, he asks: Has Dasein *as a whole* been brought into the fore-having of the interpretation (as is required for primordiality)? Why does he raise this question again? Has it not been settled by the elaborate analyses developed in chapters 1–2 of Division Two? What is behind the question? What provokes it?

Two problems provoke the question.

A. In the previous analysis, Dasein's Being-a-whole has been exhibited only in terms of Being-toward-the-end. Here there is the assumption that the end (death) is what determines Dasein's wholeness, delimits Dasein as a whole. But is this so? Isn't death just *one* of the ends that delimit Dasein's wholeness? Must we not also ask about that other end, which is a beginning—namely, *birth*?

B. But is it sufficient *merely* to ask about the beginning and end? Must we not also ask about Dasein's way of extending ("stretching along," *Erstreckung*) from birth to death? Is it not just such an extending (such a "connectedness of life") that really constitutes the whole delimited by beginning and end? Must this not be brought into the analysis if there is to be an assurance of primordiality? What Heidegger wants, then, to show is: that temporality (as exhibited) provides the basis for genuinely taking up these problems.

Heidegger refers to the ordinary understanding of the connectedness of life; namely, the view that it consists of a sequence of experiences, running from birth to death. The immediate problem for such an understanding is that in such a sequence, the only experience that is actual is the one that is present *now*. So the sequence of experiences gets replaced by the sequence of "*nows*"—*and* Dasein is regarded as hopping through the series while somehow preserving its identity throughout this perpetual change of experience.

But clearly, this approach is inadequate, for it turns Dasein into something present in time. So, over against this, Heidegger poses an existential concept of this connectedness, this extending. Dasein does not successively fill up a stretch of life "between" birth and death. *Rather*, Dasein extends itself in such a way that the "between" "lies *in the Being* of Dasein" (BT 374/357). That is, Dasein *is* in such a way as to be the "between," in such a way as to be the "extending" from birth to death.

Furthermore, birth (understood existentially) is not something past (something no longer present), just as death is not something outstanding (something not yet present). Rather, birth is "within" the extending, instead of being some event that befalls Dasein and is then "left behind."

Heidegger expresses the character of birth more precisely: "*Das faktische Dasein existiert gebürtig* [as born, bornedly]" (BT 357).[1] The stress here is on "factical"—that is, facticity, thrownness. Heidegger is saying: as *thrown* existence, Dasein is *born* existence. In other words, for Dasein to exist on the basis of its thrownness (as thrown basis) is the same as its existing on the basis of "born-ness" (as born basis). Said in yet another way, birth (existentially understood) coincides with thrownness. What both concepts express is Dasein's not having brought itself into its "there."

---

1. As noted, when this citation occurred earlier, the passage is cited in German. See n. 1, p. 169.

So birth and death fall "within" the Being of Dasein—*and so* their connection (the connectedness, the extending) must be understood in terms of the unity of the Being of Dasein; specifically, in terms of the unity of thrownness and Being-toward-death. *But* this amounts to saying that the connectedness (extending) is to be understood in terms of *temporality* since temporality is precisely what grounds the unity of care.

Heidegger formulates this notion in a precise way: "The specific movement of the *stretched out stretching itself along*, we call the *happening* of Dasein [Die spezifische Bewegtheit des *erstreckten Sicherstreckens* nennen wir das *Geschehen* des Daseins]" (BT 375/358). The *structure* of such happening (*Geschehen*) Heidegger calls historicity (*Geschichtlichkeit*). The task, then, is to show (through detailed analysis) how temporality makes possible Dasein's historicity. That is, Dasein is historical because it is temporal, and not conversely.

We should also mention that in the course of the analysis, Heidegger develops the concept of *fate* (*Schicksal*). This simply expresses the character of happening as a handing-over of possibilities to oneself (a unity of heritage and choice). In turn, this concept can be related to Dasein Being-with-others—and then one gets the concept of *destiny* (*Geschick*).

III. Temporality and Within-time-ness (*Innerzeitigkeit*)

In the final chapter, the primary task is: to show how the everyday experience of time arises on the basis of Dasein's temporality. This amounts to accounting for the fact that everyday Dasein takes both history and nature as occurring *in time*—and (even more importantly) that Dasein reckons with time and regulates itself according to time. (Expressed in an ordinary way of speaking about time: we "have the time," "take the time," "lose time," "waste time"—and sometimes we "run out of time"!)

This time, Heidegger calls it "*die besorgte Zeit*" (time of concern). It is the time of concern in two senses:

A. It is the time that belongs to the sphere of circumspective concern, the time that is "constituted" within this sphere.

B. It is the time *with which* Dasein can be concerned, can reckon—the time to which Dasein's concern can be, in a sense, directed.

So the task is to show how the "time of concern" arises from primordial temporality and what its specific character (structure) is.

Considering primarily the first of these—how it arises—we can express this relation (in a general way) by saying: time (of concern) is self-interpreted temporality. Let us try to see precisely how there is the self-interpretation of temporality and how this gives rise to time (of concern).

In circumspective concern, Dasein is involved with what is handy within-the-world. It understands these things—that is, projects them upon world (significance). It interprets them—that is, exhibits them *as* something (in terms of significance, in terms of their meaning). It discourses about them—that is, articulates the meaning-context. It expresses this discourse in language—that is, addresses itself to these things.

What is crucial is that handy beings are not objects over against Dasein such that, in addressing them, Dasein could leave out of account its own comportment toward them. Rather, in interpreting and addressing what is handy, Dasein *also* interprets and expresses *its* Being-alongside the handy. That is, in Dasein's comportment to the handy, in circumspective concern, there is *self-interpretation* and *self-expression*. (For example, I say "I need that tool over there"—"over there" expresses Dasein's Being-alongside, its existential spatiality.)

The fact that there is such self-interpretation and self-expression is based on the character of Dasein as *self-disclosive*: in every kind of comportment, Dasein is always also disclosed to itself with some degree of self-transparency. *But* Dasein *is* fundamentally temporality. *Thus* temporality is always disclosed to Dasein. Specifically, Dasein always understands, interprets, and expresses its temporality. However, Dasein can do this in various ways, with different degrees of transparency. And so: temporality *as* expressed and interpreted is not necessarily manifest *as primordial* temporality. We may say, then, that in Dasein, there is a self-interpretation of temporality through which temporality can become manifest in various forms.

The time of concern is temporality as interpreted and expressed within the sphere of circumspective concern. That is, the time of concern is the self-interpreted temporality manifest in the sphere of concern. In other words, it is the form that self-interpreted temporality takes in the sphere of concern.

What is this form? To determine it, we need to answer two questions: What is the character of the temporality that interprets itself here, and how does it interpret itself?

1. The temporality that interprets itself here is that mode of primordial temporality that Heidegger previously (Division Two, chap. 4) identified as the temporality of circumspective concern: it is a *making-present* that *retains* and *awaits*.

Without going into details, the general sense is this:

    a. It is an *awaiting*—which is *toward* the system of involvements.

    b. It is a *retaining*, namely—of what is then involved in the equipment.

    c. It is a *making-present*—in such a way that Dasein is absorbed in its equipmental world, engaged with the handy.

2. But how does this temporality get interpreted? That is, what is the horizon, the context of meaning within which it gets interpreted and expressed? It is that horizon that serves for all interpretation in everyday concern—namely, the *world*. So Dasein interprets its temporality in terms of the world, in connection with handy things and events within the world:

    Present (making-present)→now, that . . .
    Future (awaiting)→then, when . . .
    Having-been (retaining)→formerly, when . . .

For example:

    Now that I reach for the hammer—
    so that shoes will be finished *then when* someone comes for them—
    I find it as it was *formerly when* I used it (for some definite purpose).

This interpretation Heidegger calls an assigning of time (*Zeitangabe*). The sense is: Dasein assigns its primordial time (temporality) *to* its factical Being-in-the-world.

And by bringing it into the world, Dasein gives time to itself, gives it to itself as something with which it can be concerned (can reckon). Through such "assigning," the time of concern comes to have what Heidegger calls the structure of datability. This is the first of the four structural characters that he goes on to derive (spanned, public, worldly).

But now—we are almost out of time, and it is time for a very brief concluding remark.

Conclusion

We have come—even if finally by a series of leaps—to the end of the published part of *Being and Time*. This part ends with a long series of questions—a series that concludes with these questions: "Is there a way leading from primordial *time* to the meaning of *Being*? Does *time* itself reveal itself as the horizon of *Being*?" (BT 437/415)

These questions, and the others that precede them, are not merely rhetorical.

They express a questioning.

And, indeed, Heidegger's engagement in this questioning led him to hold back the remainder of the work—namely, the division in which the matter would have been "turned around" from "Being and time" to "time and Being"—that is, in which the movement from the Being of Dasein (care) to temporality (Division Two) would have been followed by a movement from temporality to Being. As he later explains in "Letter on Humanism," the questionable division was held back because an adequate saying of the turning did not succeed with the help of the language of metaphysics.

But this does not mean that he abandoned the thinking of *Being and Time*—rather that he found himself compelled to persevere in the *questioning* that *Being and Time* had initiated.

In a text written in 1964 and first published in 1966 under the title "The End of Philosophy and the Task of Thinking," Heidegger writes of his "attempt, undertaken again and again since 1930, to give the questioning in *Being and Time* a more originary form. This means: to submit the beginning of the question in *Being and Time* to an immanent critique."[2]

Here we may appropriately recall again the question with which we began our attempt to interpret *Being and Time*—the question: Where does *Being and Time* begin?

And in this connection, we may then say: Heidegger's thought moves away not from *Being and Time* but rather back to its beginning—in order to attempt a more originary beginning, a beginning more accordant with the beginning (ἀρχή) of the *Sache* itself.

---

2. See n. 1 on p. 183. Martin Heidegger, "Das Ende der Philosophie und die Aufgabe des Denkens," in *Gesamtausgabe*, vol. 14 (Frankfurt am Main: Vittorio Klostermann, 2007), 69. In English, "The End of Philosophy and the Task of Thinking," in *On Time and Being*, trans. Joan Stambaugh (New York: Harper and Row, 1972), 55.

Editor's Afterword

THE PRESENT VOLUME of *The Collected Writings of John Sallis* presents John Sallis's lectures on Martin Heidegger's *Being and Time* from three separate occasions. The lectures were presented during the 1985–86 academic year at Loyola University of Chicago, the fall semester of 1999 at Pennsylvania State University, and the fall and early-spring semesters of 2021–22 at Boston College. The fourteen years separating the beginning of the two earlier courses are significant in that many of the *Gesamtausgabe* volumes appeared in that interval as well as a second translation of *Being and Time*. While the additional *Gesamtausgabe* volumes make no appearance in the Sallis lectures, there is certainly an awareness of them throughout the lectures. Of course, by the time of the Boston College lectures, not only had a great many more and important volumes of the *Gesamtausgabe* appeared, but a much-improved second edition of the SUNY translation of *Being and Time* had also emerged (in 2010).

What is published in the present volume is a synthesis of the manuscripts of the three separate lecture courses. The Loyola manuscript consists of 350 pages in Sallis's own, clearly legible handwriting; the Penn State manuscript consists of 224 pages of the same handwriting; and the Boston College lectures consist of two separate manuscripts of 161 pages and 45 pages, respectively. For the most part, each manuscript is written in complete sentences, albeit in the form of a sophisticated conceptual outline.

Very few editorial decisions were required, except for the following. While Sallis typically works from Heidegger's German text, he nevertheless cites mainly from the available English translation. In the Loyola course, that translation was, of course, the one produced by Macquarrie and Robinson from 1962; the Penn State course was that produced by Stambaugh in 1996; and the Boston College manuscripts came from the second, revised SUNY edition under the direction of Dennis J. Schmidt, published in 2010. In the text, *Being and Time* page numbers are indicated by "BT," followed by the German and then the revised, second edition of the Stambaugh translation published by SUNY Press. The organization of the text follows the original manuscript, and its organization is identical to Heidegger's *Being and Time*, thus the divisions and chapters follow Heidegger. This organization will make it very easy to read the Sallis text alongside Heidegger's original. While the publication is a synthesis of the three lecture courses, I have relied on the 2010 translation, although that translation has occasionally been altered to either conform to the language of the Salllis lectures or to what I thought worked better as a translation. One translation item should be noted. While Macquarrie and Robinson translate Heidegger's *Vorhandenheit* as "present-at-hand" and the SUNY translation opts for "objective presence," neither of these were satisfactory to Sallis, and we thus decided on "present" or "present object." The remaining decisions consisted of synthesizing the three manuscripts into a singular, unified text and thereby making the language of the three manuscripts consistent. Finally, I have made some alterations to the language of the manuscripts in order to eliminate some occasional repetition and overuse of the em dash. On a more personal note, I studied with John Sallis at Loyola for a number of years, and these latter decisions were not always easy, as they were frequently overdetermined for me by recollecting the many pauses and the like that were introduced by Sallis for emphasis in the actual delivery of his lectures. A warm recollection of those years remains.

I would like to thank John Sallis for trusting me with the task of making these lectures available to the many people who will certainly benefit from them. It is to the advantage of present and future readers of *Being and Time* that they now possess the guidance of these lectures by John Sallis.

Index

apophantic, apophantical "as," 49, 95, 100
Aquinas, Thomas, 110
Arendt, Hannah, 8
Aristotle, 1, 2, 8, 11–13, 28, 30–32, 48, 93, 102, 109, 110, 178n2, 179
attestation, 136–49, 153
attunement (*Befindlichkeit*), 73, 86, 87–89, 91, 100–107, 127, 133, 139, 144, 145–46, 158, 160, 164, 182
Augenblick (moment of vision), 162, 163
authentic, authenticity (*Eigentlich, Eigentlichkeit*), 29, 56, 80, 82, 92, 94, 96, 102, 105, 107, 115, 117, 128–34, 135–40, 141, 144–59, 150, 153, 161–63, 171–73, 179
awaiting (*Gegenwärtigen*), 161, 162, 163, 175–76, 178, 185

Befragte (what is questioned/interrogated), 15–16
Being-alongside, 108–9, 124, 132, 156, 175, 185
being-false, 49
being-guilty, 141–42, 144–46, 148, 150–52, 156
Being-in, 59–63, 73, 78–79, 84–103, 107, 109, 146
being-true, 49, 112
Being-with, with-Dasein (*Sein-bei*, Mitsein, Mitdasein), 59, 77–80, 84, 132
Biemel, Walter, 9, 74
birth, 134, 158, 168–69, 177, 183–84

care, 29, 36, 60–61, 65, 80–81, 93, 96, 101, 102n2, 104–8, 109, 123–28, 138–39, 142, 144, 150–59, 161–62, 168, 169, 174, 180, 181–86
categorial, categorial intuition, 13, 35, 38–42, 43, 44, 59, 68
circumspection, circumspect (*Umsicht, umsichtig*), 67–70, 74, 75, 93, 165, 167, 174–75, 182–85
clearing (*Lichtung*), 85–87, 93, 100, 102
conscience, 118, 136–53

datability, 175–79, 186
death, 115, 118, 119–34, 135, 147–49, 150–58, 161, 168–69, 171–73, 179, 183–84
demise (*Ableben*), 123, 129
destiny, fate (*Geschick*), 60, 118, 173, 184
disclosedness (*Erschlossenheit*), 109, 110–13, 124, 126–27, 129, 130–31, 133, 136–37, 145–48, 152, 153, 158, 161, 162–63, 165, 176, 182
discourse (λόγος), 48–49, 59, 86, 100–103, 118, 137–38, 146–48, 150, 158, 160, 163, 175, 184

ecstasis, ecstases, 158, 160–64, 165, 176, 181–82
ecstatic, 165, 178–79, 182
Erfragte (what is to be ascertained in questioning), 15–16
everydayness, 28–29, 44, 57, 65, 70, 77–81, 85, 87, 94, 102, 104, 105, 107, 117, 124, 128, 129, 137, 140–41, 144, 158–59, 160–67, 174n1, 181
existence, 21–22, 26, 31, 52, 55–56, 59, 61, 77–79, 83, 84, 86, 98, 102–3, 108–9, 117, 120, 124, 126–28, 131–33, 137, 140–41, 144–45, 147, 151, 155–57, 165, 169, 172, 181, 183
existential, 22, 28, 31, 57, 59–60, 61, 64, 68, 73, 77–79, 84, 85–86, 88–92, 97–98, 100–101, 104, 107, 108, 110, 112, 117, 119, 120, 123–49, 151, 154–55, 158–59, 160, 164–66, 168–72, 175, 178, 181, 183, 185
existentiell, 22, 64, 80, 82, 123, 130, 133, 135–36, 143, 145, 147–49, 150, 153, 160
expecting (*Erwarten*), 131

factical, 64, 78, 133, 144, 147–48, 152, 161, 169n1, 172, 176, 183, 185
facticity, 60–61, 87, 107–9, 124, 156–57, 169, 181, 183
falling (*Verfallen*), 102–3, 105–9, 113, 124, 127–29, 139–40, 156–58, 160–63, 181
for-the-sake-of-which (*Worumwillen*), 90–92, 165, 182
fore-conception (*Vorgriff*), 95–99, 116

189

fore-having (*Vorhabe*), 95–99, 116–17, 119, 133, 168, 183
fore-sight, foresight (*Vorsicht*), 95–99, 116–17
fore-structure (*Vor-struktur*), 95–99, 116–17, 133, 135, 147, 153
freedom, 107, 133, 172–73
fulfillment, 15, 24, 26, 38–39, 41, 49, 63, 112, 122, 151, 153
future, 24n3, 155–57, 160–64, 171, 176, 179, 181–82, 185

Gefragte (what is asked about), 15–16
guilt, guilty, 118, 140–46, 148, 150–52, 156

hermeneutical, 95, 97, 116–17
hermeneutical "as," 94, 100, 115
historical, 26, 30–31, 110, 158, 170–71, 184
historicity (*Geschichtlichkeit*), 31–32, 158–59, 168–73, 174n1, 177, 181–82, 184
horizon, 7, 10–11, 16, 27–29, 48, 53, 57, 65, 70, 102, 117–18, 164–65, 170, 175, 177, 178, 180, 182, 185–86
Husserl, Edmund, 2, 8–9, 19, 35, 40, 42–46, 78, 112

in-order-to (*Um-zu*), 66–72, 90, 94, 164–65, 182
inauthentic, inauthenticity (*Uneigentlich, uneigentlichkeit*), 56, 82, 92, 94–97, 102, 117, 128, 130, 133, 136, 155, 158, 160–63, 173
indefiniteness, 106, 129, 139, 148, 153, 172
innerworldly, 68, 71, 78, 80, 96, 106–8, 166, 177
intelligibility (*Verständlichkeit*), 96, 100–101, 153
intentionality, 35–39, 43–45, 112
intuition, 35, 38–44, 48, 89, 93–95

Kant, Immanuel, 1, 24, 32–33, 40, 42, 52, 73, 89, 93, 109, 158

language, 40, 43, 65, 70, 73, 99–101, 113, 134, 164, 175, 180, 182, 184, 186
Leibniz, 108

making-present (*Gegenwärtigen*), 156, 161–63, 175–76, 178–79, 181, 185

meaning (*Sinn*), 1–2, 5–7, 13–18, 23, 25, 27, 29–34, 39–42, 45, 48–51, 57, 63, 64, 79, 95–98, 109–11, 118, 121, 143, 146, 152, 153–59, 161, 163–65, 168, 173, 174, 180, 181–86
method, 19, 25–26, 33–34, 43–44, 46, 51, 57, 60, 111, 150
mineness (*Jemeinigkeit*), 56, 60, 78, 120, 125, 132, 140
mood (*Stimmung*), 60, 87–89, 102, 143

nearness (*Nähe*), 74
negativity, negative, 48, 142–44, 151–52, 156–57
Nietzsche, 1, 2, 7, 108
not-yet, 117, 120–22, 124, 129
nothing, 2, 106–7, 109, 120, 125, 128, 131, 138–39
now, 155, 161, 169, 176–79, 183, 185

ontic, 22, 64, 69, 71, 102, 104, 109, 130, 133–35, 145, 147
ontological, ontology, 7, 10, 12, 18–19, 22–34, 43, 51–53, 55, 58, 64–66, 68, 71–72, 77–79, 86, 89–90, 93, 96–97, 100, 102, 104, 108–10, 112, 117, 123–24, 128–30, 133, 135–37, 143–44, 147, 150, 153, 159, 165, 167–68, 178

phenomenology, 2, 8, 26–27, 34–52, 63, 75, 97, 104, 165–66
Plato, 2, 5, 11–12, 25, 93, 173
possibility, 11, 56, 71–72, 75, 80, 84, 89–92, 96, 104, 106–9, 112–13, 119–20, 123–37, 143–48, 150–56, 160–61, 164–65, 172–73, 177, 180–82
presence, 33, 37, 55, 60, 65, 69, 77, 92–94, 97, 99–100, 142–44, 188
projection, 73, 91–92, 96, 102, 107–9, 118, 142–43, 148, 150–54, 160, 162, 165, 172, 181

reading, 8, 55, 115
reference, 66–71, 78–79, 94, 97, 116, 120, 123, 178–79, 181
region, 18, 22, 43, 44–45, 56–57, 74–76, 106
relevance (*Bewandtnis*), 70–72, 94, 100
repetition (*Wiederholung*), 6, 10, 25, 29, 58, 152, 158–59, 160, 162–63, 173, 188
representation, 37, 63, 98, 111–12

resoluteness (*Entschlossenheit*), 118, 135, 146–59, 161, 163, 168, 171–73, 181
reticence, 146, 148, 150

schema, schemata, 15, 164–65, 182
science, 18–19, 22, 50, 160, 165–67, 170
selfhood, 81, 158
significance (*Bedeutsamkeit*), 70, 72, 89–92, 94–96, 100, 106–9, 154, 161, 165, 175, 178–79, 182, 184
situation, 2, 22, 116–17, 134, 145, 147–48, 152–53, 161, 172
space, spatiality, 42, 59–60, 73–76, 85, 158, 163–64, 175, 185
statement (*Aussage*), 49, 95, 98–100, 110–13, 178
stretching-along (*Erstreckung*), 158, 168–69, 183–84
structure, 7, 14, 16, 18, 22, 28, 35–36, 37, 43–45, 47, 51, 53, 59, 64, 66–68, 70, 74, 78–79, 84, 86, 89, 91–103, 105, 108–9, 116–17, 119, 124, 127–34, 135–36, 139–40, 144–48, 150, 153, 157, 160, 169, 171, 174, 176–77, 184, 186
subject, subjectivity, 17, 20, 24–25, 32–33, 35–37, 42–45, 57, 62, 64, 71, 75–78, 82, 84, 89, 98, 108–9, 158, 166, 170–71, 179

temporality, 24n3, 29–31, 115, 118, 150, 153–80, 181–86
they (*das Man*), 29, 78, 81–82, 84–85, 102–3, 105, 107–9, 128–29, 132, 136–41, 146–49, 151–53, 158, 172
thrown, thrownness, 73, 87–88, 91, 101, 103, 107–9, 127, 134, 139–44, 147, 156, 162–65, 169, 171–72, 177, 182–84
totality, 40–41, 59, 64, 66–75, 84, 94–96, 99–101, 108–9, 116, 154
truth, 28, 31, 39–40, 49, 73, 109–13, 146, 152, 165

uncanniness, 139–41, 144
understanding, 6–8, 10–11, 14–17, 20–23, 25, 27–30, 32–34, 42, 45, 57, 59, 72–73, 77, 83, 85–86, 88–97, 100–103, 104–9, 111, 118, 125–27, 131–34, 140, 142–46, 148, 150, 154, 158, 160–64, 166–68, 170, 176, 179, 182–83

whither, 74, 87, 103, 164, 182
whole, 7, 38, 41, 53, 59, 88, 90, 101, 104–5, 108–9, 116–17, 119–34, 135, 142, 146–49, 150–59, 168, 183
worldliness, 59, 64–76, 78, 84, 89, 92, 94, 106

JOHN SALLIS is Frederick J. Adelmann Professor of Philosophy at Boston College. He is author of more than twenty books, including *Chorology*, *Songs of Nature*, and *Kant and the Spirit of Critique*.

JEFFREY POWELL is Professor of Philosophy at Marshall University. He is the editor of *Heidegger and Language* and coeditor of *Aesthetic Reason and Imaginative Freedom: Friedrich Schiller and Philosophy*. He is cotranslator of Heidegger's *The History of Beyng*.

For Indiana University Press

Tony Brewer, Artist and Book Designer
Dan Crissman, Trade and Regional Acquisitions Editor
Anna Francis, Assistant Acquisitions Editor
Brenna Hosman, Production Coordinator
Katie Huggins, Production Manager
David Miller, Lead Project Manager/Editor
Dan Pyle, Online Publishing Manager
Pamela Rude, Senior Artist and Book Designer
Stephen Williams, Marketing and Publicity Manager